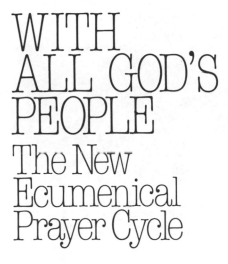

WITH ALL GOD'S PEOPLE

The New Ecumenical Prayer Cycle

WITH ALL GOD'S PEOPLE

The New Ecumenical Prayer Cycle

Compiled by John Carden

WCC PUBLICATIONS, GENEVA

Cover design: Rob Lucas

ISBN 2-8254-0943-x

© 1989 WCC Publications, World Council of Churches,
150 route de Ferney, 1211 Geneva 2, Switzerland

Printed in Switzerland

The edition for the United States of America will be published in 1990 by *Twenty-Third Publications*, Mystic, Connecticut.

Contents

Foreword

At the very heart of the ecumenical movement is the reality of prayer. Jesus prayed that we may all be one, united in God in the mystery of the Trinity. That is the basis and the goal of our search for unity.

Prayer is our pathway to unity. What we seek in and through the ecumenical movement is a communion that we cannot articulate in words because it belongs to our life in God. It is through prayer that we both seek and celebrate that communion.

Intercessory prayer is of the essence of the church's vocation. Like Abraham interceding for Sodom and Gomorrah, and following the example of Jesus' priestly prayer in the Gospel of John, we raise our hearts and minds to God in worship and adoration, and we intercede on behalf of all with whom we share the world and all its joys and sorrows. Through the daily discipline of intercession we affirm our solidarity with Christians all over the world, brothers and sisters living in diverse situations and experiencing diverse problems.

The Vancouver Assembly of the World Council of Churches in 1983 reaffirmed the centrality of worship. Participants experienced there the power of prayer. They interceded for churches everywhere and for the nations and peoples of the world. A larger number than ever before at such gatherings were able to be part of one eucharistic community, sharing as they did in the memorable celebration of the Lima Liturgy, which tries to embody in liturgical form some of the ecumenical theological convergence achieved through the years.

It is out of such ecumenical worship experience that this edition of the Prayer Cycle has been prepared. It represents an attempt to identify with God's people in every place and to present before God their specific needs and aspirations.

With All God's People includes prayers from many countries. It enables us to journey in prayer through every region of the world and through every week of the year. It enables us to pray together, *with* all God's people and *for* all God's people, from within our concrete contexts.

Many member churches and Christian groups have their own prayer cycles which follow their liturgical tradition and calendar. They have litanies and liturgies around denominational and congregational concerns. These serve an important purpose. But there is also the need to grow in an ecumenical spirituality of prayer. As churches and Christians we are committed together to the search for full visible unity. During and within that search we must celebrate the unity that God has granted us; and we must hold up before God all the partners in this ecumenical pilgrimage in their disparate situations. Committing one another to God, we draw closer to one another and we grow in unity together.

For many people the first edition of the Ecumenical Prayer Cycle, *For All God's People*, published in 1978 and later translated into some twenty languages, was their first introduction to ecumenical prayer. *With All God's People* continues that tradition; it seeks to inform our public worship and private prayer with ecumenical concern and content. It demonstrates the old ecumenical conviction: *Lex orandi lex credendi.* Churches and Christians, men and women, live by a faith embodied in a variety of credal and doxological affirmations, but they enter the presence of God together, for and with one another.

In the process of preparing this volume, we have received a great variety of worship material from many sources. Available now at the worship resource centre of the WCC at its Geneva headquarters, it indicates the richness of the liturgical traditions among our member churches and of the themes and styles of prayer Christian people resort to in our time.

The WCC offers this book to member churches and Christian groups in the conviction that it is responding to a demand for a spirituality that is contextual, local and ecumenical.

Where there is no prayer for unity there can be no vision of unity. Let the Spirit so guide us that our human voices praying to God for the salvation of the world and the unity of the people of God may be heard and answered.

EMILIO CASTRO

About this Book

Published in 1978 and subsequently translated into a number of languages, the first Ecumenical Prayer Cycle, *For All God's People*, has been widely used by many different churches, groups and individuals all over the world. The present volume is a successor to it. The revised title carries with it an idea very familiar in WCC circles, that of staying together, struggling together, growing together and praying together; and which, applied to the EPC, implies an effort not just to pray *for* all God's people, but also to understand, to stand alongside and to pray in solidarity *with* our fellow Christians around the world.

With All God's People takes its shape and content from the interaction of many different people, and from formal and informal dialogue with churches and councils of churches and with individual friends in the ecumenical movement in different parts of the world. We are grateful to those many people who provided inspiration, who have allowed us to use their prayers and words, who have made corrections, or in any other way participated in the process of preparing this new book.

The cycle

It is obviously an aid to our sense of Christian solidarity and to the growing sense of interdependence on the part of all human beings if we can find some way of praying together on a regular and agreed basis. Certainly solidarity is one of the recurring themes of this book, as of the ecumenical movement as a whole, and is articulated most forcefully by churches which are under pressure of one kind or another, and most appreciatively by individual Christians in situations of isolation and privation.

This ecumenical prayer cycle is offered by the member churches of the WCC as one method of enabling Christians to broaden and also to focus their prayer and concern, and to familiarize themselves with, and bring into the local family, people of different parts of the world. Intended for the use of individuals and local congregations as well as for places of daily corporate prayer and ecumenical formation such as religious communities, ashrams, theological colleges and lay training institutes, the weekly material can be used over the course of the week as it is in the Ecumenical Centre in Geneva. Alternatively — especially in the case of congregations who use the EPC as the basis for their Sunday intercessions, and find it difficult to assimilate more than one country on any given Sunday — the region can be prayed for as a whole, or, as is done in the GDR, one country of the week each year, over what adds up to a three- or four-year cycle. Some use the book as a resource, as the hub of the wheel rather than its perimeter, and when, for whatever reason, a particular country comes to their attention, perhaps in connection with their own confessional cycle, turn to the EPC for material for prayer. It is hoped that the index which lists countries and regions and also themes of prayers will be helpful. The aim of the cycle is to provide a system and discipline for those who would value it, and a resource book for all who are concerned in whatever way to pray with all God's people.

Format

While some may regret the loss of the more ordered approach of the first edition, in the interest of freshness and variety, and in order to do some justice to regional differences, the compilers were encouraged to approach different weeks in different ways. This means that the layout for each week is not standard. For various reasons some weeks seem to call for more explanatory or factual material than others, and the amount of prayer material made available varied greatly.

Language

As its title suggests, the EPC is designed to include all, and inclusive language is therefore used throughout in respect of people. Since we are praying alongside those, both young and old, of every race and language, and using the prayers which they themselves use, there is a rich and varied way of addressing God using such names as Father, Mother, Grandfather, Parent, Elder Brother, Weaverwoman and so on, and certainly many prayers which acknowledge that God has feminine attributes. For some, the word Lord may present problems. In one of his books Kosuke Koyama instances Philippians 2, in which Christ is shown as affirming his lordship by giving it up. He goes on: "Christians live in such a Lord and their lives must point to such a strange lordship." In praying the prayers and making them our own, it is hoped that users will feel free to appropriate these varied ways of addressing God or to transpose them into forms with which they feel more at ease.

Information

Prayers emerge out of, and are related to, given situations, and it is the blending of information, facts and history with prayer, which provides one of the most satisfactory elements in ecumenical spirituality and makes this a book of living prayer rather than a bookish anthology. Within the limits of time available, care has been taken to check the accuracy of the information, and the compilers apologize for any mistakes. However, it must be remembered that situations can change quickly, and in the case of a few countries, very significant changes have indeed already taken place. In some instances these are matters for thanksgiving. Users of the prayer cycle will wish to take these changes into their prayers.

Population figures throughout the book are all taken from one standard source, taking the latest official figure available and rounding it up to the next decimal point. This means that for most countries the figure given is too low, as populations are mostly rising and often rapidly. Religious statistics are more difficult. In most cases use has been made of Barrett's forecast figures,* but wherever statistics have been made available by the local Christian council these have been used.

The prayers

While an effort has been made to achieve a degree of typicality in the prayers that have been chosen, and thus enable users to identify with the words and ways of different countries, the compilers have also had in mind the totality of the cycle and have sought to choose prayers not only for the sake of their local flavour but also because of what they contribute to the whole. So it is that Finland's prayer of blessing of a computer, or Canada's meditation on a crucified woman, are to be regarded as the gifts of those countries to the spirituality of the whole church rather than as being necessarily typical of the country concerned. Likewise prayers for those affected by AIDS are included under USA and Uganda because both of these countries have experience of AIDS, are open about it, are relating it to their Christian faith, and therefore share this pain and this problem with the rest of the world.

While in an increasingly interdependent world an ever-increasing number of prayers reflect common themes — peace, unity, cities, young people — some very striking differences of need and of emphasis are emerging. Elements of questioning, anger, anguish, penitence, silence,

---

* *World Christian Encyclopedia*, ed. David B. Barrett, Nairobi, OUP, 1982. Also used for general information: *The Europa Year Book: a World Survey, 1987*, London, Europa Publications Ltd.

solidarity, affirmation and rejoicing are all to be found, some more typical of certain areas of the world than others.

Every effort has been made to trace and acknowledge the origin of the prayers, and where these have not knowingly been adapted, to reproduce them in the form received. However, like birds released from captivity, prayers once published take on a life of their own and enjoy the freedom of the universe. Flying in different environments, they sometimes acquire new meanings. This has surely happened in the case of a number of the prayers in this book, and as they continue to be used in many different situations and settings that process will undoubtedly continue and add to their richness.

Symbols

"Am I to believe that God's concern for the people of Taiwan, for instance, or Korea, began only 60, 80 or 90 years ago when we western missionaries arrived with the gospel of Jesus Christ?" asks Emilio Castro. To which of course the answer is "No". As far as this book is concerned, a number of things follow from that. The compilers have tried firstly to acknowledge the earlier history of each country and to affirm the dignity and rights of original inhabitants, and secondly to affirm their belief that God also speaks in and through those of other faiths and all cultures. A third thing, which follows from the recognition of God's presence and activity in those who belong to largely non-literary cultures, is that God also speaks through visual images and symbols. It was at our very first meeting in Taizé that a Ghanaian member of the group challenged us to look at the possibility of introducing some non-literary elements into this new edition. To a West African the symbol on page 188 communicates immediately the need for unity and harmony in a way in which words can never do. Some of the symbols in this book, like the cross of St Thomas and the one from Taxila, speak of a very early Christian presence in those lands. Others relate to more contemporary concerns. All stand as tokens for a great deal of sharing which could be enriching. In response to the need for the world church to become fully ecumenical Walter Hollenweger, professor of mission at Birmingham University in England, posed the question as to whether a proverb, a song, a snatch of poetry, a dance, a story, a parable was ever taken as seriously as a committee resolution. And if not, why not? His inference was that it is just those things that move human beings most deeply, that stir the imagination, that evoke the teaching of Jesus and inspire the spirit of prayer more unerringly and deeply than many more formal utterances.

Maps

The seven regional maps used in this book are based on the traditional Mercator's projection. Many may find it helpful to bring the perspectives of the Peters' or North/South map to bear on their prayers for the world. A number of well-known medieval pilgrim maps view the world as centred on Jerusalem, and show the continents of Africa, Asia and Europe as radiating from that centre. This insight has been adopted in this publication to the extent of singling out Jerusalem, the place of our Lord's passion, resurrection, ascension and the promise of his continued intercession, as the point of departure for users of this ecumenical cycle of prayer.

Updating

One of our colleagues here at the Ecumenical Centre said recently that "with things moving so quickly, every day away from Africa is one more day out of date". Applied to the EPC this suggests the need for constant updating on the part of the user. Users are invited to share in updating and renewal by submitting corrections, up-to-date information, prayers and liturgical material to the Worship Resource Centre of the Sub-unit on Renewal and Congregational Life.

Services for ecumenical occasions

A companion volume to this one provides worship material suitable for meetings of an ecumenical character, either during a particular season of the church's year or in relation to a particular theme. These services are intended to be drawn upon and adapted according to local needs.

* * *

This prayer cycle has been compiled under the guidance of a task force specially constituted for the purpose, made up of members of staff of the World Council of Churches. The work was carried out under the general direction of the WCC Sub-units on Faith and Order, and Renewal and Congregational Life. In the earlier stages, the Rev. Dr Hans-Georg Link played a major role.

JOHN CARDEN
Consultant for the EPC
Renewal and Congregational Life

Jerusalem

Lord, dear Lord,
I long for Jerusalem;
The city built high in heaven
but also the one built on the rocks
over there in Israel.

In all the countries and churches included in this cycle of prayer, there can hardly be a single believer who cannot identify with the prayer of this Ghanaian Christian; and few of us indeed who, in times of privation and difficulty, have not taken comfort in the thought of the heavenly city; or, at some time or another, have not walked in imagination the streets of Jerusalem, re-living those events in the life of Jesus so central to our faith.

Lord God,
then I would see, in my mind,
how he was pushed and lashed
through city streets to Golgotha
and see there how he died for us.
I'd mourn and weep
and mourn — but I would know!
I'd see how the temple curtain was torn,
and feel the earthquake under my feet.
Then Easter when he rose from the dead.
Rejoicing, dancing and clapping
I would shout:
He is risen!
He is risen!

Since that first resurrection morning it is to Jerusalem that pilgrims have come; and it is from Jerusalem that our cycle of prayer begins, following the ever-increasing spread of the church since Pentecost to the present time. Over the centuries, the church's growth has been aided by countless preachers and evangelists, as well as by other social and political forces which have scattered Christians across the world.

Jerusalem remains also the meeting place of the three great monotheistic faiths: Judaism, Christianity and Islam, each with its centres of devotion, hospitality and scholarship and its own institutions of service. Due to the uncertainties of the future and the present political reality, many Christians and Muslims have left Jerusalem. In terms of the local Arab Christian community, for example, numbers have diminished since 1967, when there were an estimated 27,000, to something like 7,500. They belong to a number of different confessions, but are mostly Eastern Orthodox, Roman Catholics, Melkites, Lutherans and Anglicans. There is a small community of Christian converts from Judaism.

Pray for this living presence in Jerusalem

As in all greatly revered pilgrimage places, special sensitivities are involved, and relationships between the different Christian confessions in Jerusalem, as well as between the different faiths and peoples are often marked by conflict. Now, as ever, there is need to pray for the peace of Jerusalem, the city which gave rise to that great expression of the mother love of God.

O Jerusalem, Jerusalem,... How often would I have gathered your children together as a hen gathers her brood under her wings, and you would not!

The figure of a pelican feeding her young with her own life-blood is to be seen in the "Upper Room" in Jerusalem, and is an ancient reminder of the self-giving love of God in Christ. To him we pray:

Blessed Jesus,
lifting up holy hands perpetually for all humankind;
breathe by thy Spirit such love into the prayers that we offer,
that they may be taken into thine, and prevail with thine. Amen.

Pray

for the city of Jerusalem distracted and divided until this day, yet still pregnant with promise for the cities of the world

for its present-day children and for all who seek the common good of its diverse people

Gather them together, O Lord

for men and women of peace and reconciliation in every community
Gather them together, O Lord

for the custodians of holy places; for priests and pastors and for the continuing life of local congregations
Gather them together, O Lord

for the Christians of many backgrounds and traditions, who take part in the Palm Sunday walk, but find other steps towards unity less easy to take
Gather them together, O Lord

Lord Jesus, we pray for the church which is one in the greatness of your love, but divided in the littleness of our own. May we be less occupied with the things which divide us, and more with the things we hold in common. Amen.

Jesus comes to Benares
As he does to Mecca
and to Jerusalem and to Rome
In each place
he raises his hand in peace
And in each place
he is crucified again.

The Christian Conference of Asia

Jesus, ride again into our cities, temples,
Upper Rooms and Gethsemanes.
Give us sight so that this time we might recognize you. Amen.

Prayer for peace

Week 1

Egypt • Israel and the Occupied Territories • Jordan • Lebanon • Syria

Egypt

Population: 48.6 million, and increasing by at least one million annually.

Language: Arabic.

Government: Multiparty republic.

Religion: Muslims 85%; Christians 15%, mostly members of the Coptic Orthodox Church who number some 7 million. The ancient Greek Orthodox Patriarchate of Alexandria also has its roots here. There are considerably smaller Evangelical Coptic, Armenian, Catholic, Anglican and Protestant communities.

If the unforgettable words in St John's Gospel "And the word was made flesh" were written originally to meet the needs of Hellenic Jews in Alexandria, and if — as is firmly believed in Egypt — St Mark himself visited Alexandria and preached the gospel throughout the country, then there must have been a Christian presence in Egypt from a very early date. Unquestionably Egyptian Christians died in thousands in the bitter persecution of the 3rd and 4th centuries, and formed the nucleus of the great desert communities, an experience which fortified the Coptic Church for the years to come. The rise of Islam brought problems and opportunities which continue to this day.

Intercessions and Prayers

O God of the ever present crosses,
help us, your servants.

4th century Egyptian

O Master, Lord God, Almighty, the Father of our Lord, our God and our Saviour Jesus Christ, we thank you in every condition, for any

Supplement to
WITH ALL GOD'S PEOPLE
The New Ecumenical Prayer Cycle

To live is to change. So, too, with prayer. Not only are we changed as we pray, but the specifics of our praying must also change, for God's world is ever in flux.

The major changes in many parts of the world in recent months and years inevitably affect prayer informed by this cycle. Pending the next complete revision, this leaflet adapts the 1990 text in the wake of the tides — and tidal waves — of historical change since then.

Inevitably, this little update will be overtaken by events between the time it went to the printer (November 1992) and the time it is used. And it is impossible to catalogue all relevant changes (population increases, the advent of multiparty democracy in many countries, etc.).

Still, it is a modest effort to keep the *Ecumenical Prayer Cycle* current. It is suggested that you make a notation of each of these additions and replacements at the appropriate point in the book. In the years to come, you will probably want to add your own updates.

Let us continue to pray — *for* and *with* all God's people.

— *WCC Publications*

WEEK 1, *add after the first three lines on p. 12*:

In the early 1990s, however, some of the worst aspects of the previous decade and a half seemed to be changing for the better.

Fighting decreased. Independent militias, which had long held sway in different areas, had submitted to government authority. Elections were held. It was possible for many to return to home areas from which they had been driven during the period of sectarian struggles.

Still, in late 1992 the Syrian army remained in many parts of Lebanon, and some worried that Syria exercised undue control over the Lebanese government. And a band of Lebanese territory along the Israeli border continued effectively under Israeli control.

WEEK 2, *add at the end of the text on p. 22*:

The Gulf War and its aftermath: The invasion of Kuwait by Iraq in August 1990, the subsequent high-tech war against Iraq in January-February 1991 (waged under UN auspices with at least the token involvement of dozens of countries, but with a dominant role played by the United States) and the aftermath of both have had major economic, social, and political consequences.

Some were intended and foreseen, some not. Though Iraq and Kuwait were most affected, so was the rest of the Middle East and, to varying degrees, other parts of the world.

One aspect of these continuing ramifications was the confrontation and threats of war in mid-1992, as Iraq refused for a time to let a UN team search in a particular building for information about Iraqi military capability.

The invasion and war, continuing tensions and disputes involving Iraq and other nations and charges of Iraqi government oppression of Kurds and Shiite Muslims raise serious and difficult questions for church people and others.

On what grounds in our time can war be justified? If it can be, what are the limits? How can or should the United Nations operate in this post-Cold War period? When, if ever, is outside intervention justified — and in what form — to protect human rights within a given country?

These issues, as well as the host of people whose lives were lost or seriously disrupted in connection with the invasion, war and aftermath call for Christian prayer and other action, in particular during this week.

WEEK 13

Replace the text after the italics on p. 98 through the first three lines on p. 99 with:

In 1974 a military revolution deposed Emperor Haile Selassie. It was followed by unrest, many deaths and detentions, considerable discrimination against church people and notable interference with church activities.

Moreover, major famine during the 1980s added to the suffering of millions in the country.

The post-Selassie government was itself overthrown — after years of costly fighting — in 1991. The Ethiopian People's Revolutionary

Democratic Front played the major role in the new, transitional administration.

The EPRDF victory also signaled success for the Eritrean People's Liberation Front. It led a 30-year campaign for independence for Eritrea, land along the coast which was federated with Ethiopia when European control of Eritrea ended after World War II. That federation was terminated at Ethiopian behest in 1962.

An internationally supervised referendum in 1993 is expected to confirm Eritrean independence.

In the new situation in Ethiopia and Eritrea, church people and institutions have many adjustments to make. They need prayer and other support as they rebuild and renew after nearly two decades of persecution and other pressure.

Before the intercessions and prayers on p. 101, add:

In the early 1990s, multi-sided civil war and intense famine produced ghastly reports of conflict and death in Somalia. At one point in mid-1992, upwards of a third of the population was estimated to be on the verge of starvation.

Hundreds of thousands of Somalis tried to escape the deprivation and carnage by fleeing across the water to Yemen or south to neighboring Kenya. But these nations, faced with difficult internal problems of their own, did not always fully welcome the new, desperate arrivals.

WEEK 16

Before the intercessions and prayers on p. 117, add:

In the early 1990s, civil unrest increased in Madagascar, with church people playing a notable role in attempting to overcome it.

At the end of the section on Malawi, p. 119, add:

In the early 1990s, conflict between Malawi's president-for-life and church leaders and others became more public and pronounced. Some church people called for significant political and social changes and criticized aspects of the rule of the president. In turn, the government accused some church leaders of subversion and of being in league with external enemies.

WEEK 20, *add before section on Poland, p. 149*:

Modern Czechoslovakia was formed after the end of World War I in 1918 from parts of what had been the Austro-Hungarian empire. During World War II, Nazi Germany occupied the Czech part of the republic and set up a puppet state in Slovakia.

United again after the end of World War II and during the 40 years of communist rule which lasted till late 1989, parliamentary leaders of the Czech lands and Slovakia began in 1992 to negotiate a peaceful separation, under which the two states — the Czech Republic and Slovakia — would formally began to function separately on 1 January 1993.

WEEK 21

New title of week: ALBANIA, BOSNIA-HERZEGOVINA, BULGARIA, CROATIA, MACEDONIA[1], SLOVENIA, YUGOSLAVIA (SERBIA AND MONTENEGRO)

Page 153-154, replace section on Albania with:
Christian impulses reached what is now Albania early on in Christian history.

For centuries, Albania was part of the Ottoman empire, and subject to Islamic influence. Traditionally, about two-thirds of Albanians are Muslims, the remainder Christians (roughly two-thirds Eastern Orthodox, one-third Roman Catholic).

Though communist countries in general restricted religion, the communists in Albania, who came to power in 1946, went even further. In 1967, religion was outlawed. All religious institutions were closed, and strict penalties were imposed on anyone found practising religion, even in private. In this early post-communist period it is thus difficult to know with certainty what portion of the people maintain a

---

[1] The name "Macedonia" has been a focal point of tension, particularly in Greece, where fears have been expressed that its use is a first step towards an effort to expand that republic into the adjacent Greek province of Macedonia. This has led to delays in international recognition of the independence of the republic.

sense of religious identity, Muslim or Christian.

The communist government was also isolationist, so for more than four decades, Albania, the poorest country in Europe, was almost completely cut off from the world outside.

In such circumstances, the church and other independent, non-state institutions re-emerged with not inconsiderable difficulty in the early 1990s.

Pages 155-156, new section title and section text:
Bosnia-Herzegovina, Croatia, Macedonia, Slovenia, Yugoslavia (Serbia and Montenegro)
Combined population: about 25 million
Main languages: Croatian, Macedonian, Serbian, Slovenian
Governments: multi-party republics
Religion (in the countries together): Christians, three-quarters; Muslims, one-tenth; a few Jews

Born of a movement to unite southern Slavs, Yugoslavia emerged as one country from part of what was the Austro-Hungarian empire till 1918. Invaded by Italian and German forces in 1941, and torn by civil war between rival resistance movements, Yugoslavia emerged as a communist federal republic in 1945. By 1948, it had broken with the main body of communist nations, led by the then-Soviet Union.

Subsequent Yugoslav communist practice, in terms of religion and other aspects of life, was considerably less controlling and restrictive than that in most other communist countries.

In the early 1990s, after the demise of communist rule, long-standing ethnic and other hostilities which had simmered below the surface in communist times burst forth. By late 1992, what had been one country which federated six republics had become five separate countries.

Serbia and Montenegro together continued as Yugoslavia. Serbia also includes two semi-autonomous regions, Kosovo and Voivodina. The former, very important in Serbian history, is now populated mainly by ethnic Albanians.

Macedonia experienced difficulty obtaining international

recognition, largely because of Greek objections to its name[2].

Independence for Slovenia — the westernmost part of what was Yugoslavia — came relatively peacefully. Croatia separated from Yugoslavia with rather more bloodshed.

But it was in Bosnia-Herzegovina where bloody ethnic rivalries played the biggest role in producing the largest flood of refugees and displaced persons in Europe since World War II. Mid-1992 estimates ran as high as 2.5 million.

"Ethnic cleansing" was the euphemism for efforts to produce ethnic homogeneity in different parts of Bosnia by driving out — or killing — members of the "wrong" ethnic group, even though they may have lived peacefully side by side for years.

Two of the Bosnian minorities — Croats and Serbs — have a neighbouring state as some sort of advocate and protector. But lacking such, the largest Bosnian minority, Slavic Muslims, were especially disadvantaged in the "ethnic-cleansing" process (though some international Muslim aid did come on their behalf).

There were some public efforts by church leaders in the region and beyond to help stop the fighting, but they showed no more notable success than attempts by local politicians and representatives of the European Community and United Nations.

Moreover, each major form of Christianity among south Slavs is especially identified with one of the two largest ethnic groups — Eastern Orthodox with Serbs, Roman Catholics with Croats. This has not made it any easier for church people to take positions which might seem to contradict prevailing ethnic sentiment.

Numerically much smaller forms of Christianity — Old Catholic, Lutheran, Reformed, and others — also exist in the five countries which emerged from the former Yugoslavia. Some are associated especially with minority ethnic groups such as Slovaks, Hungarians, or Germans.

Besides its Serbian form, Eastern Orthodoxy also exists in Albanian and Bulgarian varieties. Some Orthodox church leaders in Macedonia have sought independence from the Serbian Orthodox Church, though

---

[2]See note 1 above. It should be noted that the use of names of countries in the *Ecumenical Prayer Cycle* does not imply any political judgement on the part of the World Council of Churches.

that aspiration is not recognized officially in other parts of the Eastern Orthodox world.

WEEK 23

New title of week: BELARUSSIA, RUSSIA, UKRAINE; KAZAKHSTAN, KIRGIZSTAN, TAJIKISTAN, TURKMENISTAN, UZBEKISTAN; ESTONIA, LATVIA, LITHUANIA; MONGOLIA; MOLDOVA; ARMENIA, AZERBAIJAN, GEORGIA

Pages 165-168, replace section on USSR with:

BELARUSSIA, RUSSIA, UKRAINE

In 988, Vladimir, grand prince of Kiev, was baptized. In 1988, the 1000th anniverary of his baptism was celebrated, marking the coming of Christianity to what is now three independent states — Belarussia, Russia, and Ukraine.

The centre of church and political life shifted from Kiev to Moscow in the 13th century. In 1589, an Eastern Orthodox patriarchate was established there.

Descendants of those who resisted patriarchal reforms of worship in the 17th century continue as groups of Old Believers.

The patriarchate was abolished later in the 17th century, and not re-established till early in this century. In 1917, the communist revolution ended the empire of the Russian tsars, which had close official links to the church. In its place came the Union of Soviet Socialist Republics. A difficult transitional period followed, as the church adjusted to radically changed church-state relationships.

With the church playing a major patriotic role in World War II, its room for manoeuvre increased somewhat, though major restrictions and controls continued in subsequent decades. Now, in the post-communist situation, the church, with the rest of society, finds it must get used to a wide variety of changes in attitude, style and assumptions.

Eastern Orthodoxy is by far the largest form of Christianity in these three countries, maintaining the allegiance of tens of millions of people, even after 70-plus years of official atheism.

Baptists arrived in the 18th century. The Pentecostal movement spread in the 1920s. Baptists, Mennonites, Adventists and Pentecostals were joined in one church body in 1944. A Lutheran church body also exists, with members concentrated in parts of Siberia.

Roman Catholics live especially in parts of Ukraine and Belarussia. Most of them are Eastern Catholics (Uniates). Their worship forms and social customs are virtually the same as those of their Orthodox neighbours, but Eastern Catholics are in communion with the pope.

The history of Eastern Catholicism is controverted, and it remains a sore point in Eastern Orthodox-Roman Catholic relations. Notably in the Ukraine, Eastern Catholics have re-emerged vigorously from an illegal, underground existence (their church having been officially merged into Russian Orthodoxy in 1946).

Also at issue in terms of inner Orthodox life in the Ukraine is whether or not Ukrainian Orthodoxy should be autocephalous (completely self governing), or continue under some degree of Russian jurisdiction.

KAZAKHSTAN, KIRGIZSTAN, TAJIKISTAN, TURKMENISTAN, UZBEKISTAN

These five central Asian republics have a predominantly Islamic religious heritage. Except for Tajikistan, their languages are related to Turkish. One legacy of the years of Soviet rule are significant ethnic Russian minorities, notably in major cities.

ESTONIA, LATVIA, LITHUANIA

Part of the Russian empire till the end of World War I, the post-war independence of Estonia, Latvia, and Lithuania was ended by Germany and the Soviet Union in World War II.

The demise of the Soviet Union meant independence once again for the three, which resumed their more traditional orientation toward other nations which border the Baltic.

Lutheranism is the main form of Christianity in Estonia and Latvia, and links with the church in Sweden and Finland are notable. Roman Catholicism is numerically dominant in Lithuania. Eastern Orthodox, Reformed, Methodists and Baptists are also present in the republics.

Mainly as a result of Soviet policies, there is a notable Russian ethnic minority presence, particularly in Latvia. Not all members of Russian and other ethnic minorities feel so much at home now that the countries are independent. This has further complicated the countries' problems as they have sought to re-establish their independence under market forces after years as a small part of a sprawling centralized communist state run from Moscow.

MOLDOVA

Moldova is largely Romanian in ethnic heritage. It became part of the Soviet Union in connection with World War II. Now that it has emerged as a separate state in the wake of the Soviet demise, it has cultivated ties with neighboring Romania. Some advocate a union of Moldova and Romania. However, the presence of a notable ethnic Russian minority in part of Moldova complicates such proposals.

ARMENIA, AZERBAIJAN, GEORGIA

The Armenian form of what is now Oriental Orthodoxy became the official church of Armenia in the 4th century. The monastery in Etchmiadzin, near Yerevan, the Armenian capital, is now the worldwide administrative centre of the Armenian Apostolic Church.

An estimated 3 million Armenian Christians live in the republic, another 1.5 million in other parts of what was the Soviet Union and another 2 million in a worldwide diaspora, notably in Turkey, Lebanon, other parts of the Middle East and the United States.

The suffering of Armenians under the Ottoman Empire, notably what Armenians commemorate as the genocide of an estimated 1.5 million Armenians in 1915-16, is a major part of the modern Armenian historical consciousness.

Azerbaijan is a predominantly Muslim republic, though the disputed enclave of Nagorno-Karabagh is a centre of Armenian Christianity. Fighting between Armenians and Azeris has marred the first years of their new independence.

Christianity also arrived early in what is now Georgia. Today, the Georgian Orthodox Church, with an official membership of about five million, is an autocephalous (completely self-governing) member of the Eastern Orthodox family.

Over the centuries, Georgian Christians have lived under Arab, Mongol, Russian and Soviet rule. Now, along with the rest of society, they are adjusting to the new conditions of national independence and post-communist renewal and reform. A secessionist-minded Russian minority concentrated in one corner of Georgia has complicated efforts at national unity in the post-Soviet period.

WEEK 24, *add at end of text on p. 173:*

At the beginning of the 1990s, a horrendous civil war raged in Liberia. It was marked by atrocities including a massacre of people gathered for safety in the main Lutheran compound in the capital Monrovia.

A ceasefire was eventually put in place, but disputes between rival factions were not definitively settled, and reconciliation and rebuilding have proved difficult.

WEEK 28

New title of week: CAMBODIA, LAOS, VIETNAM
Page 199, new section title: Cambodia
Page 200, add before last paragraph:

In the early 1990s, UN-sponsored peace accords seemed to be moving Cambodia slowly towards a more peaceful situation and stable government. Nevertheless, the intentions of the Khmer Rouge remained unclear, and the peace process was not without snags and difficulties.

WEEK 29, *replace lines 4-14 on p. 206 with:*

In the early 1990s, opposition to the military government (which took power in 1988) became more pronounced, symbolized by the prolonged house arrest of Nobel Peace Prize winner Aung San Suu Kyi. Outside observers accused the government of grave violations of the human rights of political activists and ethnic minorities.

Over the years the church in Myanmar has exhibited resourcefulness and vitality as it lives with the daily question of what it means to be a Christian in a land which has what has been described as "the strongest, most true-to-the-original type of Buddhism" in the world. To some extent, the church has coped by linking Christian and national unity — working together ecumenically and supporting national unity through ecumenical activities. Theological education for church members at large continues to be an important ecumenical activity.

WEEK 36, *replace paragraph after affirmation on p. 247 with:*

Another large Caribbean island, Hispaniola, which now includes the countries of Dominican Republic and Haiti, is thought to be where European explorer Christopher Columbus landed in October 1492. His arrival is the symbolic beginning of Europe's contact with the Americas and its native peoples.

It was in the context of European domination, exploitation and often extermination that Christianity was first spread in much of the hemisphere. Such a mixed legacy inevitably coloured many activities and programs which marked the 500th anniversary of the landing.

What is now Haiti gained independence from France following a slave revolt in the early 19th century. Today it is among the poorest countries in the region. After years of brutal dictatorship by the Duvalier family, prospects for change and renewal came to be symbolized by the election in 1991 of Jean-Bertrand Aristide, a Roman Catholic priest, as president. Before long, however, he was forced into exile. In 1992, thousands of Haitians tried to flee their country in boats, but they were generally returned, to an uncertain fate, by US authorities.

In the Caribbean, church divisions reflect those of the Old World. That one or another tradition is notably strong numerically seems related mostly to which colonial power controlled a given area. Some have criticized parts of the contemporary Caribbean church for being too oriented towards the former colonial power.

WEEK 38

Bottom of page 265, add before italics:
On 1 January 1992 peace accords were finally signed between the government and forces fighting it. This followed efforts for peace in which church people played a notable part. Now, prospects seem much improved that the violence and uncertainty with which many Salvadorans have lived so long will decrease.

Page 266, add after paragraph on Panama:
In December 1990, US forces invaded Panama, and removed the country's strongman, Manuel Noriega. He was subsequently tried in a US court and convicted of charges involving drug trafficking.

To whatever extent many in Panama might have been glad to be rid of Noriega, the daily economic and social life of most Panamanians does not seem to have changed for the better since the invasion. And the question remains unsettled of when, if ever, it is legitimate for one country to topple the government of another.

WEEK 43, *add at end of text on p. 295*:

Developments in the early 1990s: All three countries were marked by unrest and turbulence during the first years of the 1990s. In Rwanda and Burundi, traditional tribal and ethnic tensions flared. But in the former, at least, efforts at a ceasefire and reconciliation between government and anti-government forces seemed to be bearing some fruit in late 1992. In Zaïre, efforts for greater democracy met with opposition from the long-ruling government, though it seemed that some progress on that front was being made.

PAGES 302-303, *note the following changes to text and map*:

1) CEC membership now includes Albania, and numbers 121.

2) The Single European Act, in effect from the beginning of 1993, applies to the western European countries which form the European Community (numbering 12, probably at least till 1995).

3) Countries 11 and 12 are now united as Germany.

4) Country 7 is now ten European countries (north to south, west to east): Estonia, Latvia, Lithuania, Belarussia, Ukraine, Russia, Moldova, Georgia, Armenia, Azerbaijan.

5) Country 26 is now five countries (northwest to southeast): Slovenia, Croatia, Bosnia-Herzegovina, Yugoslavia (= Serbia and Montenegro), Macedonia.

WEEK 44

New title of week: GERMANY
Page 304, new data:
    population: about 80 million
    language: German
    government: federal republic
    religion: Christians about 80 percent, about equally divided between Roman Catholics and Protestants (Lutherans, Reformed, United), plus small numbers of other traditions; Muslims 2-3 percent; very few Jews; notable minority of atheists, especially in former East Germany

Pages 304-305, replace text starting with the last sentence which begins on p. 304:

The division of Germany was formalized with the founding of two German states in the years after 1945 — the German Democratic Republic in the Soviet occupation zone and the Federal Republic of Germany in the US, UK and French occupation zones. That division persisted till October 1990. Then, a united Germany was formed with the incorporation of the GDR into the FRG.

During the latter part of 1989, pro-democracy demonstrations in the GDR gathered momentum — often with church support or encouragement — and a peaceful revolution ended communist rule. In November 1989, the Berlin Wall — a powerful symbol of the separation not only of the two Germanys, but also of two competing world systems — was opened for virtually unrestricted passage for the first time since it was built in 1961. Within a year it was almost completely torn down.

The union of the two German states has not been without difficulties, notably for the people of the former GDR. West Germany was one of the wealthiest countries in the world. East Germany was relatively less well off — though still quite wealthy compared with most of the world. In addition, its lifestyle was less hectic, and in some ways more secure, than that of the west.

Some in the east feel that their western compatriots look down on them or fail to appreciate what it was like to live for 40 years with GDR socialism. Some in the west judge those in the east as insufficiently hard-working and prone to unjustified nostalgia about some aspects of GDR life.

In the wake of German unification, church organizations have also reunited, notably the Evangelical Church in Germany (EKD), which federates 24 Lutheran, Reformed, and United *Landeskirchen* (regional church bodies).

During its two decades of separate existence, the Federation of Protestant Churches in the GDR formulated a theology of "critical solidarity" with the governing authorities, an effort to be "the church in socialism." It was able to offer a certain free space for the discontented, becoming in some respects an agent of radical change. When major change finally did come, church people played a significant role in seeing that it came relatively peacefully.

Both the EKD and the Roman Catholic Church in Germany, and related agencies, are heavily involved in social service and development work at home and overseas. The relatively large number of refugees and temporary workers in Germany is one notable area of domestic social concern.

Another is helping people cope — especially in the former GDR — with problems associated with the political and social changes of the last few years. These include rising unemployment, general social insecurity and unsavoury aspects of the communist era, such as cooperation by many — more or less closely or willingly — with the Stasi, the state agency which spied on GDR citizens.

Periodic great gatherings of tens of thousands of church people — the *Kirchentag* and *Katholikentag* — are an important feature of German church life, and have spawned or influenced similar gatherings in other countries.

Historically, the two principal forms of German Christianity — Roman Catholic and Protestant — have to some extent defined themselves over against the other. In the modern ecumenical era, that is rather less the case, notably on the official level, and in groups where Christians work ecumenically on social and political issues.

Both the Protestant and Catholic Churches in Germany are full members of the Federation of Christian Churches. With them as full or associate members of that federation are many smaller German church bodies — Baptist, Methodist, Moravian, Pentecostal, Old Catholic, Eastern Orthodox, Oriental Orthodox and others. These bodies can be vigorous, taking creative advantage of their historic distance from the state.

WEEK 50, *replace introductory paragraph on p. 335 with:*

On south-central Africa's western and eastern coasts respectively are Angola and Mozambique, part of the Portuguese colonial empire for nearly 500 years. After prolonged armed struggle, each became independent in 1975.

For several years, each was ruled by a single-party Marxist government. By the early 1990s, however, Marxism had disappeared in fact if not in name, and in common with many other countries in Africa the single-party systems were giving way to multi-party arrangements.

In Angola, a long civil war followed independence. In the south, the devastation from that conflict was exacerbated by incursions of South African forces, and also by drought.

Similarly, externally supported rebel forces wreaked havoc during the early years of Mozambican independence. However, an agreement signed in Rome in August 1992 between government and anti-government representatives offered some hope that the fear, uncertainty and destabilization associated with the conflict could be coming to an end. That would offer the country a chance to devote more attention and resources to many pressing economic and social problems.

WEEK 52

Page 348, replace the last four sentences with:
Namibia became independent on 21 March 1990. Since then, it has remained a multiracial democracy with an active opposition, a vigorous free press, and a national spirit of reconciliation. However, in the first post-independence years, the economy showed signs of weakness, and the worst drought in 30 years greatly affected the subsistence agriculture and grazing of cattle and sheep on which most Namibians depend.

Working together in the Council of Churches in Namibia, the various parts of the church have continued their pre-independence concerns with aspects of national development, and played a part in efforts to heal the wounds of the long war for independence.

In 1992, there were also signs that unity among Namibian Lutherans was making progress, after setbacks in previous years. (Lutherans are the largest grouping of Christians in Namibia, but have been divided on racial and other grounds.)

Pages 350-351, replace the paragraph crossing the page with:
With changes of leadership and policy in the white ruling party at the turn of the decade, there were signs that the goal of a non-racial, democratic South Africa could finally be at hand.

In the wake of government action to lift bans on political organizations, release political prisoners, allow exiles to return and rescind emergency regulations, representatives of the government and the African National Congress — the main organizational actor over the years in the struggle against apartheid — held talks in 1992 designed to lead to constitutional changes.

These talks had their ups and downs, but their general trajectory in the second half of 1992 seemed positive for those favoring non-racial democracy. Nevertheless, neither all blacks nor all whites supported those negotiating on their behalf; and political violence has reached horrendous proportions. While some of it can be attributed to political rivalry between supporters of the ANC and those of the Zulu-based Inkatha Freedom Party, there is considerable evidence pointing to complicity of the security forces in much of the violence. The white minority government of President F. W. de Klerk has failed to take action to stem the rising tide of violence, prompting accusations that sustained violence serves its political purposes.

*condition and in whatever condition. For that you have covered us,
preserved us, accepted us, had compassion on us, sustained us, and
brought us to this hour.*

Coptic Orthodox prayer of thanksgiving
which precedes all acts of worship

Today, give thanks

for the ordinary people of Egypt who remain cheerful in the face of
adversity, aspiring only to live a decent and reasonable life

for the lives of all the saints, known and unknown, from apostolic times
until now (for Copts the Book of the Acts of the Apostles does not
conclude with Amen, but continues in the lives of today's saints)

for the movement of renewal in the church; for classes and Sunday
schools; for the hospitality of monasteries and an expanding diakonia;

for the provision of Christian literature and cassettes and for the spiritual
enrichment they provide in the lives of the people

Today, share

with the church in Egypt its concern for work among uprooted country
people come to the cities, for a ministry to quarter of a million university
students, and for the work among the Zabbaleen living on and by means
of the rubbish dumps of Cairo

In my faith is comprised the love of the city and its inhabitants.

Sufi saying

*Lord, give us such a faith as will encompass cities the like of Cairo,
and loving prayers that will uphold and serve its 10 million people.*

Today, pray

for the bulk of Egypt's population cultivating the land of the Nile delta,
often for little reward

*We pray, Lord, for the rising of the water of the Nile this year. May
Christ, our Saviour, bless it and raise it, cheering the earth and
sustaining us, his creatures. And may the rising water remind us of the
Living Water freely given to all who repent and believe.*

From the Coptic Orthodox liturgy

for the Fellaheen and countless others who have left the countryside to
seek for labouring jobs in the cities and in surrounding countries;

separated from their families, doing hard work and often underpaid, the Christians among them are sustained by the presence of the Coptic Church or other Christian fellowship

Wherever there are two, they are not without God.
And where there is only one, I say I am with him.
Raise the stone and you will find me, cleave the wood, and there am I.

Recovered from the rubbish heap at Oxyrhynchus in Upper Egypt,
these words — claimed to be one of the promises of Jesus —
seem particularly applicable to Egypt's scattered manual workers

Accept, our Lord, from us — at this hour and all hours — our supplications; make our life easy; direct us to behave in accordance with your commandments. Sanctify our spirits; purify our bodies, straighten our thoughts; cleanse our desires; heal our sicknesses; forgive our sins; and save us from all evil, sorrow and heartache. Surround us by your holy angels that we may be kept in their camp, and guided so as to arrive at the unity of faith and the knowledge of your glory, imperceptible and boundless.

Seven times, each Egyptian day is punctuated by the Horlogion commemorating
the resurrection, the sentencing of Jesus and the coming of the Spirit,
the crucifixion, death, deposition and burial of Jesus,
each recollection concluding with the above prayer

God of grace and providence, Lord of our going out and of our coming in, we pray for Egypt, shelter of the Holy Family from the old tyranny of Herod and first resting place beyond the manger of the eternal glory. Bless her land and people, once entertaining unawares the earth's redeemer. Make the church in Egypt the patient means of thy purpose and ready custodian of the peace of Christ, ever left with his servants and ever passing through and from them to the saving of the world. We pray in his name. Amen.

Kenneth Cragg, sometime assistant bishop in Jerusalem

Israel and the Occupied Territories

Pray not for Arab or Jew,
for Palestinian or Israeli,
but pray rather for yourselves
that you may not divide them in your prayers,
but keep them both together in your hearts.

A Palestinian Christian

	Israel	*West Bank and Gaza*
Population:	4.3 million, including E. Jerusalem, Israeli residents in certain other areas under Israeli military occupation, and non-Jews in the Golan.	1.4 million.
Languages:	Hebrew, immigrant languages from all over the world.	Arabic.
Government:	Parliamentary state.	Under Israeli military administration.
Religion:	Jews 85%, Muslims 12%, Christians 3%.	Muslims 90%, Jews 5%, Christians 5%.

Something of the reality of this complex situation is apparent from these figures, but sensitivity and understanding are needed to appreciate the strength of feeling for this land, and the pain which is endured by many who live there. Each with an intense longing for the same particular land Israeli and Palestinian struggle for a secure national autonomy.

Since the 19th century the Zionist movement has been dedicated to the creation of a Jewish state and the physical return of Jews to Palestine. Given added impetus by the holocaust in Europe, and increasing immigration, both legal and illegal, of Jews into Palestine, the state of Israel came into being in 1948. The early years were marked by idealism; and in the task of developing the land and building a nation the life-style of the kubbutzim made a significant contribution. For some the current situation represents God's promises fulfilled through faith and hard work. Today, however, there are many in Israel who question the incursion into neighbouring territory, Jewish settlement on the West Bank, and the sub-human treatment of Arabs living under military administration.

Initially in 1948 some 750,000 Palestinian Arabs, by far the majority population, fled or were expelled; and the annexation by Israel of East Jerusalem, the West Bank and Gaza in 1967 produced a further wave of refugees. There are now about 2.5 million Palestinians scattered through the Middle East — many of them living in refugee camps — and rather fewer living in Israeli-occupied territory and Israel proper. Dispossessed, or suffering severe discrimination and harassment, these are the victims of the Jewish return. For them the situation represents a betrayal by the world community.

Of local Christians, concentrated in Galilee and the Occupied Territories, most are Arab; and fellowship between them and Hebrew converts is not easy. Palestinian Christians belong to a wide variety of religious communities, worshipping together Sunday by Sunday, running clinics and schools, and involving themselves in social service and reconciliation projects of one kind or another. Sometimes they are puzzled by the preoccupation of visiting tourists with holy places, and their seeming lack of interest in the living church. Always they are in need of encouragement and the assurance of understanding on the part of their fellow Christians. It is they who, at no small cost, maintain a Christian presence in the land in which Jesus lived.

Intercessions and Prayers

As Christians, especially do we pray for that land sanctified by Our Lord's footsteps, that it may become the crossroads of peace and fraternity.

Christian prayer for peace, Pope John Paul II, Assisi, 1986

We pray

that God will heal the pain of those who have suffered the loss of family or of land; that bitter hurt may be transformed into healing and love

for all those, Jew and Arab, who have the courage to meet together in the quest for understanding, reconciliation and peace

for Palestinian Christians who more easily than most can reproduce a pattern of life close to that of Jesus, and yet who find that today, it is his experience of rejection and homelessness, and of living in a land ruled by aliens, that is the hardest to bear

for all Jews in Israel, that sensitivity and goodwill may prevail in the affairs of their country; and for those in diaspora

for Muslims and Druze, with their belief in one God, and devotion to the land of their forbears

For all peoples, that thy light may shine upon them, that the spirit of justice and mutual forbearance may be established among them, the spirit of love and peace.
To Thee we cry, O Lord, hear and have mercy.

Melkite petition

Lord,
after all the talking; questioning; agonizing over your land,
grant that some compassionate breakthrough may occur. Amen.

O Lord Jesus,
stretch forth your wounded hands in blessing over your people,
to heal and to restore,
and to draw them to yourself and to one another in love. Amen.

Prayer from the Middle East

Jordan

Embracing the region traversed by our Lord in his journeys through Decapolis, the river bank where Jacob wrestled with the angel, the mountain from which Moses saw the Promised Land, the country of Ruth, and the range of hills which gave rise to the question "Is there no balm in Gilead?", the present-day nation of Jordan, being largely a Muslim nation, puts a rather different emphasis on its history. With a large influx of Palestinian refugees, very few economic resources of its own, and a geographical position which makes it both vulnerable and strategic, its preoccupation is the quest for peace in the Middle East. It is a quest shared by Muslims and Christians alike.

Population: 2.7 million (including Palestinians).

Languages: Arabic, English.

Government: Constitutional monarchy.

Religion: Muslims 93%, Christians 5%.

Amman has largely replaced Beirut as the business centre of the area, and much political initiative arises here. Christians enjoy freedom of worship, and the church has made a major contribution in education and other forms of service. The majority of local Christians are Greek Orthodox, but there are also sizeable Armenian, Latin, Greek Catholic and Anglican communities, and some small but thriving Protestant groups and churches. The Coptic Orthodox Church ministers to a large community of Egyptian labourers. Filipino, Sri Lankan and Indian workers, mainly engaged in domestic work or in hospitals, are connected with various churches.

In response to the question "Is there no balm in Gilead?" a number of signs can be instanced: parish priests quietly and humbly working among their people; a new camp-site for young people being constructed in those same Gilead hills; a vocational training school for the deaf, and a Mother Teresa home for the very deprived. In addition, other agencies run schools, clinics and centres of various kinds, both inside and outside the refugee camps.

Intercessions and Prayers

We pray

for political and church leaders, and all others who, often tired and discouraged, continue to work towards a solution to the Palestinian problem and peace in the region

for the people of Jordan — Bedouin herders, farmers, city-dwellers — outnumbered by their Palestinian neighbours

for Palestinians who continue to mourn the loss of home and land, that their sadness and unassuaged longing may find comfort and resolution

"The problem in so many parts of the world", says one who worked with Palestinian refugees, "is still threefold; first to comfort and relieve, then to inspire patience founded on hope, and thirdly to provide a happy issue out of affliction." A traditional prayer, much used locally, sums it all up in one sentence:

> *We commend to thy fatherly goodness all those who are in any ways afflicted or distressed in mind, body, or estate; that it may please thee to comfort and relieve them, according to their several necessities, giving them patience under their sufferings, and a happy issue out of all their afflictions...*
>
> Prayer Book of the Arab Evangelical Episcopal Church

We remember with gratitude the many signs of balm in Gilead, and *pray* that they may continue to bring healing and wholeness to those who are deeply wounded by the vicissitudes of life.

> *O God, send into the hearts of the people of Jordan and its neighbour-ing lands, the spirit of Jesus; and upon us all be peace. Amen.*

Lebanon

Linked in the Bible with images of glory, wealth and the sheltering cedar tree; later regarded as the commercial, financial and tourist centre of the Middle East; Lebanon today has a different kind of notoriety. Beirut, once the country's pride and joy, has been described as "one of the most violent capitals in the world"; and with 44 warring groups, about one out of every twenty people has been injured or wounded.

Population: Approximately 2.7 million (excluding Palestinian refugees in camps).

Languages: Arabic, Armenian, French, Kurdish and others.

Government: Parliamentary republic.

Religion: Muslims (Shiah and Sunni) and Druze: Christians (Catholic, Orthodox, Protestant); the present ratio widely held to be 60-40, the majority being Muslim.

Lebanon became independent in 1944. It is characterized by great religious and cultural diversity, and probably contains the closest juxtaposition of different communities within a small area of any country in the Middle East. When the republic was established in 1943, the various communities agreed on a system of power sharing based on their relative proportions in the population at that time. This system worked for many years. However the influx of Palestinians, and the higher rate of population increase in Muslim communities upset the ratio. Israeli reprisals for Palestinian resistance activity added to the tension, and civil war broke out in 1975.

The majority of Christians in Lebanon are Maronite Catholics. This church, tracing its roots to the early undivided church at Antioch, claims unbroken communion with Rome. Seeking refuge in the 9th century, Maronites settled in the mountains of Lebanon. There are many other Christian communities of whom the Greek Orthodox, Greek Catholic and Armenian Apostolic are the largest. Lebanon has become an important centre for the Armenian community.

Life today in war-torn Lebanon reflects the extraordinary capacity of the Lebanese to carry on living more or less normally in the midst of such a situation. "It is as though we live in a huge coal mine", says Frieda Haddad of the Greek Orthodox Diocese of Mount Lebanon, "which nevertheless hides in its depths a shining diamond." Some cannot see it like that, and have become disillusioned and despairing. On the other hand, one priest from Beirut observed that Christians in the city were asking as never before: "What is God saying to us in all this?"

Intercessions and Prayers

Let us join our prayers and presences to those of that great company of witnesses called upon in this invocation:

Come in peace, prophets of the Spirit, who have prophesied concerning our Redeemer.
Come in peace, chosen apostles, who have preached the good news of the Only-begotten.
Come in peace, martyrs, friends of the heavenly Bridegroom.
Come in peace, all you Saints, friends of the Son.
Offer to him your prayers for us, that he for whose sake you travailed may be compassionate to us at your intercession, O holy ones.

Maronite liturgy

Pray

for peace; and for a change of heart in all those who seem intent on keeping the conflict alive

that Lebanon may be spared unwelcome intervention from outside, and may be given peaceful initiatives from within

for all of whatever nationality who are held hostage, and for their desperately anxious families

for all families in Lebanon who have lost loved ones

Lord Christ, give me some of your Spirit to comfort the places in my heart where I hurt... Then give me some more of your Spirit, so that I can comfort other people.

Terry Waite

Pray also

for the life and work of the Middle East Council of Churches still going on in Beirut

for the Near East School of Theology, continuing to train men and women for Christian ministry for the young people of Lebanon "suffering most from despair, needing most to have grounds for hope"

for renewal in worship and family life; and that in this time of testing, the different communities may grow closer to each other

"At mid-day at the sixth hour, the hour of crucifixion, the praying church in the East lives each day anew this ultimate hour in which God's love for us was made fully manifest in the cross of Calvary." It is a rather special hour in Lebanon where every day involves a living out of the cross and resurrection.

Lord God, lover of peace and concord, look down with mercy upon Lebanon, that tormented country. Preserve its people and guide its rulers. Bless the peace-makers and those who love justice. May Lebanon become again in your loving purpose a place of unity in diversity, where men and women may learn to reverence life and humankind as your creation. Amen.

Syria

Population: 10.3 million.

Languages: Arabic; Kurdish, French, Armenian, Turkoman, Circassian, Aramaic and others are also spoken.

Government: Socialist republic.

Religion: Muslims 90%, Christians approx. 8%, Druze approx. 3%.

Modern Syria became independent in 1946 and the socialist republic was proclaimed in 1973. Syria is unique among Arab countries in that, despite the large majority of Muslims, it is a secular state. Historically Syria has links with Lebanon and has played an active part in attempting to secure some kind of cease-fire in that country. Internally, although the administration keeps a tight rein, medical and educational facilities, never before widely available, are now enjoyed by the whole population.

Ancient Syria covered a wider area and included Antioch where "the disciples were first called Christians" (Acts 11:26) and which became one of the great centres of the early church associated with St Peter and St Paul. Division occurred in 451 when the family of Oriental Orthodox churches (Armenian, Coptic and Syrian) separated. There are Armenian and Syrian Orthodox communities in Syria today and the Syrian Orthodox Church (see also week 49) has its see in Damascus. This church, which has suffered greatly through the centuries, has remained very close to the Jerusalem tradition of the ancient church. The ongoing (Greek) Orthodox Church of Antioch, whose membership is Arab and liturgical language Arabic, is now the largest Christian body. Catholics belong to six different rites. Most Protestants are members of either the National Evangelical Synod of Syria and Lebanon, or the Union of Armenian Evangelical Churches of the Near East. The churches are doing lively work in the field of Christian education.

Foreign missionaries were expelled in 1963 and Syrian nationals are not permitted to change their legal registration from Muslim to Christian. Syrian Christians, after the manner of St Paul, faithfully playing their part in the life of the local church, have been joined in recent years by others of diverse nationality and background, whose informal and joyful worship must surely delight the heart of the apostle.

Intercessions and Prayers

O glorious apostle Paul, who can describe your bondage and your tribulations in the cities? Who can tell the hardships and efforts you went through while preaching Christ in order to win all men and women and offer the church to Christ? O apostle Paul, founder of churches, pray that the church may be strengthened by you until the end of time.

From the Melkite liturgy

Christians in Syria give thanks
for a long and rich history

and pray
that it may be constantly maintained and passed on to their children, and that they may be ready, like their countryman Ananias, to welcome and embrace others

Today there are signs of new vitality in the Syrian church.

Thanks be to God

To me who am but black cold charcoal
grant, O Lord,
that by the fire of Pentecost,
I may be set ablaze

A prayer after St John of Damascus

In peace let us make our supplication to the Lord — Lord have mercy

For the peace that is from above, and the love of God, and the salvation of our souls, let us make our supplication to the Lord — Lord have mercy

For the peace of the whole world, and the unity of all the holy churches of God — Lord have mercy

For them that bear fruit and do good deeds in the holy churches of God, that remember the poor, the widows and the orphans, the strangers, and them that are in need; and for them that have desired of us to make mention of them in our prayers — Lord have mercy

For them that are in old age and infirmity, the sick and distressed, and them that are vexed in spirit, their speedy healing from God and salvation — Lord have mercy

For them that lead their lives in celibacy and asceticism, and in venerable marriage, and them that carry on their struggle in the caves and dens and holes of the earth, our holy fathers and brothers and sisters — Lord have mercy

For Christians that sail, that journey, that are strangers, and for our brothers and sisters that are in bonds and exiles, and imprisonment and bitter slavery, their peaceful return — Lord have mercy

For good temperature of the atmosphere, peaceful showers, pleasant dews, abundance of fruits, fullness of a good season, and for the crown of the year — Lord have mercy

And for every Christian soul in affliction and distress, and needing the mercy and succour of God, and for the conversion of the erring, the health of the sick, the rescue of the prisoners, the rest of them that have departed afore, our brothers and sisters — Lord have mercy

That our prayer may be heard and acceptable before God, and that his rich mercies and pities may be sent down upon us, let us make our supplications to the Lord — Lord have mercy

The divine liturgy of St James

Week 2

Countries of the Arabian Peninsula
Iran • Iraq

O God, I haven't recognized thee as thou ought to be recognized.

Prayer of Muhammad

The Arabian Peninsula

Tradition holds that the apostle Bartholomew first brought the gospel to Arabia; and scripture tells us (Acts 2:11) that Arabians were present at Pentecost. By whatever voice and means, Christianity certainly came to this area very early. A bishopric existed in Bahrain in the 3rd century, and by the 4th and 5th there were well-established Christian communities along the mainland coast. The spread of Islam in the 7th century virtually extinguished Christianity in the peninsula although a legend exists of a small group of Christians, who had survived a thousand years without a priest, greeting the chaplain of a 15th century Portuguese ship which called into Muscat. More recent evangelistic effort, both Roman Catholic and Protestant, began in the latter half of the 19th century, first in Aden (then under British rule) and shortly afterwards in the Gulf, with an emphasis on medical and educational work. Evangelism has never been permitted in Saudi Arabia. The presence of large numbers of immigrant workers, many of them Christians, means that there are probably more Christians in the Arabian Peninsula today than there have ever been.

Saudi Arabia (population 10.9 million) is the focal centre of Islam. The Prophet (570-632 AD) was born and died here. Each year over a million Muslims come from all over the world on the Hajj which every devout Muslim hopes to make at least once in his or her life-time. The strictly orthodox Wahhabi movement, dedicated to the reform of Islam, originated here, and indeed was the centre of the first Sa'udi kingdom. The present-day monarch is the religious head of the country, and custodian of the holy shrines. Islam is the only permitted religion. However, from 1970 onwards, hundreds of thousands of immigrant workers from many lands have entered the country, men and women, separated from their families; they work long hours and face an insecure future. Meetings for worship are not officially permitted, and clergy are not allowed into the country, but groups meet informally for Bible study and prayer. The groups are constituted largely on a language basis, confessional differences becoming insignificant in this situation. "I'm Catholic really," said a recent resident, "but that was a long time ago. We've been to Saudi Arabia since then. Now we're just Christians."

Since the discovery of oil, *the Gulf States* (Kuwait, Bahrain, Qatar, United Arab Emirates, and Oman) have developed rapidly. Employment possibilities have brought large numbers of workers, especially Middle Eastern Arabs, Indians and Pakistanis, as well as Europeans and Americans. In Qatar and UAE the immigrant work force far outnumbers the local population. It is the Christians among these expatriates who largely constitute the church in the Gulf, although there are a few local Christians in some areas. A wide range of confessional churches is represented: Orthodox, Catholic, Mar Thoma, Anglican, and various Protestant bodies; but in many instances congregations are ecumenical. Here, where local people observe Indian and Pakistani congregations meeting regularly and faithfully, Christianity is seen as an Asian religion. The freedom, or otherwise, of the church to worship openly varies in the different states. In some there are church buildings, in some not; and everywhere house groups are important. In general open evangelism is not permitted, although in some areas the church is allowed to run schools, clinics and hospitals. Throughout the Gulf a ministry is exercised through Family Bookshops.

In the south-west corner of the peninsula is the *Yemen Arab Republic* (North Yemen), the ancient biblical kingdom of Sheba. A relatively high rainfall and fertile soil mean good agricultural potential, but a large part of the work force is in oil-rich countries sending home much needed money. The country has suffered civil war and intermittent warfare with neighbouring South Yemen. Since the country's Jewish residents emigrated to Israel, the local population (9.3 million) has been 100% Muslim. At the invitation of the government a number of Roman Catholic and Protestant bodies are assisting in clinics and hospitals, and Mother

Teresa's Sisters of Charity have opened homes for the aged and helpless. Proselytization is not allowed.

The *Peoples' Democratic Republic of Yemen* (South Yemen) is a single-party Marxist state in which 99.5% of the population (2.3 million) are Muslim. There are tiny Hindu and Christian minorities. In 1973 all missionaries were expelled except one Catholic priest who remained to minister to the foreign community. Since then "he has presided over the church in Aden, maintaining a place for Christian worship, and a large heart to welcome Christians of any background".

The YAR/PDRY Yemen council, established in 1981 and scheduled to meet every six months, is working towards the reunification of Yemen.

Intercessions and Prayers

Give thanks to God

for a Christian presence on the soil of this peninsula; and for all acts of mercy undertaken in the spirit of Jesus

that just as myrrh (traditionally believed to have come from Salalah in Oman) was offered at Christ's epiphany, so the gifts and devotions of contemporary dwellers in the region are being offered to Christ

> *O God, who by a star guided the wise men to the worship of your Son; we pray you to lead to yourself the wise and the great of every land, that unto you every knee may bow, and every thought be brought into captivity; through Jesus Christ our Lord.*
>
> Epiphany collect from the Church of South India, adapted

Call upon God

for all migrant workers in the Gulf and other parts of the Middle East

for Christian house groups, composed of many nationalities and allegiances, seeking to "sing the Lord's song in a strange land"

that Christians of the land may be encouraged and renewed

for today's "apostles" to the Arabian peninsula — visiting bishops, itinerant pastors and other enablers — who provide much-needed links with otherwise isolated congregations

> How often it happens that special destiny is given not to the great and complacent majorities, but to the little bands of people who never

succeed so well as to be able to forget the Source of their strength and life.

Christians in the Arab East, Robert Brendon Betts

For all such we pray

We pray, O Father, for the land that nurtured the prophet Mohammed and for the people who follow his path. Guard them from the temptations of affluence; lead them into the ways of peace; and help them to see the fullness of your revelation in Jesus the Lord.

Iran

Population: 48.2 million.

The Christian witness in Iran has been unbroken since the 3rd century, carried on mainly through the Assyrian Church of the East. At the turn of the 16th-17th centuries, Shah Abbas the Great invited Armenian craftsmen to beautify his capital city (Isfahan), thus introducing an Armenian community together with the Armenian church. Two-thirds of the Christians of contemporary Iran belong to these two ancient churches. Roman Catholic missionary orders came in the time of Shah Abbas, and again in the 19th century — along with Protestants and Anglicans.

Zoroastrianism came to birth in Iran in approximately the 6th century BC, later becoming the state religion and a symbol of national and cultural identity. There is still a Zoroastrian minority. The Bahai faith also originated here. Bahais have been persecuted almost since the faith began, particularly so under the present regime.

Iran, formerly Persia, and with a long history of civilization, has experienced tragic turmoil in recent years. Since the Islamic fundamentalist revolution of 1979, many Iranians have left. "There is hardly a major city in the West in which there are not a great number of Iranian wanderers in search of a second home." In addition, the costly war with Iraq means that most families have lost a male relative. News of the church trickles out. Traditional missionary work is no longer possible, Christians are allowed to worship but sometimes meet with difficulties, and clergy cannot travel freely. "Priests these days are a very rare commodity. If one is found anywhere, even of a different denomination, demand on his time is enormous — very much like a medical doctor appearing in a place where they have had no doctor for a long time —

patients won't leave him alone — like our Lord himself who sometimes could not get away from the crowds..."

Intercessions and Prayers

God protect this country from foe, famine and falsehood.

2,000 year-old Persian prayer

Give thanks

that in the long history of Iran to the present time, there have always been men and women of faith, integrity and courage ready to withstand both foe and falsehood even at the cost of their own lives

for the faithful life and worship of the ancient churches of Iran

> *Thou who didst spread thy creating arms to the stars, strengthen our arms with power to intercede when we lift up our hands unto thee.*

Armenian liturgy

We intercede

for the leaders of Iran and Iraq, that in the name of One who is most compassionate they may take steps to end the bitter conflict between them

> *O God, thou hast not endowed conscience with material force to compel from human beings a reluctant obedience. So grant them inwardly a spiritual compulsion, in which they will follow it out of choice and delight... O God, guide thy servants who have gone almost irretrievably astray. Thou are the Hearer and the Answerer.*

City of Wrong, Kamil Hussein

for all who are victims of repression

for the church in Iran: "Our condition is very much like the condition of Peter," writes a group of Irani Christians, "when, with his eyes on Christ, he was able to walk on the water, but at other times would sink to the depths crying 'Lord, save me'."

> *The cross of our Lord protect those who belong to Jesus*
> *and strengthen your hearts in faith to Christ*
> *in hardship and in ease, in life and in death,*
> *now and for ever.*

Blessing given by Simon, a Bishop of Iran,
at the time of his martyrdom in 339 AD

Iraq

Traditionally the Garden of Eden, certainly one of the oldest civilizations in the world, laid waste by the Mongols in 1256, and thereafter under some kind of foreign domination until achieving independence in 1932, Iraq is currently a country at war. Since 1980 bitter conflict with Iran has drained the nation, and drastically reduced oil exports, a potential source of wealth. Predominantly Arab, but with Kurdish and other minorities, this socialist republic allows religious freedom. Islam is the state religion and about 95% of the population of 14.2 million are Muslims.

Jewish communities in Mesopotamia were evangelized in the 1st century, traditionally by St Thomas; and the church was later strengthened by the work of Assyrian missions. Islam increased in importance in the 7th century but the church continued. In 1552, in consequence of an internal split, a large segment of the Assyrian Church became linked with Rome, and this Chaldean Catholic Church is today by far the largest Christian community in Iraq. There are other ancient churches of Mesopotamian origin. Roman Catholic missions date from the Crusades, and sustained Protestant work from this century.

Today's Christians number about half a million. Their participation as Iraqi nationals in the war effort has brought them greater acceptability, and they contribute in all areas of society.

Litany for Iraq

For lasting peace in this war-torn land — From you, O Lord

For wisdom and compassion for all in authority — From you, O Lord

For comfort for families separated or bereaved — From you, O Lord

For the release of captives — From you, O Lord

For refreshment for the weary and healing for the sick — From you, O Lord

For continuing faithfulness of the ancient churches of this land — From you, O Lord

For tenacity of spirit for small Christian groups — From you, O Lord

For the mutual enrichment and support of those of different Christian traditions — From you, O Lord

You, Lord of all, we confess;
You, Lord Jesus, we glorify;
For you are the life of our bodies
And you are the Saviour of our souls.

> The response in the litany and this hymn both come from the Chaldean liturgy.
> The ancient hymn celebrates Christ the source of resurrection
> in all situations of death and deprivation.

O Lord, we beseech you grant your blessing and guidance to all who are seeking to bring peace to the Middle East; stir the conscience of the nations, and break the bonds of covetousness and pride; make plain your way of deliverance, through Jesus Christ our Lord. Amen.

Week 3

Cyprus • Greece • Turkey

Lord, who through a vision to your servant John on Patmos revealed yourself amidst the seven churches of Asia, encouraging, reproving and challenging those first Christian communities; continue to walk, we beseech you, to this same end, amidst today's churches in Cyprus, Greece and Turkey; and grant that we all may be heedful of your presence and obedient to your commands. Amen.

Cyprus

The island is currently divided into Greek and Turkish sectors, with a United Nations peace-keeping force present. The British continue to maintain military bases on the island.

Population: Approximately 666,000 of whom 80% are Greek Cypriots and 19% Turkish Cypriots. Britons, Armenians, and others account for the rest.

Languages: Greek, Turkish, English, Armenian, Arabic and others.

Government: Republic.

Religion: Christians 80%, Muslims 18.5%.

Greek colonies were established in Cyprus in the 2nd millenium BC. Since then the island has had a troubled history, being occupied and ruled in turn by Romans, Byzantines, Arabs, Franks, Venetians, Ottomans and the British. The people won their independence in 1960 after a five-year guerilla war conducted by Greek Cypriots. Since independence there has been tension between the two Cypriot communities, and in 1963 the Turkish Cypriots ceased to participate in government. Following a coup inspired by the Greek military junta, the armed forces of Turkey occupied the northern sector in 1974; 200,000 Greek Cypriots and 55,000 Turkish Cypriots were displaced from their homes and the economy was devastated. A de facto partition has existed since then. In a unilateral declaration of independence, the Turkish Republic of Northern Cyprus was declared in 1983. Only Turkey has recognized this government.

Founded by the apostles Paul and Barnabas, the Eastern Orthodox Church of Cyprus to which 96% of Christians on the island belong, has been officially recognized as autocephalous since the 5th century. Since Ottoman rule the archbishop has had considerable political significance as head of the nation. For ordinary people religion centres on home and family as well as liturgical and sacramental life, and local priests are close to their people. Family life here, as throughout the region, is a source of great stability. The fate of the refugees from the north constitutes a major concern of the church. The Armenian Apostolic Church has been represented here since the 11th century, and the Maronite Church since the Crusades. There are a number of small Protestant groups. Roman Catholics and Anglicans are mostly expatriate.

Cyprus today has become something of a meeting place for the Middle East. Numerous Christian organizations have opened headquarters here, and it provides a venue for regional meetings, as well as a haven for rest and refreshment. The tourist industry is considerable, bringing prosperity but also social problems. Arabic Christian literature is printed and stored here for distribution in neighbouring countries.

Intercessions and Prayers

We pray

for the restoration of the freedom and independence of Cyprus and for the peaceful unity of all the people of the island

that Cyprus will be a meeting place for many, and that the peace of God may flow out to other troubled lands

> *O God of peace, good beyond all that is good, in whom is calmness and concord: Do thou make up the dissensions which divide us from one another, and bring us into unity of love in thee; through Jesus Christ our Lord.*
>
> Liturgy of St Dionysius

In spite of the impression that the Middle East gives to the West of great instability, of being just about to break out into some great conflagration, underneath there is a great deal of stability, and many forces that pull together.

A bishop in Cyprus

We give thanks

for religion; for home and family life; for traditional values and all else that unites and stabilizes in the life of the people of Cyprus

for the haven this island provides for those of many nationalities

We identify

with Orthodox Christians of Cyprus in giving thanks for St Barnabas:

> *O Barnabas, who art equal unto the angels (1), thy godly and blameless soul (2) dwelleth in the Jerusalem which is above (3), and thy body that bore much torment hath Cyprus for its earthly resting place, the which thou didst bring unto the faith. Thy spirit joyeth on high with the angels before the throne of the invisible God (4), delighting in the sweet vision of his unassailable glory, thyself made godlike (5) in a union with the consubstantial Trinity: and below thy precious relics (6) spring forth health and cure (7); and thy shrine is called "the place of healing", for as such hath it long endured through the often working of thy power. Wherefore, being united with us invisibly at this present time, watch over us in God from the heavenly height; and forasmuch as thou art tender-hearted, keep from us all wrath that is laid upon us for our sins; shield us from the crafts of the devil, and entreat that peace be upon us and great mercy (8).*

(1) Luke 20:36; (2) 1 Thess. 5:23; (3) Gal 4:26; (4) Rev. 14:5; Col. 1:15; (5) 2 Pet. 1:4; Ps. 82:6; John 10:34; (6) cf. 2 Kings 13:21; (7) Jer. 33:6; (8) cf. Gal. 6:16

From the service to St Barnabas the Apostle, founder of the Church of Cyprus; the work of Hilarion, Archbishop of Cyprus 1624-1682

Greece

Population: 10 million of whom 95% are ethnic Greeks; Turks are the largest indigenous minority.

Language: Greek.

Government: Parliamentary republic.

Religion: Christians 98% of whom the vast majority are Greek Orthodox, Muslims 1.5%, a very small Jewish community.

St Paul's obedience to his vision of the Macedonian urging him to "Come over...and help us" (Acts 16:9,10) marks the beginning of

Christianity in this land. Then part of the Roman Empire, later under Ottoman rule for nearly 400 years, Greece fought in the 19th century for independence. The church took an active part in the struggle, and after liberation declared independence from the Ecumenical Patriarchate of Constantinople which was still under Ottoman rule. Autocephaly was officially recognized in 1850. In recent years, following German occupation, the country has suffered civil war and a period of rule by military juntas before the present parliamentary democracy became established in 1974.

The Greek Orthodox Church is the established religion of Greece, and has a profound influence in the nation. Monastic communities have played an important part in the spiritual life of the people, particularly the communities of Mount Athos which, in Byzantine times, was a great centre of theological learning. The twenty monasteries, which remain under the jurisdiction of the Ecumenical Patriarchate, form a self-governing unit within the country.

The Catholic Church is represented by three different rites of whom the Latins (the most numerous) have been here since the Crusades. The main Protestant body is the Greek Evangelical Church. Jehovah's Witnesses entered the country in 1900 and now have a relatively large following. There are strict rules about proselytization.

Apostolic Service, the church's organization for home missions, together with other movements, is active in evangelistic and educational work, and there are important theological faculties in Athens and Thessaloniki.

Intercessions and Prayers

Kyrie eleison — Lord, have mercy

In the English language "mercy" has a rather limited and constricting meaning. In Orthodox use however, and according to its meaning in modern Greek, it has none of this narrowness, but conveys the sense of every good thing that God wills for creation.

For the land and people of Greece — Kyrie eleison

For the authorities in church and state — Kyrie eleison

For monastic communities, and especially those for women, which are growing today — Kyrie eleison

For theologians and priests of the future, studying in theological schools and faculties — Kyrie eleison

For all Orthodox parishes, priests and people — Kyrie eleison

For the activities of organizations and groups devoted to strengthening and deepening the spiritual life of the church — Kyrie eleison

For the bond established by Greek Orthodox young people with their counterparts in North America, Western Europe and the Middle East — Kyrie eleison

For the small Helleniké Evangeliké Ekklesia; its lay participation, and its Sunday School and youth movement — Kyrie eleison

Lord Jesus Christ,
Son of the living God,
have mercy on me,
a sinner.

> The constant rhythmic use of this prayer to Jesus originated in Sinai, but from the 10th century onwards it has been practised mainly at Mount Athos

Grant, O God, that the Christians of the Orthodox Church who preserved for the world the Jesus Prayer, may themselves live by that mercy and enjoy its fruits.

Turkey

Population: 50.7 million, of whom 80% are ethnic Turks. There are a number of other groups and some 600,000 Iranian refugees.

Language: Turkish.

Government: Republic.

Religion: Muslims 99%, Christians less than 0.5%.

Present-day Turkey incorporates the territory of much of Paul's missionary journeys and the Seven Churches of Revelation. The early ecumenical councils and the first serious divisions of the church took place in this region. Constantinople (Istanbul), capital of the Byzantine empire, was for many centuries one of the greatest centres of Christianity and from here missionary work extended in many directions. Muslim invasions and the establishment of the Ottoman empire greatly reduced the number of Christians, but at the beginning of the first world war the population was still 20% Christian. The massacres and deportations of Armenians and Chaldeans, a massive exodus of survivors, and the forced exchange of Greek Orthodox Christians from Anatolia for Turkish Muslims from Greece have drastically reduced the Christian presence.

The Republic of Turkey was established in 1923, and a programme of modernization begun. In spite of the large Muslim majority it became a secular state. Incidents of social disorder resulted in much loss of life, and periods of military rule have been repressive. Democratic government was re-established in 1983, but the military still hold considerable power.

The principal centres of Christianity today are Istanbul and the southeastern part of the country, although there are scattered and isolated Christians in other areas, often without church or priest. Numerically the largest church family is the Oriental Orthodox — Armenian in Istanbul, and Syrian in the south-east. Of great significance is the Ecumenical Patriarchate of Constantinople which holds the highest honour for Eastern Orthodox Christians and was one of the first participants in the ecumenical movement. There are Catholic communities of five different rites, and the United Church Board for World Ministries (USA) is involved in educational and medical work.

Intercessions and Prayers

We give thanks

for the continued presence of the Christian church in Turkey, small as it now is

for the ways in which individual Christians and Christian-inspired organizations can be of stimulus and service to the community

We pray

for all depleted and fearful Christian communities, and for courage and integrity for individual Christians

> *Our thoughts rest for a few moments with them, and we pray that your love and compassion may sustain them always.*

Week of Prayer for World Peace

for relationships between Christians and Muslims in Turkey

For our Muslim brethren who repeat your name of grace, in their fasting, their praying and their almsgiving with faith and piety. Receive their worship and cause the light of your Holy Spirit to shine upon them and illumine in their hearts the way of love and redemption and peace,
To you we cry, O Lord.
Hear and have mercy.

Petition: Melkite rite

To God be glory;
To the angels honour;
To Satan confusion;
To the cross reverence;
To the church exaltation;
To the departed quickening;
To the penitent acceptance;
To the sick and infirm recovery and healing;
And to the four quarters of the world great peace and tranquillity;
And on us who are weak and sinful may the compassion and mercies of our God come, and may they overshadow us continually. Amen.

A prayer from the old Syriac,
used by Christians in Turkey, Iran, and South India

Week 4

Algeria • Libya • Morocco • Tunisia

Lord of the lovers of humankind,
who for your sake broke the alabaster box of life:
quicken your church today with the ardour of the saints,
so that by prayer and scholarship
by discipline and sacrifice,
your name may be made truly known.

Collect for Raymond Lull of Tunis:
Calendar of Middle East Saints

Once one of the most significant centres of Christianity in the Roman Empire, North Africa was the home of such early saints and scholars as Cyprian, Tertullian and Augustine. The Mediterranean coastal plain of this region has been invaded and settled by Phoenicians, Romans, Vandals, Byzantines, Arabs and Europeans successively, some of whom integrated the local population into their way of life. Many of the indigenous Berbers, however, remained nomadic pastoralists, carrying out frequent raids from the mountains and the desert beyond.

Christianity persisted on into the 6th century, but had begun to decline well before the Muslim invasion. Later Christian work, from the 13th century onwards, has produced a number of martyrs, notably Raymond Lull (a lay Franciscan) and some of the early White Fathers. The White Fathers and the White Sisters were organized in Algeria in the 19th century to carry on missionary work throughout Africa.

Charles de Foucauld, whose dramatic conversion was prompted by his experience of observing Muslims at prayer, lived a hermit life among the Tuaregs. Protestant work dates from the 19th century. Radio programmes and Bible correspondence courses operated from outside the area are features of contemporary evangelistic effort.

Algeria

Population: 20.5 million of whom about 1.7 million are migrants in Europe.

Languages: Arabic, French, Berber.

Government: Single-party socialist republic.

Religion: Muslims 99.5%, Christians 0.3%.

Attached to France for just over a century, Algeria gained independence in 1962 after an 8-year war which left the country drained. However in recent years it has experienced rapid industrialization and economic expansion. With few exceptions the Algerian people are Muslims.

The church is mainly composed of former French colonialists who stayed on, and Europeans and other expatriates working or living in the country, some of whom have taken Algerian nationality. The majority are Roman Catholics. Three Protestant bodies — the North Africa Mission (interdenominational), the Methodist Church of the USA, and the Reformed Church — joined together in 1973 to form the Protestant Church in Algeria. There is also an Orthodox community. Although the Christian churches have no legal status and proselytization is forbidden, Muslim-Christian relationships are good, and there is freedom to worship. Service to the community is a major emphasis of all the churches.

Following the death in 1916 of Charles de Foucauld in Tamantasset deep in the Algerian desert, others have continued to go to the Sahara to be a Christian presence similar to his. A more organized attempt to follow in his footsteps led to the founding in 1933 of the Little Sisters and Brothers of Jesus, who retain a link with Algeria and the Sahara but now locate their "desert" wherever the poorest, most helpless and underprivileged of this earth are to be found.

Libya

Population: 3.7 million.

Languages: Arabic; English and Italian are also spoken.

Government: Single-party socialist republic.

Religion: Muslims 98%, Christians 2%.

Formerly an Italian colony, Libya was the scene of bitter fighting in the second world war and was subsequently administered by France and Britain until 1951 when it became independent. Islam, the state religion, is regarded also as an ideological alternative to capitalism or communism, and thus has added significance for Libyan nationals.

The Christian church is almost entirely expatriate. A major confessional body is the Coptic Orthodox Church of Egypt. There are also Catholics (Eastern rite) and Orthodox from Greece and the Middle East, Presbyterians from Korea, and Roman Catholics, Anglicans and other Protestants from various countries. Missionaries were not permitted entry after the 1969 revolution but in more recent years some Roman Catholic nursing sisters have been invited in. The very few local Christians are nurtured by informal means. Communication between expatriates and local people on matters of religion is difficult.

Morocco

Population: 20.5 million, including 164,000 inhabitants of Western Sahara.

Languages: Arabic, Berber, French, Spanish.

Government: Modified constitutional monarchy.

Religion: Muslims 99%. There are about 60,000 Christians and half that number of Jews.

After being divided into French and Spanish protectorates for nearly half a century, Morocco became independent in 1956. Islamization, among the Berbers also, has been profound in this area. Islam is the state religion. The exercise of monotheistic religions is guaranteed by the constitution. The fact that Christian leaders supported the move towards independence has created considerable goodwill towards the churches. All over the country Christian churches enjoy hospitality and respect which are traditional values in Morocco. A number of church-related and other Christian humanitarian organizations are working in areas of social service, health care and development, and thus contribute in solidarity and mutual respect to the country's most urgent needs. The Moroccan Council of Christian Churches incorporates the Roman Catholic, Greek and Russian Orthodox, and Anglican churches and the Evangelical (Reformed) Church of Morocco.

The disputed territory of *Western Sahara* (formerly Spanish Sahara) was ceded to Morocco (and Mauritania) in 1976. The claim of the

Sahrawi Arab Democratic Republic for the territory is recognized by a number of countries. The proposal has been made for a referendum, and has to be worked out with the assistance of the United Nations.

Tunisia

Population: 7.3 million.

Languages: Arabic, Berber, French.

Government: Republic.

Religion: Muslims 99.5%. There are small Christian and Jewish minorities.

Formerly a French protectorate, Tunisia became independent in 1956. In spite of relative political stability, unemployment and a high rate of population increase have led to hardship, and there have been times of civil unrest. The people are renowned for their hospitality and the government for moderation in foreign relations.

The church today is small and almost entirely expatriate. Most Christians are Roman Catholics, but there are also Greek and Russian Orthodox churches, and a number of very small Protestant congregations. Missionaries are not allowed in the country, but the government shows tolerance to foreign religious minorities.

Intercessions and Prayers

Lord, let me offer you in sacrifice the service of my thoughts and my tongue, but first give me what I may offer you.

St Augustine of Hippo, born 354 at Tagaste in North Africa,
died 430 in Hippo

Another day of sand and prayer. I tried to remember some of the 99 names of God handed down to us by the tradition of Islam. And I wondered whether the 99 names revealed God or hid him. Perhaps they do both.

I recall some names I particularly like. God the Merciful, the Compassionate, the Peaceful, the Faithful, the Tolerant. But the one I like best is God the Patient.

Nevertheless, none of these names struck me as apposite in my situation in the desert. I felt that yet another name had to be added to the list: God the Difficult. In the desert I was always wrestling with a difficult God.

Abu Hurayra affirms that whoever knows these 99 beautiful names of God will enter heaven. But I am inclined to believe that the one who knows the hundredth name of God is more likely to get there first. After all, the road that leads to heaven is narrow and difficult.

Meditations on the Sand, Alessandro Pronzato

We give thanks

for the North African saints and scholars and hermits of the early centuries — Augustine and Monnica, Tertullian and Cyprian — whose experience was also of a difficult and demanding God

for missionaries such as Raymond Lull, Archbishop Lavigerie and the White Fathers and Sisters, Charles de Foucauld and all who have followed them; some in martyrdom, and others by patient presence in the deserts and towns of North Africa

for all small Christian congregations in North Africa today who continue to bear these countries on their hearts and in their intercessions

My brother, bridge the Christian centuries and touch us now.
Least calm of all the saints,
your white-hot African blood
not stilled by your conversion to the faith.

Ranging among Algerian hills you tasted all
our depth of self-despair
before you reached in middle-life
the calm of sin forgiven.

We need your strength in our slow decadence to understand
re-birth through pain and hope
and on this Gadarene hillside
the sovereignty of God.

A prayer in honour of St Augustine of Hippo

We pray

for wisdom, integrity and compassion for the rulers of these lands

for local Christians, often isolated, some able to meet in small groups; that they may be faithful in the circumstances in which they are set

for Christian expatriates of all nationalities in these different countries, and for the churches to which they belong for a Christian-inspired consortium in Tunisia offering personnel for community service and development projects

Almighty God, whose Son our Saviour Jesus Christ taught us that to serve the least of his brethren is to serve him; we give you thanks that Simon from Africa was there to help Jesus our Lord to carry his cross, and we beseech you to grant us compassion like his and a ready willingness to serve the weak and helpless as though we were serving Jesus.

Collect for Simon of Cyrene; Calendar for Middle East Saints

for the church's ministry through orphanages and homes for people with disabilities, the poor and the destitute

that the churches may mirror the proverbial hospitality of these lands, and may reach out to those who are lost and lonely

for the dialogue between Christian and Muslim being promoted in Tunis, and for all informal contact and conversation between Muslims and Christians

"Islam... takes God with awful seriousness," writes Dr Hendrik Kraemer. "Whoever has listened with his inmost being to the passionate call that vibrates through those well-known sentences: Allahu Akhbar (God is Great) and La Sharika Lahu (He has no associates), knows that Islam has religious tones of elemental power and quality. The apprehension of the naked majesty of God in Islam is simply unsurpassed..."

Almighty God, grant that we may listen with deep attention to those awesome words from the minarets of the Muslim world, and listening, hopefully gain a hearing for those other resonances of your divine nature embodied in the life and death and resurrection of Jesus Christ. Amen.

As the needle naturally turns to the north when it is touched by the magnet, so it is fitting, O Lord, that your servant should turn to love and praise and serve you; seeing that out of love to him you were willing to endure such grievous pangs and sufferings.

Prayer to Jesus by Raymond Lull, stoned,
Bugia, Algeria, 30 June 1315

Give, O God, peace and harmony to the Islamic nations of North Africa. Strengthen in faith and witness the Christian minorities that live and work among them. And hasten the time when your Son may again be known in these ancient lands as Lord and Saviour.

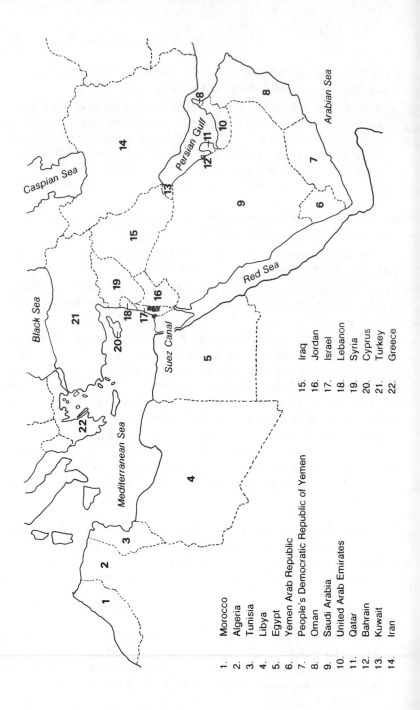

1. Morocco
2. Algeria
3. Tunisia
4. Libya
5. Egypt
6. Yemen Arab Republic
7. People's Democratic Republic of Yemen
8. Oman
9. Saudi Arabia
10. United Arab Emirates
11. Qatar
12. Bahrain
13. Kuwait
14. Iran

15. Iraq
16. Jordan
17. Israel
18. Lebanon
19. Syria
20. Cyprus
21. Turkey
22. Greece

Middle East Council of Churches (MECC)

The 12 million or so Christians in the region are today the heirs of rich Christian traditions, which by remaining indigenous to the areas where Christianity began, link the world church historically with its origins.

David Kerr, quoted in *MECC Perspectives*

A further link with this rich Christian tradition was established in 1974 when, on the inception of the Middle East Council of Churches, member churches of an earlier ecumenical body were joined by Oriental and Byzantine churches. Thus, with the inclusion also of the Church of Cyprus, and churches from Iran, the council ceased to be a forum only for the Arab churches, and began to reflect some of the richness and diversity of the whole Middle East. Its geographical area now stretches from Iran to Morocco and from Turkey to the Gulf. With its main office still in Beirut, but with regional offices in Egypt, Cyprus and Bahrain, the MECC represents about 75% of the Christians of the region.

Over the years the principal concern of the MECC has been the continuity of Christian presence in this area, with renewal, the quest for Christian unity, and the pursuit of justice and peace as integral parts of that concern. Its programme units and its related organizations concerned with theological education, with the study and observation of Middle East Christianity, and with the production and sale of literature, all stem from this same concern. A more wide-ranging brief is to facilitate the link between the world church and its origins through visits and prayer. "The solidarity we are seeking between our churches and churches everywhere", declares Gabriel Habib, MECC general secretary, "must mainly be manifested through prayer, with full awareness of the suffering and joy of the members of Christ's body, the church, to which we all belong..."

God bless the countries of the Middle East
Guard their children
Guide their leaders
Grant them peace with justice
for Jesus Christ's sake. Amen.

Week 5

Hong Kong • Macao
People's Republic of China • Taiwan

(The listing and description of the Peoples' Republic of China and Taiwan in this way are done for the sake of convenience acknowledging the present reality. This in no way reflects any policy of the WCC on issues related to China.)

Hong Kong

Christ
Look upon us in this city
and keep our sympathy and pity fresh
and our faces heavenward
lest we grow hard.

These words of Thomas Ashe provide the inspiration
for St Thomas' Clinic, Hong Kong

With a population of 5.5 million the British Crown Colony of Hong Kong has one of the highest population densities in the world, swollen even more by waves of refugees. It comprises Hong Kong island, and Kowloon Peninsula and the New Territories on the mainland. Chinese and English are the official languages, but Cantonese is widely spoken. The majority of people are Buddhists. Christians number about 8% of whom just over half are Roman Catholics. There are many Protestant denominations. Christianity came to Hong Kong mainly from China, and acted as the social conscience, promoting educational and social services of every kind. Such work continues today on a scale unique in Asia.

In recent years Hong Kong has gone through a period of uncertainty and anxiety during which China and Britain negotiated the future of the territory. An agreement providing for the reversion of Hong Kong's sovereignty to China and turning it into a highly autonomous Special

Administrative Region of the People's Republic in 1997, was officially signed in December 1984 by the Chinese and British governments. The church fully supports this and is playing an active part in the drafting of the Basic Law and encouraging a new political awareness among the people. A source of comfort and encouragement, it looks for a spirituality to match its involvement in society. Searching for an authentic Chinese Christian identity some recall the earlier use of Chinese thought-forms, symbols and practices. Others define their identity in much more contemporary Western terms and are actively commited to the use of the media as a stimulus to faith and a means of sharing it with others. Hong Kong has been described as "a place of baffling contradictions — anxiety and hope, insecurity and indomitable courage".

Intercessions and Prayers

Heavenly Parent, as the miry bottom of the pond helps the lotus flower to grow, so may our often unlovely environment encourage growth in us. And as the lotus blossom in all its radiance rises above the mire, so help us to transcend our earthly environment to become heavenly personalities worthy to be called your children. Amen.

Prayer of a Chinese Christian

Give thanks

for the Sino-British Agreement about the future of Hong Kong

for the church's obedience to God's calling to be a servant people, especially during recent uncertainties

for the gifts of the Spirit constantly at work in the lives and affairs of Chinese people

Pray

for the many refugees whose future continues to be uncertain

for those who work towards a new and suitable government structure in Hong Kong, and for the emerging political leadership for those who work among the mass of the population especially in the field of civic education

> *Pray for us, brothers and sisters in Christ,*
> *that we may not fail in the oil of comfort,*
> *the wine of justice, the involvement of the patient mule,*
> *and the generosity which, having given, promises more,*
> *until recovery is complete.*

A plea from Hong Kong

> *O God our Father,*
> *We thank you for the daily bread. We thank you for the providence which has sustained this restless city where millions have found their home. The restlessnesss has sapped our strength, and often times tempted our eyes towards the vulgarity of life. But we thank you for the hard-earned daily bread which sustains our bodies and our pride.*
>
> *On the verge of rejoining China's mainstream destiny we come to you with trembling hope and fearful joy.*
>
> *Lord of the churches, make us one. Help us love one another as you have loved us, so that all may come to know we are yours.*
>
> *Lord of history, make us strong. Help us live this day as if it is tomorrow, so that the past no longer binds the future.*
>
> *May your will be done in this city. May you be pleased with this land and this people on which to build a concrete token of your kingdom.*
>
> *In Jesus' name. Amen.*

Raymond Fung, Hong Kong

Macau

Population: Approximately 0.5 million (of whom 2-3,000 are Portuguese).

Languages: Portuguese, Cantonese, English, Burmese.

Government: Special territory under Portuguese jurisdiction.

Religion: Buddhists 66%, Christians 15% (mostly Roman-Catholics, but with a small Protestant, mainly Baptist, community).

Lying opposite Hong Kong, and comprising a small hilly peninsula on the mainland and three nearby islands, Macau was established by the Portuguese as a trading post with China in 1557. It was used as a stepping stone for missionaries entering China; notably the Jesuits, and later (1807) the Presbyterian Robert Morrison who here had his vision of "millions who shall believe".

In 1976 Macau's status as an overseas province of Portugal was redefined, and in 1999 the territory is due to be transferred to the Peoples' Republic of China. In recent years the population has been greatly swollen by refugees. Gambling, dog-racing and the Macau Grand Prix are tourist attractions, facing the church with all the opportunities and problems innate to such a situation. From an early date the Roman Catholic Church has played a major role in education. The churches remain active in education and social work, but numbers — certainly in the Protestant community — are steadily diminishing. Commenting on the return of the territory to China in 1999, and the consequent loss of government subsidies, the Roman Catholic bishop has declared that the church must become "more a church of the poor".

Give thanks to God

for Macau's long association with the Christian faith

Pray

for the encouragement and renewal of the church

> *God the Father*
> *the voice of John the Baptist challenges us to repentance*
> *and points the way to Christ the Lord.*
> *Open our ears to his message, and free our hearts*
> *to turn from our sins and receive the life of the gospel.*
> *We ask this through Christ our Lord.*
>
> Mass, Feast of St John the Baptist, Patron Saint of Macau, Roman Missal

People's Republic of China

Population: 1 billion.

Languages: Putonghua, various local dialects, and languages of minority groups.

Government: Socialist republic.

Religion: Traditional religions and philosophies of China are Buddhism,

Confucianism and Taoism. Today many are atheists. There are significant Muslim and Christian communities.

Chinese civilization and culture has a continuous history of over 5,000 years. The last of the dynasties was overthrown and a republic established in 1911. Following a traumatic period of international and civil wars Communist forces took over in 1949 and the People's Republic was proclaimed.

Christianity entered China with the Nestorians in the 7th century, but disappeared after about 200 years. At the time of the Mongol occupation it appeared again temporarily, but it was not until sea routes were discovered in the 16th century that the Roman Catholic Church began to take root in China. The first Protestants arrived early in the 19th century when a considerable missionary impact followed the expansion of Western commercial and political interests.

With the establishment of the People's Republic churches and institutions receiving foreign funds were registered at a government bureau, all foreign missionaries left or were expelled, and the Three-Self Movement (self-government, self-support, self-propagation) began to take root. The Cultural Revolution (1966-76) led to the closure of all churches and theological colleges, and Christians as well as others suffered greatly. The church — like the grain of wheat — went underground.

Now new fruits are appearing. The government has adopted a policy of religious liberalization. The emerging church has developed an independence and discovered a sense of selfhood hitherto unknown. The Catholic Church continues to function apart from Rome. Among Protestants, united in the China Christian Council, denominational labels have ceased to be relevant. Local churches, while using a variety of liturgies, regard themselves as post-denominational churches. Structure and form, and pattern of ministry have yet to emerge, but the churches rejoice in using a new common hymnal. Church buildings are reopening. Many have been closed or used for other purposes for as long as thirty years; and the task of restoration, compensation and negotiating their re-use demands much patience. The rebuilding of relationships, and more particularly the working out of the church's relationship within the world Christian community requires much sensitivity.

The Three-Self Movement provides a framework for Christians to participate with the government in the task of nation-building. "Christians need to care for the welfare of the people of the whole world...," says Bishop K.H. Ting, "it means for us caring for China, not exclusively but

as our point of departure, the first stage in our love for humankind." In this period of rebuilding after the trauma of the Cultural Revolution, reconciliation and forgiveness, and selfless service to others are dominant themes. "Although dynamic and growing," says Emilio Castro following a visit, "the Christian church today in China is a small island in a sea of one billion people — but a joyful island."

Intercessions and Prayers

We reverently worship
  the mysterious Person, God the Father;
  the responding Person, God the Son;
  the witnessing Person, the Spirit of Holiness.
We worship the Holy Trinity
Three persons in one.

Ancient Chinese ascription, used in worship by the Nestorian Church

Let us rejoice with present-day Chinese Christians
in their recovery of freedom to worship and to speak openly of their faith
that the historical experience of the churches in China has brought to Christians a wider experience of God's presence and activity
in their opportunities to participate in the tasks of reconciliation and rebuilding in nation and neighbourhood

Reconciliation is a theme that can speak to the mind and heart of the Chinese people. And reconciliation, we think, is *the* permanent theme of Christian theology.

Bishop K.H. Ting, Chairman of the China Christian Council
and the Three Self National Committee

Help each one of us, gracious God,
to live in such magnanimity and restraint
that the Head of the church
may never have cause to say of us:
This is my body, broken by you.

Prayer from China

Let us pray with Chinese Christians
at the local level
meeting for worship; some in church buildings, and many in homes and other meeting places

for all believers bearing witness to Christ in the places where they live and work

for the pastoral care and Christian nurture of growing congregations, and the faithful work of a largely elderly ministry

and more widely

for the work of the China Christian Council and the Chinese Protestant Three-Self Movement

for the theological training programmes in Nanjing, Shanghai, Beijing, Hangzhou and Fuzhou; for men and women in training, and for the establishment of an appropriate form of ministry

for efforts to relate theology to life, and to make the Christian gospel understandable and acceptable in the New China

for the Amity Foundation for the promotion of education, health and social work

> *O God, teach us to be understanding friends*
> *to our fellow Christians in China,*
> *that endeavouring to sit where they sit*
> *and to kneel where they kneel*
> *we may share their vision and their hope.*

> *God, creator of heaven and earth and giver of human life, we thank you for the witness to your truth, your goodness and your beauty which the long history of China has borne. We thank you for the church in China which is bearing witness to Christ in ways beyond our hopes. Strengthen ties that bind Christians together beyond national boundaries. Help us to accept the idea that all local churches are part of your church universal and are witnessing on its behalf and with its blessing. To the glory of Jesus Christ in whom all riches abide. Amen.*

A contemporary prayer from China

Following the foundation of the People's Republic, and in response to what they describe as "secular revolutionary goodness", Chinese lay Christians have been challenged to re-examine their understanding of Christ and their expression of the Christian faith in China. Turning to St John and the epistles to the Ephesians, Colossians and Hebrews they affirm the pre-existent, risen, ascended, upholding and sustaining Christ "who liberates and enables us":

> *Now may the God of peace who brought again from the dead our Lord Jesus, the great shepherd of the sheep, by the blood of the eternal covenant; equip you with everything good that you may do his will, working in you that which is pleasing in his sight, through Jesus Christ; to whom be glory for ever and ever. Amen.*
>
> Hebrews 13:20-21

Taiwan

Population: 19.3 million.

Languages: Mandarin, Hoklo, Hakka, various tribal languages.

Government: Republic.

Religion: Chinese religions and philosophies are widely practised. Christians 5% (Protestants — of whom the majority are Presbyterians — 3.6%, Roman Catholics 1.4%), Muslims 0.5%.

Comprising one large and several smaller islands off the coast of the Chinese mainland, Taiwan is the second most densely populated country in the world. The original inhabitants — less than half a million — are considerably outnumbered by Hoklo and Hakka-speaking people who arrived from south-east China over the last four centuries. In 1949 Taiwan became the refuge of the Nationalist Chinese government bringing in over 2 million Mandarin-speaking mainlanders. This Kuomintang regime has continued to dominate the local population ever since.

Roman Catholic priests arrived in Taiwan from South China in 1859. The Presbyterian church, established in the 1860s, is mainly a church of the original inhabitants and therefore of the rural areas and small towns. The years 1945-60 saw the arrival of other Protestant churches, and considerable growth in the Chinese church in the citites. More recently there has been both a resurgence of Chinese religions, and a growing secularism, but the work of the Protestant churches has continued to grow in the rural and mountain areas in spite of an acute shortage of pastors. The Presbyterian Church in particular has come into conflict with the government on major issues concerning human rights. Long prison sentences have been imposed on pastors and laypeople, whose courage and faithfulness must rank among the most challenging and inspiring of this century (see *Testimonies of Faith: Letters and Poems from Prison in Taiwan*).

Intercessions and Prayers

If the Lord is in prison with me,
what do I fear?
Lonely and solitary though I am,
  I believe
  I praise
  I give thanks.

If the Lord is in prison with me,
why do I grieve?
The Lord knows my trouble and pain,
to him I entrust my heart and my all,
  I believe
  I rejoice
  I sing.

Hsu T'ien Hsien

Praise God

for the witness of the Presbyterian Church in Taiwan in the struggle for freedom and justice for the people

Pray

that the peoples' desire for their integrity, and for democracy in their state may be recognized

for the many who work under bad labour conditions

for aboriginal children lured into prostitution, and for all who strive for its prevention

that in the midst of much materialism the church may continue to speak to the deep needs of the people of Taiwan

Gracious God,
let your will for Taiwan be known,
Hakka, Mainlander, Taiwanese, Tribal...
Let all be partners in shaping the future
with a faith that quarrels with the present
for the sake of what yet might be.

Prayer from Taiwan

The biblical prayer most frequently used by leaders of the Presbyterian Church in Taiwan on behalf of their president, his government and the whole people of Taiwan is that found in Micah 6:8

You have shown us, O God, what is good.
Enable us, we pray,
  to act justly,
  to love mercy,
  and to walk humbly with you. Amen.

Week 6

Democratic People's Republic of Korea
Japan • Republic of Korea

If I had not suffered,
I would not have known the love of God.

If many people had not suffered,
God's love would not have been passed on.

If Jesus had not suffered,
God's love would not have been made visible.

Mizuno Genzo, Japan

Japan

In history books Japan is an ancient country whose traditions reach back into the mists of mythology. Yet few countries belong so actively to the here-and-now of the modern world. In this hyper-active, industrialized, technological country 90% of the population regard themselves as middle-class, a situation unique in Asia. Since mountains account for about 85% of the total land area of which only 17% is arable, most people live in the cities.

Population: 120.3 million.

Language: Japanese.

Government: Parliamentary democracy, with constitutionally limited monarchy.

Religion: Buddhism, Shintoism and Confucianism are the traditional religions and philosophies, and are often practised together. Many syncretistic "new religions" have sprung up in recent years. Less than 1% of the population is Christian.

Christianity was first brought to Japan in 1549 by Francis Xavier. At first the church grew rapidly, but later was outlawed, and hundreds of Christians were martyred. In spite of persecution the church survived in secret through more than two centuries of isolation (see Shusaku Endo's historical novel *Silence*) until Japan became open to foreign trade in the mid-19th century, and a process of modernization began. Many Catholic and Protestant missionaries entered the country. In 1861 Nicholas Kassathin, later canonized, established the Orthodox Church in Japan. In 1887 the Nippon Sei Ko Kai (Anglican Church) was formed by the uniting of three separate Episcopalian missions. The church again suffered during the second world war and was required to conform to the militaristic regime. In order to fulfill the requirements for recognition many Protestant groups joined together in 1941 to form the Nippon Kirisuto Kyodan (United Church of Christ in Japan).

At the end of the second world war the religious laws were abolished, and a number of bodies withdrew from the Kyodan which, however, remains the largest of the Protestant churches and seeks to work out its life and witness in the ecumenical context. Nearly half of Japan's Christians are Roman Catholic. Significant, albeit small in numbers (5,000), the Korean Christian Church in Japan ministers to the descendants of Koreans forcibly brought to Japan during the annexation of Korea between 1910-45.

In addition to many social issues the Christian churches as well as other groups are concerned about the discriminatory practice of fingerprinting foreign residents, including the 800,000 Koreans who were born in Japan. The NCC of Japan has led a campaign against it. "As a Catholic I feel that fingerprints are given by God," says Kim Myong Shik. "They are beautiful. It is to defy the will of God to use them for purposes which are violent... This is the message and the prayer addressed by Jesus to me: this is why I personally refuse to be fingerprinted."

Confession of responsibility during the second world war is deeply felt by Japanese Christians and is embodied in a resolution, seeking the forgiveness of God and of all people, adopted by the Kyodan. "Indeed, even as our country committed sin, so we too as a church fell into the same sin. We neglected to perform our mission as a 'watchman'." The importance given to the Yasukuni Shrine — a Shinto war memorial symbolic of Japan's pre-war militarism — has long been protested by Christians. Seen by many as a sign of increasing militaristic patriotism, it is interpreted as a threat to peace. Peace and the need for international cooperation are deeply felt concerns.

*"I will write peace on your wings,
and you will fly all over the world."*

Praying for peace for all victims of war as she folded paper cranes, these words were composed by Sadako Sasaki, child victim of atomic radiation in Hiroshima.

They serve as a continuing stimulus to prayer for peace.

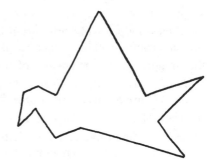

Intercessions and Prayers

Starting the new day with a Japanese Christian

Try to read into this prayer some of the circumstances you know to apply to members of the Japanese Christian community who may use it. Nearly all of them start their new day and do their work in artificial light in the midst of city smog. Ask, therefore, what kind of renewal and freshness they seek from God; what kind of work they do (there is a high level of employment in Japan); what form of captivity it is that holds them, and what kind of justice and freedom they seek.

*Eternal God
We say good morning to you
Hallowed be your name.
Early in the morning, before we begin our work
we praise your glory.
Renew our bodies as fresh as the morning flowers.
Open our inner eyes, as the sun casts new light upon the darkness
which prevailed over the night.
Deliver us from all captivity.
Give us wings of freedom like the birds in the sky,
to begin a new journey.
Restore justice and freedom, as a mighty stream
running continuously as day follows day.
We thank you for the gift of this morning,
and a new day to work with you.*

Masao Takenaka, Japan

We remember

the witness for peace of Christians in Japan and the anxiety felt at signs of official endorsement of all that Yasukuni Shrine symbolizes

the struggle against the practice of finger-printing aliens

> *Lord, touch with your fingers those who are so demeaned,*
> *and restore to them their proper dignity.*

the work of Christian education in Japan

those with disability, and especially the hibakusha who continue to survive and to suffer from atomic bomb exposure

the continuing presence of the cross of Christ in the lives of Japanese people

> *O God, we do not protest even if our life is destined to lead to the*
> *cross, or if the way leads to our losing our lives. Teach us how to*
> *dispense with unnecessary things.*

Toyohiko Kagawa

"Those who would pray for the Christian church in Japan might do worse than start with the yellow pages in the telephone directory," writes a recent visitor. "Some towns list as many as 150 different churches and religious groups. Just where would a potential enquirer make a start?"

> *Lord, bless the work of the National Christian Council of Churches in*
> *Japan, the Bible Society, all uniting and community churches, the*
> *Japanese Overseas Christian Medical Service, and all who in their*
> *work for unity seek to make sense of the prayer of Jesus that they all*
> *may be one. Amen.*

Lord, make us one as You are One.

Korea

The people of the Korean peninsula have a distinctive history and culture extending over 4,000 years. Formerly an independent kingdom, Korea was annexed by Japan early in this century, and remained under Japanese colonial rule until the end of the second world war when it was divided at the 38th parallel into military occupation zones with Soviet forces in the North and US forces in the South. North Koreans entered the South in 1950; and the ensuing 3-year war hardened attitudes and generated fear and suspicion. Today the Democratic People's Republic of

Korea (North) and the Republic of Korea (South) are divided by an impenetrable barrier of reinforced concrete across which until recently there has been virtually no communication.

Even though there had been several contacts with Christianity, the first missionary work was done in the 18th century by Koreans themselves, who in the course of official visits to China came into contact with Roman Catholic priests and Christian literature. In the 19th century Christians were persecuted by the government and many gave their lives. The country was closed to foreigners. Following a treaty with the USA the first Protestant missionary arrived in 1884. Others followed and the church grew. During the Japanese occupation the church again came under pressure. Imbued with the love of God Christians continued to witness to Jesus Christ and many joined the great company of Korean martyrs.

O God,
you have made us glad
by those Koreans who,
by dying for you,
received a crown of glory.
Grant that through their example
our resolve may be strengthened
and our faith in you deepened.

Thanksgiving for Korean martyrs,
observed in Korea 20 or 26 September

Democratic People's Republic of Korea

Population: 20.4 million.

Language: Korean.

Government: Unitary single-party republic.

Religion: Buddhism, Confucianism, Taoism, Shamanism and Chundo Kyo (a syncretistic religion peculiar to Korea) are the traditional religions and philosophies. The number of Christians is unknown, but is estimated at about 10,000.

The constitution speaks of "religious liberty" but also of "liberty of anti-religious propaganda", and it seems likely that all religion is discouraged in this communist country. Many Christians fled to the South during the 1950-53 war, and there has been little contact with those in the North since. The indications are that they are continuing to meet in house churches. "Christians in North Korea have been worshipping in the privacy of homes for over 30 years," writes Erich Weingärtner. "It has become a way of Christian life and witness. To forsake the intimacy of this experience in favour of a showcase edifice would be to forsake what links them to the early church of New Testament times."

What, then, shall we pray for them — unless we pray that prayer which has always stood Christians in good stead?

Our Father
Hallowed be your name, in Korea;
your kingdom come, in Korea;
your will be done, in Korea;
Give them today their daily bread, in Korea.
Deliver them from evil, in Korea.
For the kingdom, the power and the glory are yours, in Korea,
now and for ever, Amen.

Republic of Korea

Population: 41.1 million.

Language: Korean.

Government: Republic, with power centred in the executive.

Religion: Buddhists 20%; Christians 21% of whom 80% are Protestants. Confucianism and Chundo Kyo are also prevalent.

Since the bitter war of 1950-53 South Korea has developed a flourishing capitalist economy, but a wide gap remains between rich and poor. In the face of what is felt to be a constant threat of invasion from the North, the government has been strongly autocratic, and a sizeable American military presence remains. Christians opposing the government's oppressive policies have been dealt with harshly, but changes have occurred and greater moderation has been shown recently. There continues to be considerable political ferment and student unrest. On the other hand, the church in the cities continues to flourish and grow, with congregations numbering thousands. A number of Christians belonging to these congregations serve in parliament and in the armed forces, and also take an active part in evangelism. In recent years alongside a phenomenal growth of the Protestant community with a strong emphasis on Korean initiative, there have also been major splits in most of the large denominations and a proliferation of Christian groups.

Intercessions and Prayers

"On Sunday morning in Seoul the number of Christians going in cars to their different churches is liable to cause a traffic jam."

We give thanks O God, for the rapid growth of the church in Korea. We pray that zeal may be tempered with sensitivity and that numerical growth may be accompanied by spiritual deepening. May the divided Christian communities in Korea become one in faith and purpose, that they may grow into a credible sign of that unity in love promised by Jesus to his followers.

We must not forget that today there are many people who cannot come to the big evangelistic meetings. I mean those workers who are labouring hard with beads of sweat; those young boys and girls who are continually running, like rats; those sick people who are living in the wood-and-tarpaper shacks and wondering how to get their next meal; those who are struggling to live with polluted air and water in rural and fishing villages; and those who are poor, enviously watching the luxurious life of the cats and dogs of the rich, despite the fact that they themselves were born as human beings.

Rev. Park Hyung Kyu, written shortly before one of his arrests

O Christ, whose loving eyes see those we so often fail to see, bless these your needy children in Korea.

North and South are both interested in reunification, albeit each on its own terms. Contact at government level has been sporadic and fraught with difficulties. Significantly a meeting was negotiated recently between Christians from both sides who, in spite of ideological differences, were able to celebrate the Lord's supper together, and to reaffirm the role Christians in their two countries should play in breaking down barriers.

"The story is told of an ageing South Korean pastor, who, on his death, donated his eyes to a young person needing sight. He wished his eyes to be able to see the reunification of his homeland."

Lord, with Korean Christians, we pray for the unification of their land, and the creation of a new, just and peaceful future. Amen.

Lord,
thanks to you
the dividing wall of the temple is no longer a problem for us,
but the separating walls which we continue to build
most certainly are.
So Lord,
whether we are in Berlin, Soweto,
Belfast or on the 38th parallel,
or a member of an ordinary Christian congregation somewhere,
putting up all the barriers common to human communities
the world over,
show us how we may begin instead to take them down. Amen.

Lord, break down the walls that separate us
and unite us in a single body.

Chorus of the theme song;
Fifth Assembly of the WCC, Nairobi

Week 7

The Philippines

*United through grace with all the members of your universal church,
we offer you, Lord, our being, our working, our thinking, our feeling,
our desiring; so that by these we may serve your greater glory.*

Offering of the day: a prayer used in the Philippines

Made up of over 7,000 islands, many of them uninhabitable, the
Philippine Republic is the only predominantly Christian country in Asia.
Two-thirds of the population live on the islands of Luzon and Mindanao.
The economy is mixed agricultural and industrial. There are extensive US
military bases.

Population: 55 million.

Languages: Filipino, English, Spanish and many local languages.

Government: Presidential republic.

Religion: Christians 95% (Roman Catholics 80.6%, Protestants 14%;
there are 140 different denominations and sects). Muslims 4.3%, mostly
in the south, and dating from the 14th century.

The Philippine Republic is "a young nation made up of old peoples"
who lived in a large number of independent groups in the islands for
something like 25,000 years before the advent of the Spanish in 1565.
Some then retreated to the mountains and remain today as minority tribes.
Revolution in 1896 resulted in freedom from Spain, but the country then
found itself under United States rule. It was occupied by the Japanese
from 1942-45. Independence was gained in 1946.

Under the Spaniards, political and ecclesiastical domination went
together, and within a hundred years the Spanish missionary orders had
established the only Christian nation in Asia. Protestant missions became
active round about the turn of this century, and several of them formed the
Evangelical Union to avoid duplication of work. Meanwhile a desire for

reform and nationalization within the Roman Catholic Church led to the formation of the Iglesia Filipina Independiente (Philippine Independent Church). A number of Protestant indigenous groups grew up, of which the Iglesia Ni Cristo is the fastest growing. In this century the history of the church has been one of schism, union and proliferation. The Council of Churches in the Philippines (NCCP) was formed in 1963, offering new possibilities for unity and cooperation.

Since independence the Filipino people have continued to experience exploitation, with large areas of peasant land appropriated by the government for "development" by large multinational companies, from which the poor do not benefit. In the mountains tribal minorities, both Christian and Muslim, have suffered steady encroachment of their lands. Resistance to domination of various kinds has been a continuing thread of Philippine history, and the churches are much involved in the struggle for justice and peace. Under the Marcos regime many people, including church leaders, were harassed and imprisoned. There are now a variety of people's organizations working for social change; and many facets of the women's movement, coordinated by GABRIELA, are strong.

In 1986 what began as an electoral exercise designed to shore up the sagging credibility of the martial law regime quickly became a democratic movement which resulted in a change of government, thus giving the people a new hope and a greater sense of unity. Much however remains to be done if a genuine democracy is to be realized. Land reform remains a crucial issue. In the words of Dr Edicio de la Torre: "The first half of the Magnificat has been fulfilled, and the mighty put down from their seats; but the lowly are not yet exalted." In this situation the church has an important role to fulfill. Dr Feliciano Cariño, general secretary of the NCCP, writes of a new political incarnation "requiring a renewed church that will be a companion in the making of a new society... living a spirituality of justice and freedom, rooted among the poor..."

Intercessions and Prayers

In company with the church in the Philippines

we offer thanks for
all those who proclaim and work for the betterment of the whole person
signs of awakening in the church
the hope in Jesus Christ which sustains Filipino Christians

We pray

that God's presence may continue to be felt in this changing period of Philippine history

that in days of economic stringency those who live in plenty may share with those who are without

for the struggle of women in the Philippines against sex tourism

for courage as Christians continue to involve themselves in the struggle for justice, peace, truth and freedom

> *As you annointed kings and called prophets of old, lead us to recognize our true representatives and authentic leaders: men and women*
> > *who love your people and can walk with them*
> > *who feel their pain and share their joys,*
> > *who dream their dreams*
> > *and strive to accompany them to their common goal.*
>
> *In your fire — with your spirit —*
> > *embolden and commission us*
> > *to transform our political system,*
> > *to serve your people*
> > *and to bring real glory to your name. Amen.*

Prayer from the Philippines

We pray that we may be truly sensitive to the poverty and oppression around us, of the marginalized of our society — the poor peasants, the poor estate and city workers, shanty-dwellers, unemployed youth, exploited women and children, depressed classes, ethnic minorities; of those repressed, imprisoned and put to death in the struggle for democratic and human rights — Lord hear us.

We call on you to succour them and to show us how we may participate in their struggle for justice, as co-workers together with Jesus, the servant Lord — Lord hear us.

We pray for true spiritual resources necessary for these tasks. We pray for a true awareness of the corruptible forces and influences in our society and in ourselves, and for trust in your grace and strength in building a new spirituality for our times — Lord hear us. Amen.

Prayers for Asia Sunday; the Christian Conference
of Asia, of which many Philippine churches are members

Often heavily laden with grains, sometimes bent over and broken, and so common a sight as to go almost unnoticed, the
stalk of rice in the Philippines stands symbol for burden and struggle, and for all that
satisfies and sustains. It symbolizes the
potential richness of the land, which, because of maldistribution and the profitabil-
ity of international trade, fails to reach the
hands of the very poor who continue to
struggle.

Prayer for the people of the Philippines under the symbol of growing rice.

In every country in the world local Christians take what are often very
well-known words, and praying them in their own particular situation
invest those words with new meaning for themselves and others. Such is
the familiar affirmation used at every eucharist throughout the Philippines, said with special intention for their country and its people, and in
which we are invited to join.

Your death, O Lord, we commemorate — Amen.
Your glory as our Risen Lord, we now celebrate — Amen.
Your return, as Lord in glory, together we await — Amen.

Acclamation as used by Filipino members
of Cursillos in Christianity

Week 8

Brunei • Malaysia • Singapore

May the peaceful nature of multi-racialism in our lands grow into a Christ-like family; we ask in the name of Jesus, the Elder Brother.

Prayer of a Malaysian Christian

The population of these nations is multi-racial and multifaith. Muslims form the largest religious group overall, but are outnumbered by Buddhists and Taoists in Singapore. There are appreciable Christian and Hindu communities. The indigenous people are Malays who are almost all Muslim, and other tribal races in Sarawak and Sabah (formerly North Borneo). Chinese from south-east China have migrated to the area over the centuries, and are usually Buddhists or adherents of Chinese folk religion (syncretistic), although a considerable number are Christian. There are significant Indian (mostly Hindu) and Pakistani (Muslim) communities — also Eurasian and European groups. The latter, as well as some Indians and Pakistanis, are Christians.

Christianity was brought to the region by colonialists: the Portuguese in the 16th century and the Dutch in the 17th. Areas were later annexed piece-meal by the British, and the East India Company appointed chaplains in Malaya and Singapore. Other Protestant churches were introduced, initially ministering to European congregations, but later working also among the Chinese. Methodism came from the United States and Britain, and is now the largest Protestant church in Malaysia and Singapore.

Brunei

The Sultanate of Brunei is a traditional Islamic monarchy. Formerly it consisted of most of the coastal region of the island of North Borneo, but in the 19th century its rulers ceded large areas to the United Kingdom. In 1888 it became a British protected state, and was invaded by the Japanese during the second world war. The Sultan decided not to join the Malaysian Federation in 1963, and Brunei attained internal self-government in 1971 and full independence in 1984.

The majority of the population of 200,000 are Muslim Malays, and Islam is the official religion. Other indigenous races are mostly animist. The second largest group are the Chinese and there are some Indians and Europeans. Malay and English are official languages. The Christian church is small and confined to the Chinese and expatriate population. Evangelism is not permitted but existing churches are allowed freedom of worship.

Malaysia

The Federation of Malaysia consists of 13 states, 11 on the Malayan peninsula (West Malaysia) and two, Sarawak and Sabah (East Malaysia), on the north coast of Borneo. All have a colonial history. The 11 peninsular states united under British protection, becoming the Federation of Malaya in 1948, and achieving independence in 1957. The Federation of Malaysia came into being in 1963.

The population of 14.5 million is multi-racial and proportions vary in different areas. In West Malaysia approximately 55% are Malays who are all Muslims, and about 34% Chinese. The remainder are Indians (9%), Pakistanis, Eurasians and Europeans. In Sarawak and Sabah other indigenous races and Chinese predominate over the Malays. The country received many refugees from Indo-China, especially Vietnam, some of whom have been resettled elsewhere. The official language is Malay, but others are widely spoken.

With such a racial and religious mix it is not surprising that there have been tensions and even riots in the past; nor that today, although tolerance and accommodation prevail, life is influenced by political and communal decisions made along racial lines. Terrorist activity by communist insurgents was a problem in the later 1970s and is still perceived as a potential threat.

As in some other parts of the world, a revival of Islamic fundamentalism has challenged the government to be more overtly Islamic in its policies. As a result an interfaith organization representing Buddhists, Christians, Hindus and Sikhs, and the Christian Federation of Malaysia (made up of Roman Catholic and evangelical churches as well as the Council of Churches of Malaysia) have emerged as watchdogs to protect the rights of minority religions. Islam is the state religion and evangelism among Muslims is not permitted. In West Malaysia Christians number about 7%, with three and four times that in Sabah and Sarawak where there has been considerable outreach among the tribal peoples. The church is increasingly aware of its moral responsibility to address issues like racial polarization and the disparity between rich and poor. Individual churches are steadily growing, but ecumenical activity is hampered by the use of so many different languages.

Singapore

The Republic of Singapore, with its mixed population of 2.5 million, has one of the highest per capita incomes in Asia. Natural resources are limited and the country relies on imports, but it is a thriving centre of international trade. In the colonial era it was linked with Malaya, and became part of the Federation of Malaysia in 1963, but separated two years later to become a fully independent country. It has enjoyed considerable political stability. Chinese (Mandarin), English, Malay and Tamil are official languages.

About one quarter of the population is Buddhist, and another quarter practise Chinese folk religions. There are appreciable Muslim, Christian and Hindu minorities, and some who profess no religion at all. Christians number about 12% of whom nearly half are Roman Catholics.

In this highly entrepreneurial society the pressure to succeed pushes some to breaking point. With every third person under 15, schools are overflowing and competition is keen. The social cost of high-rise, high-density living is making itself felt and there are many who live in poverty. The churches, which pioneered social action in Singapore, continue to develop new ways of responding to changing social needs.

Here, at the heart of South East Asia, is a vigorously growing church which has risen from 2 to 12% of the population in the last twenty years. Since 1972 it has been experiencing a renewal of its life and ministry. Trinity Theological College trains men and women of different denominations for ministry throughout the region in multicultural societies.

According to the Christian Conference of Asia, Christians of this region are being called to act upon their prayer and to speak courageous words and perform courageous deeds in all places where there is injustice and oppression, and the pressure of materialism. It is for doing precisely this that the CCA was asked to leave Singapore.

Intercessions and Prayers

O God of many names
Lover of all nations
We pray for peace
    in our hearts
    in our homes
    in our nation
    in our world
the peace of your will
the peace of our need.

Week of Prayer for World Peace

We identify with Christians in Malaysia in seeking to build a church in which all races may feel at home — *Lord, turn our thought into a blessing.*

We warm to the apostolic style of ministry exercised among tribal people in Sabah, and respond to their request to "give thanks to God for the Christian joy that is never exhausted, even when living through troubled times and dealing with difficult people" — *Lord, turn our thought into a blessing.*

We put ourselves in the shoes of the very small church in Brunei and are thankful that it can still minister to expatriate Christians — *Lord, turn our thought into a blessing.*

We sit with Singaporean Christians to hear afresh the story of Jesus' synagogue sermon; to rejoice where charismatic gifts have been truly experienced; and to pray with them for a spirit of questioning, disquiet and boldness at all that falls short of being good news for the poor, the needy, the prisoner and the oppressed — *Lord, turn our thought into a blessing.*

We remember men and women being trained for the ministry in the region and visualize the different situations in which they will serve — *Lord, turn our thought into a blessing.*

We think of young people under such heavy pressure to succeed and, with many of them crowding into various Christian fellowships, offering enormous potential for Christian discipleship — *Lord, turn our thought into a blessing.*

Just call me by my name is the prayer of many young people in today's Singapore and Malaysia:

1. A-lone   I   am   yet not   a-lone.   There're peo-ple all a-round.
2. To count the crowds that fill the streets sta-tis-tics are the measure;
3. A- way   from grave and name-less rut   a man for oth-ers came;

I bear a name,   yet I have none.   I'm   lost, can I   be
I am a tag   with-out a name,   a   chest wit h-out its
up-on the lives of us he put   a   price, a soul, a

found?
trea - sure. Just call me by my name. Just call me by my name.
name.

Just call me by my name,O my Lord!   Just call me by my name.

Thank you Father, for your blessing upon this land: for peace, for freedom from natural calamities; for stability of government; for tolerance between races; for freedom of worship; for rich resources beneath the soil and in the sea. But Father, prevent your children from becoming fat and lazy, and content to meet needs that do not call for much sacrifice. Help your churches to bring the good news to the poor, and to be touched by those who sit in the darkness of sin.

Prayer of a leading Chinese Christian businessman in Malaysia

In the brightness of your Son
we spend each day;
in the darkness of the night
you light our way;
always you protect us
with the umbrella of your love.
To you, God, be all praise
and glory forever and forever.

Opening recollection and benediction, from Christian Conference
of Asia resource for Delhi 1984 Asia Youth Assembly

Week 9

Denmark • Finland
Iceland • Norway • Sweden

Destroy, O Lord, the spirit of self-seeking in individuals and nations. Give to the peoples and their leaders thoughts of peace and reconciliation. For you, O Lord, can find a way where human beings know not what to do.

Prayer from Sweden

These five countries have close historical, cultural and confessional ties and all are now joined in the Nordic Council founded in 1952. The Lutheran Church is the major religious body throughout the region.

Population, language and government

Denmark: 5.1 million; Danish.

Finland: 4.9 million; Finnish, Swedish, Lappish.

Iceland: 242,000; Icelandic.

Norway: 4.2 million; Norwegian, Finnish, Lappish.

Sweden: 8.4 million; Swedish, Finnish, Lappish.

Denmark, Norway and Sweden are constitutional monarchies; Finland and Iceland are parliamentary republics.

The Christian message was brought to the Nordic countries from three directions. It was carried into Norway, Denmark and Sweden from the British Isles and from Germany. Best known of the apostles to the Scandinavian countries are Ansgar, later Archbishop of Hamburg/Bremen, and the English Bishop Henrik. The latter, accompanying the Swedish king, also carried the gospel into Finland. At the same time Orthodox Christianity was extending from Russia. Except in Karelia (the easternmost province of Finland) the Western tradition prevailed. Bishop Henrik, eventually martyred, became the patron saint of Finland. Women played an important part in spreading the faith, notably in Iceland in the 9th and 10th centuries. Christianity had spread throughout all these countries by the end of the 12th century.

The Reformation reached northern Europe by various means, and on the whole proceeded without violence, former Catholic dioceses quietly becoming Lutheran. During the 16th and 17th centuries devastating wars between Sweden and Russia brought severe persecution to the Orthodox in Karelia, many of whom fled to Russia. During the 20th century the Nordic churches have been influential in the development of ecumenism. Particularly important was the work of Archbishop Nathan Söderblom of Uppsala in the Life and Work movement.

In an area where East and West still meet, the need for disarmament and detente is felt acutely. Although their foreign policies diverge, these countries are concerted in their efforts to promote worldwide justice and international peace.

More than 90% of the people nominally belong to the Lutheran folk churches, although, with variations from place to place, relatively few attend church regularly or take part in church activities. Secularization is widespread, and in Denmark and Sweden the number of children baptized has fallen drastically, especially in the cities. The provision of Christian education for both adults and children has become an urgent necessity. In all these countries discussion is proceeding about the traditional relationship between the state and the (Lutheran) church. This could eventually lead to disestablishment. The Pentecostal movement has considerable influence, many people being active in this and the Lutheran church. In Finland and Sweden the Orthodox church, although numerically small (about 1.5%), is widespread; in Finland it is recognized as a national church.

In Denmark and Sweden especially, recent immigrations of foreign workers have brought members of other faiths; and there are considerable numbers of Turkish Muslims in Finland. The problem of refugees is a burning issue in all these countries. Small Jewish communities have been established throughout the region for centuries. In Iceland the reintroduction of traditional Norse pre-Christian religion has gained a small following.

In *Denmark* where the bond between church and culture is close, the Lutheran church embraces many different, sometimes opposing groups. Voluntary organizations and missions within the church promote renewal and outreach. Sharing in the region's long tradition of humanitarian concern on peace themes and human rights, Denmark recently opened the world's first ever treatment clinic for the victims of torture. In Greenland, Denmark's self-governing Arctic colony, 50% of the sparse population are Christian, nearly all Lutheran. Catechists mostly care for these scattered groups.

Although the church in *Finland* is not directly involved in political activity, parishes are independently active in a range of socio-ethical issues. Among a number of Christians there is a growing concern that the privileges and benefits of life in their country may be shared with the deprived and dispossessed of other lands. As a result of the cession of Karelia to the USSR, the entire population moved in 1944. Orthodox Christians (of whom 75% lived in Karelia) thus became spread throughout the country.

In *Iceland* the movement of people into the capital, and the inability of many diminished rural congregations to support a pastor, have called for new ways of working. With the whole island a single diocese and 97% of the people Lutheran, the church is looking anew at its role in society. This small church has, since the second world war, undertaken missionary work in Africa, and contributed generously to development projects overseas.

The *Norwegian* church's involvement in socio-political issues stems from its wartime experience. Because the country is so mountainous and people scattered, habitual church attendance has never been widespread, and the church faces a shortage of pastors. However membership and belief are strong and religious broadcasts provide a much-needed service. Voluntary organizations and lay movements have sprung up, and many Norwegian missionaries serve overseas.

In *Sweden* the Free churches account for 10% of the population, and as a result of the influx of refugees and foreign workers there is an appreciable Orthodox community. In this country, with its exceptionally high standard of living, many church people are expressing in positive action a new sense of responsibility for those in the third world, and the country's long-standing concern for peace is well known.

Ecumenical awareness and cooperation are growing, and the Roman Catholic Church is a member of the three national ecomenical councils of

Denmark, Finland and Sweden. In Iceland an interdenominational committee including Roman Catholics and Pentecostals organizes the Week of Prayer for Christian Unity. The ecumenical climate in Norway is changing, and there is now a forum for dialogue on theological matters.

While for many Nordic Christians today the way of holiness lies through personal piety and devotion, for others a truly contemporary spirituality involves active involvement in the struggles and needs of the world. For some people the appeal of Orthodoxy lies in its facility for uniting these and other dimensions of the Christian faith in a single whole. This diverse spiritual quest is the key to the prayers that follow.

Intercessions and Prayers

Nine "prayer strokes", three times three on the largest bell, signify the beginning of Sunday service in Denmark, followed by the prayer said together:

O Lord, I have come into your house to hear what
You, God, my Creator,
You, Lord Jesus, my Saviour,
You, Good Holy Spirit, my Comforter in life and death
will speak to me....

Father in heaven
In the evening when we prepare to go to sleep, we are consoled by the thought that you are the one who watches over us — and yet, what a desolation if you were not present and watching over us when we wake up in the morning and remain awake during the day. The distinction that we make between sleep and waking is an artificial one, as if we needed your wakefulness only as long as we are asleep, but not when we ourselves are awake.

The Prayers of Sören Kierkegaard, 1813-55

Oh God, our Father and Mother,
we confess today that your own sons and daughters in Christ have let you down.
Dominated by our fears, we have trampled and smothered one another.
We have smothered the tenderness of man and the creative thinking of woman.

Help women to discover honest and life-giving sisterhood.
Help men to open their hearts to each other in true brotherhood.
Help us to create a community of brothers and sisters
where we can live with each other in creative community
man with man, woman with woman, man with woman...

Help us to share with each other our pain and joy,
our fears and hope.
Save us from chilliness and distance,
from teaching without life,
from seeking prestige and struggling for power.

We pray for those who hesitate to confess your name.
You know them and their secret longing.
Do not let your sinful church and its fearful followers
hinder them in their seeking for you.

Taken from a prayer by Kerstin Lindqvist and Ulla Bardh, Sweden

We thank God

for the Christian church in these lands, for the rich and varied Lutheran heritage, and for the saints, missionaries and ascetics of the Orthodox church

for the invigorating contribution of the minority churches

for the spiritual intensity and depth brought by movements of revival and renewal

for the work of missionaries from northern Europe in other lands

for all movements concerned to protect the environment

We pray God

for these countries, that they may share not only their material goods but also spiritual gifts in solidarity with people inside and outside northern Europe

for Christian education in an increasingly secularized consumer society

for the strengthening and growth of trusting and sustaining relationships within families and between generations

that Christ's people may continue to fulfill their mission and service to the world, especially in their efforts for disarmament and detente for a creative response on the part of the churches to changing conditions; and a willingness to enter into new relationships with state and society

for more ecumenical openness and cooperation locally, nationally, and internationally

Pray

with and for the people of Iceland as they prepare to commemorate one thousand years of Christianity in the year 2000:

> *God, grant that in my mother tongue*
> *Thy gospel may be sounded,*
> *To rich and poor, to old and young,*
> *Its blessings be expounded,*
> *Over vale and glen*
> *By lip and pen,*
> *To each remotest dwelling,*
> *While Thy strong hand*
> *Safeguards our land,*
> *Dangers and foes repelling.*

> Regarded as among the public treasures of the Icelandic people, the 300-year-old passion hymns of Hallgrimur Petersson are commonly read aloud in homes during Lent, and recited on state radio after the evening news

Affirming that for Orthodox "knowledge and faith belong to the one wholeness of God", the Finnish Orthodox Church offers this prayer, used in the blessing of their newly installed computer in the monastery of New Valamo, and which may be adapted for the blessing of computers anywhere:

> *Lord our God, who taught wisdom to Solomon, and who by sending your All-Holy Spirit made the fishermen your disciples and proclaimers of your Gospel, you who by your word, make light to shine in darkness; grant that the work done with this computer may be to your glory, and lead to the benefit of your church and to blessing for this holy monastery.*

> *Lord, you who are the guide into wisdom, giver of understanding, teacher of the ignorant and refuge of the poor; sanctify and bless computers which you have inspired people to create. Grant that they may be used to promote truth. Grant that they may serve the unity of humankind, and the sanctification of life, peace and justice. Amen.*

In the towns of Finland an increasing number of families, having become disenchanted with apartment living, are getting together with friends and relatives to build their own houses, thus giving rise to occasions when the blessing of God is sought upon home and family life:

> *Heavenly Father, we thank you that in the building of this home many hopes and aspirations have been fulfilled. We thank you for hard work and tiredness, for protection and rest, and for all the people who have helped in this work.*

> *Come and be the Master of our homes so that family members may grow up as your children in mutual confidence and love. Grant that the homes of our land may be places of rest and relaxation for their members as well as to those who visit.*

The New Lutheran Manual, adapted

The following prayer for solidarity with women is taken from a prayer used on the Norwegian radio, 6 March 1987:

> *Lord, we bring you thanks for the care and attention you gave to women when you lived among us. We thank you for your solidarity with them, for returning human dignity to women and for inviting them to service.*

> *Lord, we pray:*
> *for women, who are victims of war, or refugees, or left behind alone with their children*
> *for women living in poverty, not having food and other necessities for themselves and the ones they love*
> *for women without education and employment, women who suffer from their economic dependency*
> *for children and young girls exploited like slaves for their labour*
> *for women despised and used for prostitution and pornography*
> *for women who are victims of drugs and alcohol*
> *for women living in oppressive cultures and systems*
> *for women subject to violence and abuse in their own homes.*

> *Lord, help them and give them strength and courage in their struggle for better lives.*

> *Lord, help all of us to show the same solidarity and care as you, help us to persist in the struggle so that your kingdom may come to every person. Amen.*

God, our Creator,
as we join the large spectrum of Christians in different churches who
are praying for refugees,
we realize that we are, in fact, asking for changes in our own society.

We pray for politicians,
that they may be willing to share the prosperity of our country with all
people — not only with their own citizens.
>   *Send to them someone who will give a name and a human face to*
>   *the refugee problem, and thus show them the inhumanity of the*
>   *legislation.*

We pray for journalists and others who work in the media, and thus
influence public opinion.
>   *Send into their experience events which will safeguard them from*
>   *cynicism and invite them to use their capacities to generate a*
>   *friendlier atmosphere towards refugees.*

We pray for the police and immigration officers at our airports,
who exercise power over the lives of people — often without a real
knowledge of their situation.
>   *Send into their lives people who are able to help them understand*
>   *the realities of the asylum seekers.*

We pray for ordinary citizens in our country,
that we may not be naive or indifferent, but join those who are working
to alleviate the lot of refugees.

God, our Creator, have mercy on us
we who are acting as if freedom, peace, and the wellbeing of our
country were meant for our benefit alone.

God, our Creator, help us to become changed people, and to change
our attitudes, as well as our legislation. Amen.

Prayer from Finland

Week 10

Republic of Ireland • United Kingdom

O Holy Spirit, giver of light and life,
free us from all that is matter-of-fact, stale, bored, tired;
all that takes things for granted.
Open our eyes to see and excite our minds to marvel.

After a prayer by Monica Furlong

Although Christianity first appeared in these islands round about 200 AD during the Roman occupation, its spread was uneven over the next 500 years, and owes much to the missionary work of many saints of both the Celtic and Roman traditions. Both of these strands have continued to contribute to the spirituality of these lands to this day.

Republic of Ireland

Population: 3.6 million.

Languages: Irish, English.

Government: Unitary multi-party republic.

Religion: Christians 99.5% (Roman Catholics 94%, Anglicans 3%, Presbyterians, Methodists and others).

From the 12th century until the 20th, Anglo-Irish relations have fluctuated through varying degrees of discord, perceived by many as centuries of English oppression. During this period the Church of England was imposed as state religion upon Ireland; and Scottish and English "planters", mostly Presbyterians and Anglicans, were introduced into Ulster (Northern Ireland) in order to settle this area under English control. Ireland became part of the United Kingdom in 1801. The 26 southern counties obtained full independent sovereignty in 1937, the six northern counties remaining part of the United Kingdom. This partition of Ireland has resulted in much bitterness and bloodshed affecting both the Republic and the United Kingdom, the worst impact being felt in Northern Ireland.

The Irish Roman Catholic Church has great importance overseas, partly as a result of large-scale emigrations, and partly because of the country's remarkable missionary contribution. Despite its strongly traditional character, it is increasingly participating in ecumenical ventures. In the Irish Interchurch Meeting Roman Catholics and Protestants are deeply committed in an ongoing initiative with permanent working departments on theological questions and social issues. The Irish School of Ecumenics is sponsored by the Anglican, Methodist, Presbyterian and Catholic churches. The Irish Council of Churches, established in Belfast in 1922, serves both the Republic and Northern Ireland, and in the Republic includes the Anglican and six Protestant churches. In both north and south matters of justice and peace as well as social problems are being increasingly handled on an ecumenical basis, and the charismatic movement is bringing some Catholics and Protestants together in a new way. Most of the recently formed Christian women's groups recruit members without reference to denomination, thus contributing to understanding and fellowship. Women play an increasingly active role in the life of all the churches, pastorally, liturgically and administratively.

Of course the traditional Catholicism of Ireland has its own immense strengths. With a long tradition of reverence for holy places and holy people, and a strong emphasis on the family and the Christian education of children, this church retains the loyalty and active participation of its members both at home and abroad. They have a reputation for homely and practical piety, and speak easily of their faith.

Intercessions and Prayers

Lord Jesus Christ, you are the way of peace.
Come into the brokenness of our lives and our land with your healing love.
Help us to be willing to bow before you in true repentance, and to bow to one another in real forgiveness.
By the fire of your Holy Spirit, melt our hard hearts and consume the pride and prejudice which separate us.
Fill us, O Lord, with your perfect love which casts out fear and bind us together in that unity which you share with the Father and the Holy Spirit.

Emerging out of the movement of charismatic renewal,
this prayer is used in both the Republic and Northern Ireland.
Unity, the newsletter of the Irish School of Ecumenics

We pray

for all ecumenical initiatives and all occasions which bring together Christians of different traditions

for the people of Ireland, for Irish missionaries, and those many other Irish men and women living and working overseas

> *Three things are of the Evil One:*
>   *an evil eye;*
>   *an evil tongue;*
>   *an evil mind.*

> *Three things are of God,*
> *and these three are what Mary told her Son,*
> *for she heard them in heaven:*
>   *the merciful word,*
>   *the singing word,*
>   *and the good word.*

> *May the power of these three holy things*
> *be on all men and women of Erin for evermore. Amen.*

15th century Irish benediction

United Kingdom

Population: 56.7 million.

Languages: English, Welsh, Gaelic and various languages of immigrant communities.

Government: Parliamentary constitutional monarchy.

Religion: The majority count themselves Christian, but there are significant numbers of Muslims, Jews, Hindus, Sikhs, Buddhists and others.

Waves of invasion in times past have resulted in a considerable mixing of peoples in Great Britain, although the Celtic groups to the west have been better able to retain their original identity and languages. Britain's history as a colonial power has resulted in a more recent influx of immigrants from many parts of the world.

The figures, 7 million adult church members (of whom approximately 2.3 million are Roman Catholics, 2.1 million Anglicans, 1.5 million Presbyterians) and 2 million of other faiths, speak for themselves, and indicate something of the secular and spiritual dimensions of multi-racial, multi-cultural and multifaith Britain. Together with increasing contact with continental Europe these contribute to the development of a new relationship with the wider international community. On the other hand, large-scale unemployment, urban decay, racial tension and a wide disparity in standards of living all contribute to the adverse sociological climate in which the church carries out its mission in Britain today.

Many movements of reform and renewal have contributed to a complex pattern of church life in which the Roman Catholic Church plays a significant part. The Church of England (Anglican) and Church of Scotland (Presbyterian) are the established churches in England and Scotland respectively. In Wales, which has no established church, a strong sense of cultural identity, owing much to the Welsh Bible and Welsh hymnody, has moulded the life of the chapels and churches. Of the other mainstream Protestant churches Methodists and Baptists form the largest groups. There are 100,000 members of Orthodox churches, and Black Pentecostal churches are growing numerically. The Society of Friends and the Salvation Army have made distinctive contributions, not least in areas of social concern and missionary outreach. Many churches are currently struggling to understand better the role of women in mission and ministry, and there is a growing consciousness among women themselves of their call to serve.

In exploring new forms of prayer and worship, in contact with those of other faiths, and in responding to the problems of inner cities the churches in Britain have been increasingly acting together. This has provided the momentum for the development of an interchurch process of prayer, reflection and debate on the nature, purpose and unity of the church involving upwards of a million people in England, Scotland and Wales. According to the general secretary of the British Council of Churches the ensuing conference was "the most representative gathering of churches since the Reformation, including Orthodox, Catholic, Anglican, Reformed, Lutheran and all the way across the spectrum to Black Pentecostals and Brethren". Under the banner "Not Strangers but Pilgrims" they are now committed to some very practical proposals for the church's ministry and unity in the years that lie ahead.

Northern Ireland has its own complex difficulties. Most Protestants wish to retain their British citizenship and are opposed to unification with the Republic, while a high percentage of Roman Catholics aspire to a united Ireland. Para-military organizations, particularly the IRA, have resorted to violence as a means of promoting their ends, with the result that thousands of people have been killed and injured and there has been widespread suffering. In this situation the reconciling role of the churches is vital, and both Protestants and Catholics have become involved in peace-making in a host of community organizations operating at the "sharp end" of things.

Intercessions and Prayers

"In contrast to the beauty and wealth of nature, in Northern Ireland especially, we are torn apart by hate and fear. Every attempt at peace comes under immediate attack and is never allowed to establish itself. Violence is always ready to erupt, bringing sorrow and shame."

We are tired, Lord,
weary of the long night without rest.
We grow complaining and bitter.
We sorrow for ourselves
as we grow hardened to the pain of others.
Another death leaves us unmoved.
A widow's tears fall unnoticed.
Our children know only the bitterness
already possessing their parents.
Our violent words
explode into violent acts
by the hands of youth
bringing destruction without thought or reason.
Lord, have mercy upon us.
Lead us to repentance that we may forgive
and be forgiven. Amen.

Presbyterian minister, Northern Ireland

God our Mother and Father, we come to you as children. Be with us as we learn to see one another with new eyes, hear one another with new hearts, and treat one another in a new way. Amen.

Corrymeela community

Let us kneel alongside those in Britain who seek forgiveness for
false pride and complacency
unthinking consumerism
insularity, and a reluctance to accept new ways

acquiescence in a society which is often ruthless in its pursuit of progress and profit; and heedless of the hurt and anger felt by its victims

> *All-merciful tender God*
> *you have given birth to our world,*
> *conceiving and bearing all that lives and breathes.*
> *We come to you as your daughters and sons,*
> *aware of our aggression and anger,*
> *our drive to dominate and manipulate others.*
> *We ask you to forgive us,*
> *and by the gentle touch of your Spirit*
> *help us to find a renewed sense of compassion*
> *that we may truly live as your people*
> *in service to all humanity.*

Janet Berry, South West Manchester Group of Churches

Let us pray

for a willingness to live lives with a bias towards the poor, the needy, the unemployed and the deprived

for the people of Wales, concerned to preserve their cultural identity and for their various churches exploring ways of recognizing each others' ministries

for the diverse ministry of the church in Scotland: in city areas, the Highlands and islands, and the Lowlands

for the church in Britain, diminished in size, beset with problems, but increasingly alert to its task

for Christians of different traditions on converging paths

> *Lord God, we thank you*
> *For calling us into the company*
> *Of those who trust in Christ*
> *And seek to obey his will.*
> *May your Spirit guide and strengthen us*
> *In mission and service to your world;*
> *For we are strangers no longer*
> *But pilgrims together on the way to your kingdom. Amen.*

Prayer for the interchurch process, Jamie Wallace

Week 11

Belgium • Luxembourg
The Netherlands

O Lord Jesus,
let not your word become a judgment upon us,
that we hear it and do not do it,
that we believe it and do not obey it.

Thomas à Kempis

These three countries have been linked together since the Middle Ages. The term "Netherlands" (the Low Countries) was originally used for the whole area, but now applies only to the northernmost country. Highly industrialized, the three have been linked together in the Benelux Economic Union since 1960.

Population, language and government

Belgium: 9.9 million; French, Dutch, German.

Luxembourg: 367,000; French, Letzeburgesch, German.

Netherlands: 14.6 million; Dutch.

All are constitutional monarchies.

Christianity was brought to the Low Countries during the 6th and 7th centuries by Celtic missionaries, who were the first evangelists and martyrs. Utrecht was one of the earliest centres, and Willibrord and Boniface among the first leaders.

At the end of the Middle Ages this area was a collection of principalities united by the fact that foreign princes inherited them one after another. One of the main causes of the separation between the northern and southern Netherlands was the Reformation, combined with rebellion against the Spanish Hapsburgs who sought to impose Catholicism. The northern area became a refuge for the followers of Luther, Zwingli and Calvin. After an 80-year war the northern provinces became an independent republic under William of Orange, the southern provinces remaining under the Hapsburgs. The south, including the southernmost part of the present kingdom of the Netherlands, has remained predominantly Roman Catholic, while Calvinism has been dominant in the north. After Napoleon the Netherlands and Belgium were united into one kingdom, with Luxembourg, a grand-duchy, also under the Oranges. Belgium became independent in 1830, and Luxembourg in 1890.

A number of international and European organizations use the major cities of the Low Countries as their headquarters, thus ensuring the presence of a sizeable international community. Immigration, especially from Mediterranean countries, has brought members of other faiths, and there are appreciable Muslim communities in Belgium and the Netherlands. The Jewish community, present in these countries for centuries, was largely decimated in the second world war.

The Christian church is predominantly Roman Catholic in Belgium and Luxembourg (89% and 96% of the population respectively). In the Netherlands about 40% of the population is Roman Catholic, 30% Protestant and 26% profess no religion at all. Church people in this area are progressive in their views. Concern within the Protestant churches, many of which have had women priests for years, with issues relating to the role of women in church and society, and changing attitudes in the Roman Catholic Church to the question of married priests and to divorce and remarriage, all indicate a readiness for change. Joseph Suenens, one-time Cardinal Archbishop of Malines-Brussels, and active in Vatican II, sees the charismatic movement and a more spontaneous prayer life as a necessary sequel, at a time when observance of the traditional forms of Roman Catholic devotion has greatly declined.

Shared experiences of suffering during the second world war and common challenges facing the churches today have resulted in increasing ecumenical contacts. The United Protestant Church has existed in Belgium since 1979, and in the Netherlands the synods of the two Reformed churches have declared themselves to be "in the situation of reuniting". The Council of Churches in the Netherlands incorporates a wide spectrum, including the Roman Catholic Church. Increasing secularism has forced the churches to rethink their role and identity in society. All have become more actively involved in political and social issues: peace and justice, nuclear disarmament, north-south dialogue, unemployment and social security, welcoming and accepting immigrants and the problems of a plural society. Although often polarized and divided within themselves, the churches perform an increasingly important role as watchdogs of government policy, and in championing the cause of the underprivileged.

Intercessions and Prayers

Grant to us, O Lord,
to know that which is worth knowing,
to love that which is worth loving,
to praise that which pleaseth thee most,
to esteem that which is most precious unto thee,
and to dislike whatsoever is evil in thy eyes.
Grant us with true judgment to distinguish things that differ,
and above all to search out and do what is well pleasing unto thee,
through Jesus Christ our Lord. Amen.

Thomas à Kempis, 15th century:
member of an informal brotherhood in the Netherlands

We thank God

for the missionaries and martyrs who brought the gospel to these lands

for the courageous struggles of the peoples of the Low Countries for freedom of thought, faith and conscience

for the protection given to Jewish citizens during the second world war and for the life and witness of many courageous Jews

for the ecumenical initiatives of the churches in these countries and especially for the contribution of Willem A. Visser't Hooft, the first general secretary of the World Council of Churches

for the many movements of renewal in both Protestant and Catholic churches

We pray God

for a greater coming together of the churches in response to the need for a joint Christian witness in a secularized society

that just and compassionate solutions may be found to tensions arising from economic pressures

for the handicapped, the unemployed, and migrant workers; and for their acceptance and integration in local communities

for a change of heart and habit on the part of all who prosper or suffer from the bondage of drugs; and courage for those who seek to break free

for the resolution of friction between the French- and Dutch-speaking communities in Belgium for the International Court of Justice in the Hague, and Institutions of the European Community in Brussels and Luxembourg; and for the church's responses to them

that initiatives taken by these countries for peace and disarmament may be fruitful

Let us pray to God who calls us in Jesus Christ to unity

for the Christian churches on earth: that they may no longer allow themselves to be separated from each other by questions and problems that have often long since ceased to be ours

for the leaders in our churches: that like the apostles they may be open to the call of the Spirit, put off all fear and may speak in words all Christians can understand

for all theologians and ministers: that they may humble themselves under the mighty hand of God and, setting aside human caution and shrewdness, may trust in the Spirit who comes to the aid of our weakness

for those men and women who can no longer understand the separation of Christians and also for those who equate the church of Jesus Christ only with their own favourite customs: that they all may recognize that it is not the way back but the way into the future that they tread together which alone can give us unity

Lord, our God,
lead us through the love of your Son
our Lord Jesus Christ
to the unity we long for.

From *Fürbitten und Kanongebete der holländischen Kirche*, 1972

O Holy Spirit of God, who with thy holy breath
doth cleanse the hearts and minds of thy people;
comforting them when they be in sorrow,
leading them when they be out of the way,
kindling them when they be cold,
knitting them together when they be at variance,
and enriching them with manifold gifts;
by whose working all things live:
We beseech Thee to maintain and daily to increase

the gifts which Thou hast vouchsafed to us;
that with Thy light before us and within us
we may pass through this world
without stumbling and without straying.

Erasmus of Rotterdam, 1466-1536

God in heaven, we beg you;
bless all who make endeavours for peace and human welfare;
take from us anxiety about the future
and let us contribute to the peace of the world
by the way we ourselves behave.

From *Fürbitten und Kanongebete der holländischen Kirche*

Go now, all of you, in peace
to the place where God has given you responsibility
and he himself will bless you,
the Father, the Son and the Holy Spirit.

Prayers, Poems and Songs, Huub Oosterhuis

Week 12

France • Portugal • Spain

Lord, grant that Christians may again find visible unity,
that they may be one that the world may believe.

France

Population: 55.2 million.

Languages: French; Breton, Basque, Occitan and Alsatian are also spoken.

Government: Republic.

Religion: Christians about 80% (Roman Catholics 76.4%, Protestants 2.4%, Orthodox 0.8%), Muslims 5%, Jews 1.4%, Buddhists 0.2%.

Christians arrived in France from Italy at an early date, and by the end of the first century groups were meeting for worship in the south. The mass baptism in 496 of the Frankish king Clovis with his warriors was significant in the spread of Christianity in the region. The Middle Ages were marked by the Crusades, the monastic reforms of Benedict of Cluny and Bernard of Clairvaux, and the political intrigue which installed a rival pope in Avignon. At the time of the Reformation the Protestant movement became strong; but as a result of the counter-Reformation and later persecution Protestants remained a persecuted minority until the Revolution of 1794. Napoleon's concordat with Rome (1802) recognized Roman Catholicism as the major religion, the Lutheran and Reformed churches being recognized a year later. Since 1905 church and state have been separate except in Alsace-Lorraine.

By far the majority church, but with a dwindling number actively participating, the Roman Catholic Church in France relies entirely on its collection boxes. It is however active, with a number of lay movements engaged in programmes of mission, education and renewal. The church takes a firm stand against racism. Secours catholique, the largest non-government organization in the country, has thousands of volunteers working with immigrants, one-parent families, and others in social need. With half a million members, the Reformed Church of France is the largest Protestant body. Although scattered throughout the country, Protestants are strongest in Alsace and in the Rhone Valley. The Protestant Federation, as well as the Roman Catholic Church, is concerned to safeguard the rights of refugees and immigrants. The CIMADE is an interdenominational organization working for the welfare of refugees, migrant workers and other displaced persons. Since the second world war the ecumenical communities of Taizé, Pomeyrol and Reuilly have increasingly become centres of church renewal. There is much joint activity and witness, ranging from the charismatic movement to ecumenical radio stations.

Portugal and Spain

Although today quite separate and independent nations, these two countries of the Iberian peninsula share a common Christian heritage. According to ancient tradition the apostles James and Paul visited here, and certainly Christianity was firmly established by the end of the 2nd century.

Muslim influence came with the Berbers in the 8th century. During the Middle Ages the Muslims, Jews and Christians living in the peninsula held one another in mutual respect. In the Christian north, the veneration of the Apostle James, the patron saint of Spain, led to the establishment of an important European centre of pilgrimage in Santiago de Compostela. In the Moorish south a special liturgy, the Mozarabic rite, developed, and is still in use today. The Christian "reconquest", which was in the nature of a crusade, took four centuries to complete, and was indirectly responsible for the declaration of Portugal as an independent nation in 1139. The coexistence of the three religious communities was destroyed, the Jewish and Muslim populations being forced to accept baptism or leave.

Reformation influences reached the peninsula through its political links with Germany. However the rigour of the Counter-Reformation made progress impossible, and it was not until the 19th century that Protestant missionaries were permitted, and a number of small Protestant congregations established.

The great voyages of discovery by Spanish and Portuguese sailors, which were also viewed as missionary journeys, marked the beginnings of the spread of Western Christianity to many other parts of the world. Regrettably they also brought the beginning of the colonial era, and the destruction of ancient cultures. The "golden age" of Spain and Portugal, albeit also the time of the Inquisition and the Counter-Reformation, bequeathed to Christians for all time the diverse spiritual treasures of saints Teresa of Avila, John of the Cross, Ignatius Loyola and others.

Portugal

Population: 10.2 million.

Language: Portuguese.

Government: Republic.

Religion: Christians 98% (Roman Catholics 97%, Protestants 0.8%). There are very small Jewish, Muslim and Bahai communities and a number of Marranos (whose forbears were compelled to accept baptism, but who nevertheless continued to keep Jewish observances).

Today Portugal is one of the poorest countries in Europe with high levels of inflation and unemployment. The illiteracy rate is also high — one of the legacies of the dictatorship which was overthrown in the 1974 "Revolution of the Carnations". Portugal's recent integration into the European Economic Community has helped to overcome its isolation.

The Roman Catholic Church, still very conservative, faces some anti-clericalism because of its previous association with the dictators. Vast numbers of the faithful continue to make the pilgrimage to the shrine of Our Lady of Fatima associated with the call to prayer and repentance. The small but vigorous Protestant churches are involved in social work particularly with children, old people and refugees. The Portuguese Council of Christian Churches links together the historic Protestant Churches.

Spain

Population: 39.4 million.

Languages: Spanish, Catalan, Basque, Galician.

Government: Constitutional monarchy.

Religion: Christians 92.5% (Roman Catholics 92%, Protestants 0.1%). Very small Muslim, Jewish and Bahai communities and some Marranos.

Spain, also recovering from a fascist dictatorship and poor by European standards, is troubled by the ongoing problem of the Basque separatist movement.

The Catholic church holds together two overlapping elements; a pious, conservatively traditional section in an increasingly progressive, socially conscious church. Many local Christian communities are socially and politically active. There is some uneasiness among church leaders about the stance of the socialist government towards religion. "It isn't easy for a Socialist government to respect liberty. There's a tendency to try and change mentalities: freedom is in danger." The Spanish Evangelical Church (Methodists, Presbyterians, Congregationalists), facing the problem of being a small minority, is concerned about the church's mission in the world and active in a number of social fields. It is on record as saying "… we place our confidence and hope in God and in the help given by the ecumenical community".

Intercessions and Prayers

Let us unite with Catholic Christians of these wine-producing countries in the words they say in their weekly mass:

> *Blessed are you, Lord God of the universe*
> *you are the giver of this wine,*
> *fruit of the vine and of human labour*
> *let it become the wine of the eternal kingdom.*

Let us join also with small groups of Protestants in these same countries in praising God for the freedom of God's word, and for the power of the scriptures to strengthen and refresh them in their daily lives.

Let us rejoice with all these Christians whenever they together thank God for all they hold in common.

> *You are always with us, Lord,*
> *You are water in the desert,*
> *the fruit of life in the garden,*
> *light at evening time.*
> *In that way you are with us, Lord.*

You are always with us, Lord,
You are the face reflected in the mirror,
the wine of joy at the celebration meal,
the sharing between friends.
In that way you are with us, Lord.

You are always with us, Lord.
You are the pilot in the boat,
the healer of the injured,
the parent in the home.
In that way you are with us, Lord.

Fr Pierre-Etienne

We thank God

for the missionary witness of the first Christian communities in these lands

for the spread of the Christian faith from Portugal and Spain to other parts of the world

for the courageous witness of many Protestant believers

for the restoration of democracy and religious freedom in Portugal and Spain

for the church's ministry among children, workers, the sick and the elderly

for the renewal and inspiration flowing from Taizé and the many other religious communities in France

We remember before God

Charles de Foucauld, priest and monk, shot in his hermitage in the Sahara by raiding tribesmen in 1916, but whose work for mission and reconciliation still goes on through the Little Brothers and Sisters of Jesus

St James, whose shrine at Santiago de Compostela has been described as "one of the most ecumenical places in Europe". With it is associated the pilgrimage emblem of the shell. Here contemporary pilgrims unite in prayer for a reconciled Europe

Lord God,
You accepted the sacrifice of St James,
patron of Spain and the first of the apostles,
to give his life for your sake.
May your church today find strength in his martyrdom
and support in the constant prayers of all the saints,
through Jesus Christ our Lord.

From the Roman liturgy

We pray

that God will heal the many deep wounds which Christians have inflicted on one another in the past

for Christians in France, exposed to the ever-present influences of secularization and consumerism

for Portuguese and Spanish migrant workers, that they may be treated with respect and hospitality in their host countries

for stability in public life, and continuing development of justice and peace in Portugal and Spain

O heavenly Father, we bend the knee before Thee on behalf of all
kings and rulers of this world, beseeching Thee to grant unto them by
thy inspiration to rule in righteousness, to rejoice in peace, to shine in
goodness, and to labour for the wellbeing of the people committed
unto them, so that, by the rectitude of the government, all faithful
people may live without disturbance in the knowledge of Thee, and
labour without hindrance to thy glory. Amen.

Mozarabic liturgy, 600 AD

that local churches may be strengthened and encouraged in their common ministry to the needs of the community

that the diverse peoples of France may live together in harmony and interdependence

You are my family, an African
you gave me a piece of bread.
You are my friend, an Algerian,
you gave me your hand.
You are my brother, a Jew,
you helped me when trouble came my way.
And you, a Chinese, you showed me the way.

Let's stand by one another, my friends,
because you, the African,
don't have a lot of bread;
to you, the Algerian,
people don't give their hand;
people make trouble for you, the Jew;
and stand in the way of you, the Chinese.

But, this bread,
   this hand,
   this help in trouble,
   this way,
will lead us to peace.

Affirmation of Patrice, a young Frenchman

Our God,
we are one in solidarity with those who live in danger and struggle.
Whether near or far, we share their anguish and their hope.

Teach us to extend our lives beyond ourselves and to reach out in
sympathy to the frontiers where people are suffering and changing the
world.

Make us one in solidarity with the aliens we ignore, the deprived we
pretend do not exist, the prisoners we avoid.

God, let solidarity be a new contemporary word for this community
into which you are constantly summoning us.

But, God, may our solidarity be genuine, and not a dishonest
manoeuvre.

May our solidarity be effective, and not just consist of wordy declara-
tions.

May our solidarity be grounded in hope, and not in the tragedy of
disaster.

May our solidarity be in humility, because we cannot bear all the
world's troubles.

God, purify us in our solidarity with others; may it be genuine,
fruitful, fervent and humble.

We ask it in the name of him who was resolutely one in solidarity with
abandoned, despised humankind, Jesus Christ, your son, our brother.
Amen.

100 prières possibles, André Dumas

All Africa Conference of Churches (AACC)

Founded in 1963, the All Africa Conference of Churches is made up of 138 member churches and associated councils in 33 countries. It represents over 50 million African Christians, i.e. more than one-third of the total Christian population of Africa. Taking legitimate pride in the manner in which God's purpose has been so richly fulfilled using the people of Africa, the AACC seeks to keep before its members matters relating to the life and mission of the church in the continent, and to promote consultation and action.

O God you who are from generation to generation the Creator of the ends of the earth and all that it contains, we of the continent of Africa bow our heads to you in humble thanks for the work that you have wrought in our lands and communities over the years.

We remember with joy the refuge which your only begotten Son our Saviour and his earthly parents took in Africa. We rejoice when we remember the journey of the Ethiopian eunuch, and his Christian fellowship with your disciple Philip in the Gaza desert.

It is a wonderful tribute to Africa that Simon of Cyrene helped to bear the heavy wooden cross upon which you hung and suffered for us sinners here in Africa and all over the world.

We can never forget the countless men and women of other lands who spread throughout Africa the gospel news of the saving grace of Christ, and now that same call comes to us to do the same.

When we think of these things our gratitude knows no bounds.

Francis Akanu Ibiam, Nigerian Christian,
one-time president of the All Africa Conference of Churches

African women these days identify with their Old Testament counterparts and give thanks for the Cushite wife of Moses (Numbers 12) and for those Egyptian midwives, Shiphrah and Puah (Exodus 1) "who feared God" and by whose compassion the children of the Israelites were saved.

Almighty and eternal God,
we fervently lift up our eyes to you,
searching for help and guidance in the midst of very many problems.

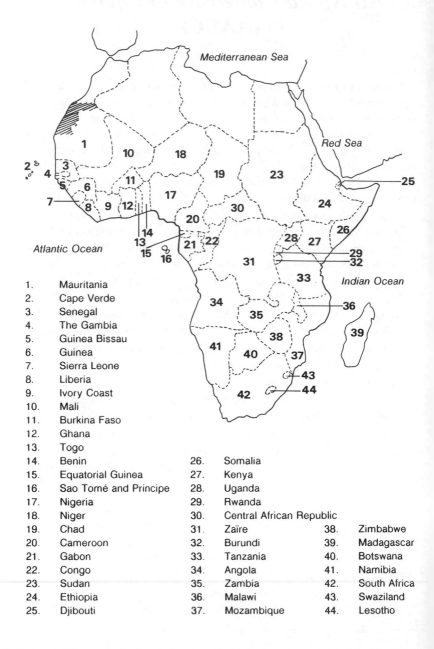

1.	Mauritania	
2.	Cape Verde	
3.	Senegal	
4.	The Gambia	
5.	Guinea Bissau	
6.	Guinea	
7.	Sierra Leone	
8.	Liberia	
9.	Ivory Coast	
10.	Mali	
11.	Burkina Faso	
12.	Ghana	
13.	Togo	
14.	Benin	
15.	Equatorial Guinea	26. Somalia
16.	Sao Tomé and Príncipe	27. Kenya
17.	Nigeria	28. Uganda
18.	Niger	29. Rwanda
19.	Chad	30. Central African Republic
20.	Cameroon	31. Zaïre	38. Zimbabwe
21.	Gabon	32. Burundi	39. Madagascar
22.	Congo	33. Tanzania	40. Botswana
23.	Sudan	34. Angola	41. Namibia
24.	Ethiopia	35. Zambia	42. South Africa
25.	Djibouti	36. Malawi	43. Swaziland
		37. Mozambique	44. Lesotho

Come and show us how to serve the refugees and the oppressed;
how to stand alongside those who struggle for social justice
and for the human rights of women and young people.
Come, liberate us from captivity to confessionalism,
and make us agents of reconciliation and unity.
Give us a will to love and serve you
through loving and serving others.
Keep us from insisting upon our own way.
Show us your way.
Enable us to grow in the knowledge of your truth.
Make us bearers of hope, and instruments of peace.
May we be living witnesses of that unity
which binds Divine Parent, Son and Holy Spirit
into one forgiving and redeeming God.

Prepared by women students in the Pan-African leadership course, Kitwe, Zambia

Week 13

Djibouti • Ethiopia • Somalia

*And in a random scorching flame of wind
that parches the painful throat and sears the flesh,
may God, in compassion, let you find
the great-boughed tree that will protect and shade.*

From a Somali prayer

Djibouti

Population: 430,000 (including refugees and resident foreigners).

Languages: French, Arabic, Somali, Saho-Afar.

Government: Single-party republic.

Religion: Muslims 94%, Christians approximately 5%. There is a small Indian Hindu community.

Formerly the French territory of the Afars and the Issas, Djibouti gained its independence in 1977. Two ethnic groups, the Issa of Somali origin, and the Afar of Ethiopian, make up the majority of the population, which has been greatly swollen in recent years by the influx of refugees from Ethiopia and Somalia. Djibouti has attempted to mediate in the conflict between its neighbours.

A volcanic desert, the inhospitable terrain provides little arable land, and about half the population are pastoral nomads herding goats, sheep and cattle. The other half live in the capital, and mostly work in the thriving free port which is a major source of revenue for the country. Djibouti is almost entirely dependent on its trade services and on foreign aid.

The majority of Christians in the country are Roman Catholics and nearly all French expatriates. There are small French Reformed, Greek Orthodox and Coptic congregations, and a handful of local Christians.

Although the church ministers mainly to expatriates, a small Christian bookshop makes the scriptures and Christian literature available to any who are interested.

Intercessions and Prayers

Lord, I am not worthy that you should
come under my roof, but speak the word only
and my soul shall be healed.

Prayer before communion, Western rite

Used in the eucharist of many different traditions, and therefore probably said by Roman Catholic Christians in Djibouti, this prayer reflects the first instance in the New Testament of faith surmounting barriers of culture, race and religion.

In its spirit we pray

for the busy port of Djibouti; and for all seafarers from this part of Africa, that they may be helped in overcoming difficulties of custom, language and race as they travel round the world

for refugees

for local Christians, that they may be sustained by the words of Jesus

In its spirit we give thanks

for all peace-making efforts made by the government of Djibouti

for the hospitality and peacefulness of its nomadic people

Ethiopia

Population: 42.2 million.

Languages: Amharic, English, Italian, Arabic and about 90 local languages.

Government: Single-party socialist state, currently under military rule.

Religion: Christians 52% (41% Ethiopian Orthodox, 10% Protestant, 1% Roman Catholic), Muslims 35%, followers of traditional African religions 10%. There are also small Hindu, Sikh and Jewish communities.

According to local tradition, the gospel was first brought to Ethiopia by St Matthew. It was brought again in the 4th century by two shipwrecked young men from Syria, one of whom was subsequently consecrated bishop by the Patriarch of Alexandria. Thus began the link with the Coptic church of Egypt which lasted until the Ethiopian church was granted autonomy in the present century. The church was weakened in the 16th century by the Muslim invasion. Jesuit missionaries also came into the country, and conflict between the two churches led to much bitterness and bloodshed. Protestant missions began work in the 19th century and there are now some 28 different denominations.

Christianity became the official religion of Ethiopia in the 4th century, and the Orthodox church became a symbol of unity binding together a diverse people and helping to maintain the country's independence over the centuries. Although one of the oldest and most conservative churches in the world, it was a founding member of the WCC. Something of this long and rich history is reflected in the church's ancient prayer over the sacrament:

O Lord our good and life-giving God
who stretched forth your holy hands on the tree of the cross,
lay your holy hand upon this paten which is full of goodness,
and on which food of a thousand years is prepared
by those who love your holy name.

Ethiopia became a socialist state in 1974 following the military revolution which deposed Emperor Haile Selassie. The revolution was followed by considerable unrest, leading to many deaths and the detention of a large number of people. In addition numerous independence movements have been active, especially in the Ogaden (claimed by Somalia) and in Eritrea; and there has been heavy fighting. The new constitution has granted a measure of autonomy to several regions. During 1984/85 the rains failed for the third consecutive crop season resulting in severe drought and famine in which an estimated one million people died and hundreds of thousands fled in search of food. Recurrent drought continues to be a serious problem, and the average daily calorie intake is still well below the FAO minimum level. With an economy based mainly on agriculture and herding, the country is at the mercy of climatic conditions.

There has been pressure on all religions since the socialist revolution, and the Ethiopian Orthodox Church especially, losing its status as state religion, was thrown into some turmoil. Nearly all foreign missionaries were withdrawn between 1975-78, and many church properties and institutions were nationalized. The importation and publication of scriptures are severely restricted. Nevertheless, both Orthodox and Protestant churches are experiencing a deepening of faith and revitalization.

Intercessions and Prayers

Yes Lord, you are the God of all.
Yes Lord, you are the King of all.
Yes Lord, you are the Almighty.
Yes Lord, you are the Governor of all.
Yes Lord, you are the Saviour of all.
Yes Lord, you are the Judge of all.
Yes Lord, you are the Life-giver of all.
Yes Lord, you are the Keeper of all.
Yes Lord, you are the Nourisher of all.

Acclamation, Anaphora of St Dioscorus,
25th Patriarch of Antioch, 451 AD

Taking strength from such an acclamation, let us pray

that Christians may remain steadfast in the face of every kind of political pressure

that churches may have freedom to proceed with the training of the priests and pastors of the future

for Christian groups meeting in homes, and their leaders

for Christian education and work among young people

for orphanages providing homes for children whose parents perished in time of famine; and for the many homeless children who roam the streets of Addis Ababa and other major cities in the region

Remember, Lord, the sick among your people: visit them in your mercy, and heal them in your compassion.

Remember, Lord, our fathers and our brothers who have travelled and who have sojourned to trade; bring them back to their dwelling-places in safety and peace.

Remember, Lord, the dew of the air and the fruits of the earth, bless them and keep them without loss.

Remember, Lord, the down-coming of the rains and the waters and the rivers, and bless them.

Remember, Lord, the plants and the seeds and the fruits of the fields of every year, bless them and make them abundant.

Remember, Lord, the safety of your own holy church and all the cities and countries of our Orthodox fathers the apostles.

Remember, Lord, the safety of humankind and of beasts and of me, your sinful servant.

Remember, Lord, our fathers and our brothers and our sisters who have fallen asleep and gone to their rest in the Orthodox faith.

Remember, Lord, the captives of your people, and bring them again in peace to their dwelling place.

Remember, Lord, the afflicted and distressed.

Remember, Lord, your servants, the poor who are under oppression, have pity upon them and stablish them in the right faith and make them a dwelling place of the Holy Spirit, through our spiritual joy and the love of humankind.

Evening prayer of the Covenant, Ethiopian Orthodox liturgy

Somalia

One of the poorest countries in the world, Somalia is a generally dry and barren land with few natural resources. Sporadic fighting in the Ogaden and recurrent drought in the region have created a major refugee problem.

Give comfort, O Lord, to all who are torn away from their homes and their loved ones by war, famine or the cruelty of their fellows; grant that we who dwell secure in this insecure world may be generous in caring for our displaced sisters and brothers.

Population: 4.7 million. Mostly pastoral nomads.

Languages: Somali, Arabic, Italian, English.

Government: Single-party socialist republic.

Religion: Muslims 99.8%. Miniscule Christian minority

The independent Somali republic came into being in 1960 with the agreed merger of British Somaliland and Italian Somaliland, at the same time as these territories obtained their independence. Both were committed to the unification of all Somali territories including those in French Somaliland (now Djibouti), Ethiopia (Ogaden) and Kenya. This aim led the country into continuing conflict with Ethiopia, and tension with Kenya which has largely been resolved. Following a military coup in 1969 the country was declared a socialist state.

After the revolution the state regarded all religion unfavourably, but the attitude to Islam has changed and this is now the state religion. The Christian church is tolerated, but is not free to evangelize. Although Roman Catholic institutions of education and social work were nationalized in 1972 the church continues to serve the local community in various ways. Following the revolution Protestant activity was also curtailed, though some workers have now been allowed to return. The majority of Christians in the country are expatriates. Most are Roman Catholics, but there are Episcopalian and Lutheran congregations. There are also small groups of indigenous believers.

Intercessions and Prayers

"Somalis were quite stunned at the thought that Christians around the world might pray for the welfare of Muslims," writes a correspondent. Specifically they asked for prayer for rain. "Natural forces... have a direct impact on their daily lives.... When rain does not come, they are forced to move or prepare for dire consequences. This gives them a special view of God's power that most Christians have never experienced."

> *O God, give us rain,*
> *we are in misery, we suffer with our children.*
> *Send us the clouds that bring the rain.*
> *We pray thee, O Lord, our Father,*
> *to send us the rain.*

In keeping with nomadic tradition, Somali people greet each other asking about peace. The resolution of border tension between their country and Ethiopia would indeed be good news to share. Given that they are not currently involved in fighting, the peace they long for embraces all of life, not least peaceful transition from one government to the next.

O God, give us peace,
give us tranquillity,
and let good fortune come to us.

Invocation for peace, rain and health:
The Prayers of African Religion, John Mbiti

Lord God,
there are places in this world some of us will never visit,
and people we have hardly ever thought of until we are reminded that
they are there, and that you know about them.
Such a place is Somalia;
the Somalis such a people.
Bless the church there, negligibly small in this world's terms.
Give it an appropriate witness,
a lively experience of worship,
and a life-style which commends the gospel. Amen.

Week 14

Sudan • Uganda

O Thou, who art the Lion of Judah,
be thou also the Lion of Africa,
and burst all the chains
that still bind our African brothers and sisters
and deliver them from all fear.

A prayer for Africa

Sudan

The Democratic Republic of Sudan is today the largest country in Africa. Formerly known as The Sudan it achieved independence in 1956.

Population: approx. 21 million.

Languages: Arabic, English, and over a hundred other languages.

Government: Multi-party republic.

Religion: Muslims 74%, followers of traditional African religions approx. 15%, Christians 9.8% (Roman Catholics 5.2%, Protestants 3.1%, Orthodox 0.8%).

The territory of present-day Sudan was the site of ancient Sudanese civilizations, notably the kingdom of Nubia which persisted for almost a thousand years in the millennium that saw the life of Christ on earth. Indeed the Ethiopian eunuch of Acts 8 was the servant of the Candace of Merowe which is now in northern Sudan. This, presumably, is how Christianity first reached the area. Certainly by the 4th century it had spread up the Nile from Egypt, and a Coptic church became established. With the spread of Islam this church became isolated and finally disintegrated. Roman Catholic missionaries came in the mid-19th century, followed by those of other denominations. Direct evangelism was not permitted in the Muslim north, but educational and medical work was

established. In the south there were no such limitations and the church grew.

The people of Sudan belong to many ethnic groups with a major division between north and south. In 1955 shortly before Sudan achieved independence, the southern provinces began to rebel against rule from the Muslim north. Successive governments, both civil and military, were unable to deal with this problem and fighting continued for 17 years. Mass killings occurred and many people fled. The church came under intense pressure. After a period of uneasy peace, fighting broke out again.

Internal rebellion, economic crisis, drought and famine, and the influx of refugees from Ethiopia, Chad and Uganda have created massive problems, and resulted in a prolonged emergency situation. The Sudan Council of Churches (Roman Catholic, Protestant and Orthodox) is coordinating the church's relief effort.

Intercessions and Prayers

"In the troubled regions of the Southern Sudan the steadfast faith of Shadrach, Meshach and Abednego, and indeed the entire book of Daniel, has taken on new meaning in recent years."

Pray

for church leaders and all Christian people in Sudan, that they may continue to be aware of the presence of God as they walk through the fire

> *O God, make speed to save us;*
> *O Lord, make haste to help us.*

Versicle and Response: *Prayer Book of the*
Church of the Province of the Sudan

Numbed by war, struggling on amidst near starvation, pastors and people try with paltry resources to be faithful to their calling; and yet, in that very situation they contrive a new hymnody. "These are the new songs of worship, the ones that rise from the struggling Christian groups... So perfectly do some of these songs meld together the sorrow and trauma of these years, with the rhythm and the words. As we sing 'Father of our Lord in heaven' it is the last, hard-beating line of each verse that leaves a chill as I see the solemn, lost faces of my Dinka brethren round the fire."

The Father of our Lord in Heaven,
Visit us for we are worried in our hearts.
We are without faith, O Lord; try to visit us all.
We are all worried; the hardships of this world are upon us.
The sin of the world has cut us away from your path.
We are left alone, we are left, we are left, we are left.

"All the problems of the rest of Africa focused on this one country with its impossible geography, impossible mixture of people... its refugee population the biggest in Africa..."

O Lord Christ,
who as a boy lived with his parents by the banks of the Nile,
have compassion on all the refugees in Sudan,
the land of the Niles;
help and encourage all those who work to relieve their distress
for your name's sake. Amen.

Pray

for political stability in Sudan; and for the leaders of the government and the Sudan Peoples' Liberation Army, the will and wisdom to negotiate peace. The universal plea from Sudan is "above everything else pray for peace"

O God,
our Creator, Redeemer,
sustain the people of the Sudan,
give food to those who hunger,
strength to those who suffer,
and peace and security to all.

Prayer of Sudanese Christian woman

God bless Sudan;
Guide her rulers;
Guard her peoples;
And grant her peace based on justice and freedom.
Help the church to be again a means of reconciliation,
and bless all who are peace-makers.

From the Sudan Council of Churches with an appeal
for prayer and fasting

Uganda

Long known as "the Pearl of Africa", the Republic of Uganda has suffered untold devastation in recent years. Of the three major ethnic groups, the Bantu are mostly in the south and west, and the Nilotic and Sudanic people in the north and east. Normally about 90% of the population is engaged in agriculture in this naturally fertile land.

Population: Approx. 13 million.

Languages: English and many ethnic languages.

Government: Parliamentary system, interim government.

Religion: Christians 65-80% (Roman Catholic and Anglican churches by far the largest). Muslims approx. 10% especially in the north-west. Adherents of traditional beliefs about 12% especially in the north-east.

Christian missionaries first came to this area in 1877, and some of the first converts to Christianity were young men being trained for future leadership at the court of the Kabaka of Buganda. They were regarded as a threat, and many were martyred. Around the turn of the century Christianity spread rapidly, and some thirty years later the revival movement spread from neighbouring Rwanda. The church pioneered educational work, and continued to play a very significant part until the government took over all schools in 1964. In the same year a joint Christian Council (Roman Catholic and Anglican) was established.

Formerly a British Protectorate, Uganda became independent in 1962. In the following years attempts were made to balance political power between the various groups, but since 1966 ethnic rivalries have come to the surface. The country has suffered several coups, a disastrous dictatorship and civil war. Anarchy and devastation have prevailed. Christians suffered especially under President Amin. The number of people massacred is unknown, and many others fled the country. People were unable to plant their crops, and drought and famine increased the hardship. The interim government formed in 1986 offers a new hope of change and betterment. In this situation the Christian message of reconciliation is vital, and the church, supporting government policies of reform and renewal, continues to offer this alternative way of life to the nation. Serious evangelism, and patient involvement in education, medical services and community development continue. Most of all, the church in Uganda is known for its prayerfulness.

Intercessions and Prayers

Praise the Lord

Martyrs gave birth to that great dynamic family of Christ in the heart of Africa 100 years ago. It is the blood of *this* martyr that will give birth to a new burst of faith and loving sacrifice that will shape the church of Uganda in the next 100 years.

> Canon Samuel Van Culin, secretary general of the
> Anglican Consultative Council, speaking of Archbishop Janani Luwum

O God, by your providence the blood of the martyrs is the seed of the church: Grant that we who remember before you the blessed martyrs of Uganda may, like them, be steadfast in our faith in Jesus Christ, to whom they gave obedience, even to death, and by their sacrifice brought forth a plentiful harvest...

> Collect for the martyrs of Uganda

Tukutendereza, Yesu	*Glory, glory, Hallelujah*
Yesu mwana gwendiga	*Glory, glory to the Lamb*
Omusaayi gwo gunaazizza;	*Oh, the cleansing blood has reached me*
Nkwebaza, Yesu Mulokozi.	*Glory, glory to the Lamb.*

> Chorus of the East African Revival movement sung on every
> conceivable occasion, on hearing the call of God,
> at a funeral, before making a journey, on joining the fellowship

Martyrdom and revival are two notable themes of contemporary Ugandan spirituality.

Pray God

for the healing of Uganda; that the bitter ethnic hatreds may be resolved; the spirit of revenge disappear; and love flow forth

for the government; and for the national reconstruction of agriculture, industry and the entire economy

for the church in Uganda, that Christians may lead the way in forgiveness, reconciliation, and in promoting fresh trust among those in the different communities

for the inner strengthening of all God's children in Uganda against all the forces that corrupt, atrophy, undermine and weaken the human spirit

O Father God,
I cannot fight this darkness by beating it with my hands.
Help me to take the light of Christ right into it.

For all in trouble, a prayer from Africa

In common with many other countries there is concern and anxiety in Uganda about the spread of AIDS.

Keep us, Sovereign Lord
from panic when crisis and panics arise.
Help us to know that though you do
not always remove troubles from us
you always accompany us through them.

A prayer from Uganda

O Lord
stablish, strengthen and settle all Christians in Uganda
and encourage in them and in us
an awareness of our common bond as members of your body.

Week 15

Kenya • Tanzania

Grant that the peoples of East Africa
may love mercy,
deal justly,
and walk humbly with their God,
and with each other. Amen.

Christianity was first brought to the coastal regions of these countries by Portuguese mariners in the 15th and 16th centuries, but failed to survive when the Arabs reconquered the area in 1730. Both Roman Catholic and Protestant missionaries came in the colonial era. Some began work on the island of Zanzibar before crossing to the mainland, and some worked initially in settlements for freed slaves. In Kenya especially there were soon flourishing Christian communities.

Kenya

Population: 20.4 million.

Languages: Swahili, English and over 15 others.

Government: Unitary single-party republic.

Religion: Christians 75% (approximately equal numbers of Roman Catholics and mainline Protestants; slightly fewer members of African indigenous groups). Adherents of tribal religions 16%, Muslims 6%.

When Africa was carved up by the colonial powers in the latter half of the 19th century, Kenya became a British colony. Independence was gained in 1963, and apart from brief periods of unrest, stability has been maintained. Some 85% of the population are engaged in agriculture and the dairy industry. The high rate of population growth together with the effects of drought has largely offset economic successes. There are many different African ethnic groups including the Kalenjin, Kamba, Kikuyu, Kisii, Masai, Meru, Miji Kenda, Luo, Luyia and Somali, as well as appreciable Asian and European communities.

The number of Christians in all denominations has grown rapidly in this century, and the East African revival resulted in a deepening of spiritual life. Arising out of an essentially African appropriation of the gospel indigenous churches have emerged, and there are now over 200 such "independent" churches. The years 1952-56 saw the Mau Mau crisis, in which a resurgence of African traditional oathing combined with rising nationalism was directed against the British and those associated with them. Many Kikuyu Christians refused to take the Mau Mau oath and were martyred. The church subsequently tended to remain aloof from civil affairs, but is now playing a more active part, and has voiced concern on a number of issues.

Nairobi is a key communications centre in East Africa, and is the headquarters of the All Africa Conference of Churches and of the Association of Evangelicals of Africa and of Madagascar, representing conservative evangelical Christians.

Intercessions and Prayers

Bwana Asifiwe!

Translated "Praise the Lord!" this is a common greeting among Kenyan Christians as they meet, shake hands and discuss the happenings of the day. Moreover, Bwana Asifiwe also speaks of a God continually watching over the activities, needs, relationships and thoughts of all in Kenya, and is therefore an ascription which passes naturally from praise into prayer.

Pray therefore

that peaceful development may continue in Kenya, and that all people may share in the material welfare of the country

We beg you, O God
to rule over this and every town and city.
Increase our blessings,
and bring us prosperity.

Prayer from Kenya

for those living in areas of famine, and for parents who must watch their children suffer

for the continued numerical growth of the church, and for unity, devotion and compassion surmounting all barriers of tribe and denomination

for all priests, pastors and teachers, that they may be given gifts to meet the spiritual needs of people; and that many may come to know Christ as Saviour and follow him along African paths

that Christians in Kenya may enter more deeply into their biblical and sacramental heritage, and rejoice in its present day relevance:

From a wandering nomad, you created your family;
for a burdened people, you raised up a leader;
for a confused nation, you chose a king;
for a rebellious crowd, you sent your prophets.
In these last days, you have sent us your Son,
your perfect image, bringing your kingdom,
revealing your will, dying, rising, reigning,
remaking your people for yourself.

From the draft eucharistic liturgy,
Church of the Province of Kenya

A litany based on a traditional Kikuyu form

Leader: *Let us pray to the God of our fathers, through Jesus Christ his Son, in the power of the Holy Spirit.*
May the bishops and leaders of our churches have wisdom and speak with one voice.

People: *Praise the Lord: peace be with us.*

Leader: *May the leaders of our country rule with maturity and justice.*

People: *Praise the Lord: peace be with us.*

Leader: *May the country have tranquillity and the people be blessed.*

People: *Praise the Lord: peace be with us.*

Leader: *May the people and the flocks and the herds prosper and be free from illness.*

People: *Praise the Lord: peace be with us.*

Leader: *May the fields bear much fruit and the land be fertile.*

People: *Praise the Lord: peace be with us.*

Leader: *May the face of our enemies be turned towards peace.*

People: *Praise the Lord: peace be with us.*

Leader: *May the path of the world be swept of all danger.*

People: *Hallelujah! The Prince of Peace is with us.*

From the draft eucharistic liturgy,
Church of the Province of Kenya

Tanzania

Population: 21.8 million.

Languages: Swahili, English and over a hundred others.

Government: Unitary single-party republic.

Religion: Christians 45% (Roman Catholic, Lutheran and Anglican denominations are the largest). Adherents of traditional African beliefs 22%, Muslims 33%, notably in Zanzibar and along the coast.

Tanzania came into being in 1964 by the merger of Tanganyika, a former German colony which gained independence in 1961, and the Sultanate of Zanzibar, a former British protectorate. Zanzibar retains a degree of autonomy. The Tanzanian people belong to very many different ethnic groups, but this has not caused significant divisions. Some 90% are farmers often at subsistence level. The socialist government implemented a new village system, Ujamaa (familyhood), which is a cooperative for farmers in which decisions are made communally and products shared according to need. Lack of technical knowledge and experienced leadership are continuing problems. Drought and adverse terms of trade have led to severe economic problems, and the country, one of the world's poorest, is dependent on foreign aid.

The Christian church is growing rapidly in Tanzania, but is not yet Africanized, and there is a relative absence of indigenous churches. There is, however, considerable vitality, with the renewed discovery of healing and other spiritual gifts, and a lively response from young people.

Churches are required to become more involved in the formation and organization of Ujamaa, and many Christians have responded willingly. The church continues to minister in a number of social and development projects.

Intercessions and Prayers

Heavenly Father,
thank you for the peace you have given us in Tanzania;
grant our leaders wisdom and honesty
to seek the welfare of all our people.
Give us strength to plant our fields
and joy in using the land you have given us.
Teach us to care for the sick and poor,
that all may know your love. Amen.

Prayer from Tanzania

We pray

for all in authority in the land, from the ten-cell leader in the village to the president in Government House, that they may display courage, honesty and integrity

for wisdom and skill for those who manage the economy; and for a fair distribution of food, fuel, soap and whatever basics are obtainable

for responsible use of the land and the forests; and for all those combating insects and other pests that eat away growing crops and stored grain

for local Christian congregations; for pastors, lay leaders and people; and their witness in the community

Good Lord:
Just as you were pleased to relax,
in the home of Martha and Mary,
abide also, we pray, in our homes.

Bestow upon them an atmosphere of Christian love
where your presence can be found,
your word made known,
your will accepted
and your purpose worked out.

Prayers for Today, for African congregations

"Here in Tanzania neighbouring churches of different areas — Roman Catholic, Anglican, Lutheran — observe the Week of Prayer for Christian Unity moving from one church to another on successive days. In this way they all share messages and experience followship outside their own church."

O God forgive us for bringing this stumbling block of disunity to a people who want to belong to one family. The church for which our Saviour died is broken, and people can scarcely believe that we hold one faith and follow one Lord. O Lord, bring about the unity which you have promised, not tomorrow or the next day, but today.

A prayer from Africa

Week 16

Madagascar • Malawi • Zambia

Let your love be like a steady, gentle rain,
not a cloudburst...

A Malagasy petition

Madagascar

"Daunting, enchanting, and almost overwhelming" is how a recent visitor described Madagascar. The country is poor, and suffers annual devastation from cyclone. The people came originally from Indonesia and the South Pacific, but others have migrated from Africa and Arabia.

Population: 10 million, and rising rapidly.

Languages: Malagasy, French. English, Swahili, Hindi, Arabic and Chinese are also spoken.

Government: Single-party republic.

Religion: Christians 46% of whom about half are Roman Catholics. Adherents of traditional religions approximately 45%, Muslims 1.7%.

Madagascar was a monarchy from the 16th century onwards, but became a French colony in 1896 and independent in 1960. The first Christian contacts in 1500 were Portuguese sailors, but missionary activity was spasmodic with no lasting results until the early 19th century. In the reign of Queen Ranavalona I (1835-61) Christians were persecuted and many put to death for their faith. However in 1869 Queen Ranavalona II accepted Christianity, and a mass movement followed.

Poverty, poor communication in a difficult terrain, and fear of change in a strongly traditional society all contribute to the problems of people and church; and, according to the Christian Council, "corruption also is still known everywhere". There are signs of a renewal of traditional culture; and also a lapsing into traditional religions in which an excessive preoccupation with the dead is a feature. The churches have been officially recognized by the socialist state, and a relationship established between the local Christian Council and the government in the sphere of education. There is growing support for the CCCM in which the Roman Catholic, Church of Jesus Christ in Madagascar (union of Congregationalists, French Reformed and Quakers), Lutheran and Episcopal churches participate. The Council is much concerned with human rights and social problems.

Intercessions and Prayers

For the early martyrs of Madagascar, and for all those who in successive waves of bitter persecution have remained faithful — *Thanks be to God*

For the present-day growing together of Christians of very varied traditions — *Thanks be to God*

For the ecumenical commemoration of All Souls Day (2 November and coinciding with Ancestors' Day); and the opportunity this gives to Christians to share with others the teaching of Jesus about life after death — *Thanks be to God*

> *Gracious Lord,*
> *in this season of fullness and completion,*
> *we praise you for all living and all dying.*
> *We thank you for that great circle*
> *in which we are united with all who have gone before us.*
> *Bring us all, good Lord, to the day*
> *when you will free our eyes from tears,*
> *our feet from stumbling,*
> *when we shall walk before you in the land of the living.*
>
> The greater family: a prayer by Gabe Huck

O God, who calls us to your service, may we be faithful witnesses to Jesus Christ through our words and through our works.

Prayer of a Malagasy Christian woman

God of goodness and love, in whom we human beings may trust in every hour of need: have mercy on all who are faced with fear and

distress by cyclone. We ask that help may be given wisely and
speedily, and this need turned into an opportunity to strengthen the
bonds of love and service which bind human beings and nations
together, through Jesus Christ our Lord.

Christian Aid. May be adapted for those
suffering any other disaster

*Heavenly Father, you who taught your Son all he knew, in a situation
where everything was in a state of transition;
we pray for today's young population of Madagascar, and for all
who look to the church for guidance and inspiration in a situation
of rapid change.*

*Lord Jesus Christ, you who were born poor, and lived and moved
amongst the poor, the sick and the needy:
we pray for all those in Madagascar who until this day keep their
faith in you alive in the face of hardship and chronic illness.*

*Holy Spirit of God, you who inspired the early church to witness with
great boldness before kings and rulers;
we pray that your church in Madagascar today may be an inspiration and challenge to the people of this Marxist-socialist island.*

Church of Jesus Christ in Madagascar, adapted

Malawi: Zambia

The area of these two adjoining countries was originally inhabited by
bushmen until the Bantu came round about AD 500. European travellers
came in the early 19th century, although the Portuguese had been around
Lake Malawi earlier. Arab and Yao slave raiders were also active in what
is now Malawi, and slavery did not end in this part of Africa until this
century. Both these countries were British protectorates (Nyasaland and
Northern Rhodesia), both became independent in 1964, and both have
since become single-party republics. English is the official language.

The first Christian missionaries to the area met with failure, largely as a
result of illness and natural disasters, but from about 1875 onwards, first
in Malawi and later in Zambia, many Protestant denominations as well as
the Roman Catholic Church became established. As a result of evangelism the church has grown steadily, and has pioneered educational and
medical services throughout the area.

Malawi

Population: 7.3 million.

Religion: Christians 65%, Muslims 16.3%, adherents of traditional beliefs 15%.

This densely populated country, predominantly agricultural and with few natural resources, is host to some 300,000 refugees from Mozambique. A proportion of Malawian men seek work in the mines of Zimbabwe or South Africa. The majority of Christians belong to either the Roman Catholic Church or the Church of Central Africa, Presbyterian, although other Protestant denominations are present. There are a number of African indigenous churches, but a relative absence of Pentecostalists. Although church and state remain separate they are partners in development, and the church is heavily involved in education, medical and social service. The Christian Council of Malawi incorporates a wide spectrum of traditions, and the church's relationship with the Muslim community is notably cordial.

Zambia

Population: 6.7 million.

Religion: Christians about 75%, adherents of traditional beliefs about 25%. Small Muslim, Bahai and Hindu communities.

The largest industrial concentration in Black Africa is along the copper belt of Zambia and the country has other mineral resources. The earlier closure of the border with Rhodesia in compliance with United Nations sanctions had a crippling effect on the economy from which it has not yet recovered. The church is concerned with the problem of refugees of whom there are about 135,000, mostly from Angola, Zaïre, Mozambique, Namibia and South Africa. The Roman Catholic Church and the United Church of Zambia (the largest of the 45 Protestant bodies) are the two largest denominations. Of the significant number of African indigenous churches, many have come in from other countries. The Jehovah's Witnesses have had an extraordinary influence in the country, and it is estimated that over 25% of the population have been involved at some stage in their lives, although many of these now belong to mainstream churches. The government has restricted the sect at various times. The

Zambian Christian Commission for Development incorporates thirty member churches including the Roman Catholic Church and indigenous bodies.

Intercessions and Prayers

At the concluding meditation of a recent ecumenical meeting in Lusaka, of leaders of movements fighting white minority domination in Southern Africa, somebody said: "We must see ourselves as a connected people. We are connected to those who have come before us, and those who will come after us. In this meeting, connections have been made in powerful and moving ways." The making and retaining of connections is the object of our prayer for Christians in this part of the world.

> *May Africa praise you, you the true God*
> *from the south even to the north,*
> *from east to west, from sea to sea.*
> *May the mighty wind bear your name*
> *through cities and hamlets,*
> *by quiet valleys and silent mountains,*
> *over moving waters and sounding falls,*
> *across the sunlit desert,*
> *over the quivering savannah,*
> *through the mysterious forest.*
> *Across the immense African land, overflowing with your praise,*
> *imprint all with your splendour which words cannot express.*
> *May your name be known and loved all over the land.*

Jerome Bala

We praise God

for the harmony existing between the different religious communities in Malawi

for the rich mineral resources of Zambia, and the opportunities for employment which these provide

for the steady growth of the Christian church in both these countries, and its partnership with government in working for the development of all God-given resources

We pray for Malawi

for the growing Christian church, for the development of African styles of worship, and for a deepening faith among Malawian Christians

for a spirit of discernment amongst the people in response to the presence of many foreign missionaries and evangelists

for the church's involvement in education, and in medical and agricultural work

for those men who have to work far from their homes and families, and for their wives and children left behind

We pray for Zambia

Your people tremble, wonder and are perplexed
as they see their nation grappling with creeping materialism,
atheism and gnawing corruption in high and low places.
Grant your church strength, wisdom and courage
to confront the people of Zambia,
and announce the good news of eternal life through Jesus Christ.

John Banda

Dear God in heaven,
We pray for the tens of thousands of refugees living in Zambia.
May they find some measure of comfort and peace and healing
in their exile.
May peaceful solutions be found to the problems and unrest
which plague their home countries.

From Zambia, a prayer for refugees, adapted

Merciful God,
from the sky you send the rain on the hills to fill the earth
with your blessing,
you make the grass grow for your cattle,
and plants grow as food for your people;
may it please you to send your abundant gifts of goodness
to spread into the homes of all your people in Zambia,
so that their hunger may be satisfied,
and none may be in want.

A prayer for drought-prone Zambia

Evening in Africa

At last, O God, the sun's heat has given way to the cool evening.
Take, we pray, the heat out of our desires and our tempers,
and in this evening hour calm us,
that we may experience the peace and serenity which come from you.
At last, O God, the sun's brightness has given way to the rich
colours of the evening.
Prevent us, we pray, from being blinded by the apparent brilliance
of human achievement.
And, in this evening hour,
help us to rediscover the varied beauty of your creation,
and appreciate afresh, in the stillness,
the value of your abiding presence.
For the sake of Jesus Christ our Lord. Amen.

Prayers for Today, for African congregations

Week 17

Brazil

O God of all youth, we pray to you:
We are young people, and we want to celebrate life!
We cry out against all that kills life:
*   hunger, poverty, unemployment, sickness,*
*   repression, individualism, injustice.*
We want to announce fullness of life:
*   work, education, health, housing,*
*   bread for all.*
We want communion, a world renewed.
We hope against hope.
With the Lord of history we want to make all things new.

A group of Brazilian young people
with a visiting peace and justice volunteer

The fifth largest country in the world, with staggering physical attributes — magnificent coastline, plateau, jungle and the great Amazon river — Brazil covers almost half the continent of South America.

Population: 135.7 million.

Language: Portuguese.

Government: Multi-party federal republic.

Religion: Christians approximately 92% (Roman Catholics 82%, Protestants 10%, Orthodox 0.1%). Most of the remainder practise various forms of spiritism. There are small Buddhist, Jewish and Muslim communities.

Originally occupied solely by South American Indians, Brazil became a Portuguese colony in 1500. The Indians, gradually retreating further into the interior, declined drastically in numbers, largely as a result of malnutrition and disease. In the three centuries of colonization some three and a half million Africans, mostly from western Sudan and Angola, were brought over as slaves. The mixing of these three racial groups has resulted in the great variety of physical attributes seen in Brazilians today. Since the 1880s considerable numbers of immigrants have come from various European countries, the Middle East and Japan.

It was a member of the Portuguese royal family who proclaimed Brazilian independence in 1822, becoming himself the first emperor. The country became a republic in 1889. Military leaders have been influential in political life, and there have been periods of military rule.

Roman Catholic missionaries accompanied the first explorers and settlers. The Jesuits in particular worked among the Indians as well as among the settlers: and in addition to churches and schools they established cooperative Indian villages. Opposition from colonists and government resulted in their expulsion in 1750. In the 19th century the first sustained Protestant work began, and the present century has seen a tremendous growth of the Pentecostal movement.

Potentially a rich country, with vast mineral and agricultural resources as well as modern industrialization, Brazil today suffers from inflation, unemployment and a massive foreign debt. Rural people remain desperately poor, and every city has its favelas or shanty towns. All over the country people are coming together to pray, to worship and to share their problems in basic Christian communities. When they read the Bible together they are able to accept for themselves the good news for the poor in a very concrete way. Writing of his experience with fellow Christians in the favelas of Sao Paulo a European visitor recently confessed: "I have never before realized what the Christian gospel meant until I saw it being lived out and practised in Brazil."

Within the Roman Catholic Church there are many bishops, clergy and laity who identify with the poor, and suffer as a consequence, often being branded as communists for their support of the underprivileged. A large part of the church, however, remains neutral in the face of the problem confronting Brazilian society; that of the tremendous disparity between rich and poor. Protestants play an important part in social work and education, and most denominations are growing. The Pentecostals, the largest of the Protestant bodies, are also active in the favelas.

The rubbish dump outside one city in Brazil supports 4-5,000 people. For many the only source of income is garbage picking. "But their potential is shown on the dump itself, where an area has been fenced off as a garden. There people have planted seeds found in the garbage. Corn, beans, pumpkins grow there; to feed their families and as a sign of hope."

Intercessions and Prayers

You know, O God,
how hard it is to survive captivity without any hope of the Holy City.
Sing to us, God, the songs of the promised land.
Serve us your manna in the desert,
and give us grace to enjoy your day of rest
as an expression of our trust.

Let there be, in some place,
a community of men, women, elderly, children and new born babies
as a first fruit, as our appetizer,
and an embrace of the future. Amen.

> Rubem A. Alves, who teaches in the Department of Philosophy,
> University of Campinas, Sao Paulo

Thank God

for all signs of hope in Brazil today

that new hope in Christ has been brought within reach of ordinary men, women and children through basic Christian communities

for the country's return to democracy after a long period of military rule

Pray God

for Brazil's truly apostolic men and women of God who in all walks of life are committed to the quest for the Holy City in the midst of much that is unholy

for Christians working among the poor, often labelled communist

> *Lord, no matter what we Christians get called, let the service of the poor and the asking of awkward questions continue together in Brazil and everywhere else.*

for cities like Sao Paulo, set to become the world's second largest agglomeration; and for all who seek to find an appropriate response to its needs

that the country's bountiful resources may be more effectively used for the benefit of all

that the anger and frustration felt by many Brazilians at unfair economic systems may be met by understanding and assistance from the international community for the Christian Council of Brazil, and for closer ties between those of different confessions

that standing firm beside Brazilian Christians we also may live by creeds which make costly demands upon us

I truly believe in the new humanity.

I believe in a different humankind, of brothers and sisters — politically I would call it "socialized". The world needs to breathe in harmony and be human. We human beings must come to acknowledge one another as all members of the human race, as brothers and sisters — what I would describe as the utopia of faith.

I do not believe in racial or class segregation: because the image of God in humankind is one and one only.

I do not believe in development for minorities, nor in "developmentalist" development for the majority: because that sort of development does not bear the new name of peace.

I do not believe in progress at any price: because the human race was bought for a price with the blood of Christ.

I do not believe in the automated technology of those who say to the computer, "You are our father": because our only Father is the living God.

I do not believe in the consumer society bent on consumption: because only those who hunger and thirst after justice are blessed.

I do not believe in the heavenly city at the expense of the earthly city: because the earth is the only path which can lead us to heaven.

I do not believe in the earthly city at the expense of the heavenly city: "for here we have no lasting city, but we seek the city which is to come".

I do not believe in the old humanity: because I believe in the new humanity.

I believe in the new humanity, which is Jesus Christ risen from the dead, the firstborn of the whole new human family.

Amen. Alleluia!

Well known for his commitment to the cause of the downtrodden and his readiness to bear the consequences of his political witness to Christ, this confession of an all-embracing hope by Dom Pedro Casaldaliga, bishop of Sao Felix, Mato Grosso, is the kind of affirmation by which many Christians stand or fall in Brazil today

Week 18

Argentina • Paraguay • Uruguay

*O God, to those who have hunger give bread,
and to us who have bread give the hunger for justice.*

Prayer from Latin America

The original inhabitants of this area were the semi-nomadic Guarani Indians. Spanish conquistadores came in the first half of the 16th century, and for three centuries the area was governed and exploited by Spain, although the ownership of what is now Uruguay was for a time disputed between Spain and Portugal. The first missionary work among Indians was begun in 1539 by Franciscans. Jesuits soon followed, and worked to both protect and Christianize the Indians. They established cooperative village communities until they were expelled in 1767. Today there are few Indians left in Argentina, and none in Uruguay.

In the early part of the 19th century independence movements developed all over South America, and rule from Spain disintegrated. Argentina became independent in 1816, Paraguay in 1811, and Uruguay in 1825. Following independence Protestant work became possible, the first contact being made in Argentina by James Thomson of the Bible Society, who was the first Protestant missionary in several Latin American countries. In the following decades waves of immigrants as well as other missionaries brought many denominations to the area.

Argentina

Population: 31.1 million.

Language: Spanish.

Government: Federal republic.

Religion: Christians 95.6% (Roman Catholics 91.6%, Protestants 2.8%, Argentinian indigenous 0.7%, Orthodox 0.4%), Jews 2%, Muslims 0.2%.

With a predominantly white population, Europeanized and increasingly secular, Argentina is more fully developed than most South American countries, but currently faces huge economic problems. In this century long periods of military rule have alternated with times of civilian government.

During the years of the last military dictatorship (1976-83) tens of thousands of people, mostly young, "disappeared". Many bodies, tortured and mutilated, have been found, but some 15,000 people still remain unaccounted for. Grief and anger about the fate of the "disappeared", and strong feelings about the course of justice for the perpetrators of atrocities dominate the thinking and feeling of many people. The Roman Catholic Church has been accused of failing to confront the regime, but many individual bishops, priests and lay people stood up for justice and human rights, and some of them also "disappeared". Mainline Protestant church leaders were actively involved in organizations for the defence of human rights.

The Roman Catholic Church enjoys a privileged but difficult position in relation to the state. Considerable renewal followed Vatican II with increased lay participation and concern for social issues. Of the numerous Protestant bodies, the Argentina Baptist Convention is one of the largest. The Evangelical Church of the River Plate incorporates people of largely Lutheran and Reformed traditions in all three countries. Pentecostal groups are active, and at least nine different Orthodox churches, both Eastern and Oriental, are present. A union theological seminary in Buenos Aires serves eight Protestant confessions in Argentina and Uruguay as well as receiving students from other countries. The Argentine Federation of Evangelical Churches has thirty member churches.

Paraguay

Population: 3.3 million.

Languages: Spanish, Guarani.

Government: Multi-party republic currently under military dictatorship.

Religion: Christians 98.5% (Roman Catholics 96%, Protestants 2%, Orthodox 0.2%, Anglicans 0.2%, Latin American indigenous 0.1%). A diminishing number follow tribal religions.

Most Paraguayans are of Indian, or at least part-Indian, origin. The majority live in the fertile area east of the River Paraguay, the Grand

Chaco region to the west being occupied by nomadic Indian tribes and cattle ranchers. Since 1814 Paraguay has experienced a succession of dictators, and some devastating wars. In the Triple Alliance War (1865-70) against Brazil, Argentina and Uruguay, more than half the population died, and losses were heavy in the 1933-35 war against Bolivia. As a result of these wars and the emigration of men to neighbouring countries in search of work, the male:female ratio today is approximately 1:2, a fact that contributes to considerable family instability.

A military coup in 1954 brought the present administration to power, and a state of siege was declared in 1955 which has continued, except for a short break, until the present time. It is the longest military dictatorship in South America. Political opponents and members of labour groups are harassed, and human rights violated. It is estimated that 60% of all Paraguayans live outside the country.

The Roman Catholic Church, subservient to the government for centuries, until the patronage system was abolished in 1967, was profoundly influenced by Vatican II, and since then has increasingly come into conflict with the government. Against a background of increasing unrest, the church consistently protests against human rights violations and abuse of power by the government. Mennonite refugees from Russia at the time of the revolution began work among the Chaco Indians, and sought help from Mennonites in the USA. This is now the largest non-Roman Catholic Christian community in the country. Since 1889 Anglicans have also been working in the Chaco region, and were the first to live among the Lengua Indians. Several other Protestant denominations are present. Since Vatican II there has been increasing cooperation between Roman Catholics and Protestants.

Uruguay

Population: 3 million.

Language: Spanish.

Government: Multi-party republic.

Religion: Christians 63% (Roman Catholics 59.5%, Protestants 2%, Orthodox 0.7%, Catholics of other rites 0.7%), atheists and non-religious 35%, Jews 1.7%.

After an initial period of political strife following independence, a time of stability ensued in which progressive social policies were implemented, and Uruguay became the first welfare state in South America. However, increasing military intervention in civil affairs led ultimately to 11 years of military rule from which the country struggles to recover. The present civilian government faces a severe economic crisis and the question of trial or amnesty for those accused of civil rights violations has been a major issue.

Many European immigrants to Uruguay were opposed to a state-related Roman Catholic Church, and by 1900 there was a substantial group of free-thinkers. The proportion of atheists and non-religious is now higher in Uruguay than in any other South American nation. Church and state were separated in 1918. In the Roman Catholic Church the earlier emphasis on evangelism has shifted more recently to social concerns, especially in relation to development problems in urban ghettos. Concern for the poor is also an issue for the Protestant churches, of whom the Pentecostals and Waldensians are numerically the largest groups. The Methodists, the first Protestant group to enter Uruguay, are active in the national ecumenical movement, and seek to deepen relationships especially with the Pentecostals and Roman Catholics.

Intercessions and Prayers

True evangelical faith
cannot lie dormant
it clothes the naked
it feeds the hungry
it comforts the sorrowful
it shelters the destitute
it serves those that harm it
it binds up that which is wounded
it has become all things to all creatures.

Menno Simons, 16th century founder of the Mennonites

Thank God

for all who share their faith in such practical ways

that in recent years Argentina and Uruguay have emerged from bitter experiences of military dictatorship, repression and violation of human rights

for all new experiences of freedom and the restoration of civil liberties, particularly on the part of the young

for the concern of the Latin American Council of Churches to promote peace in the region

Pray God

for all countries struggling under massive burdens of debt to the international community, while close at hand their own poor perish of hunger and poverty

for countries whose people have much cause to be unforgiving of each other; that for them the gospel may be about freedom, dignity and a new look in the eye. Asked what impact the gospel had made upon them as an indigenous people one Indian Christian said: "It enabled us to look Spaniards straight in the eye"

for the church in Paraguay, and especially its presence among Indians in the more remote areas

for those families who continue to hope that long disappeared family members will reappear

It must be the hardest thing, not to know what has happened,
or what wounds have been inflicted,
or what cell or grave marks the spot,
or whether there will ever be a home-coming.

Heavenly Father, the whole family of humanity is yours
and in your care,
So we remember in your presence
those who have been torn from their families,
those who have taken them away,
and those who are left...
Help us today to be signs of your care for them.

If you had a hundred sheep and lost one of them,
which of you would not leave the ninety-nine
and go looking for the lost one until it is found?

Lord, be shepherd, healing stream, and guard,
that lost ones may find peace with you.

From *Prayers for the Disappeared*,
Latin American Federation of Relatives of Disappeared Prisoners

for the people of Uruguay

*After 11 years of military government our small country has returned
to democracy. So, dear Lord, we pray that you will bless especially all
under 30, who, for the first time in their lives, were able to vote to
elect their new leader. Bless all those who were elected — the new
president facing a daunting task; the senators and deputies; the city
and regional mayors. Give to all of us the tenacity to build a new
nation and take from us feelings of bitterness and revenge.*

for the Christian Council in its task of keeping over a hundred different
Protestant churches and organizations in touch with each other and with
the needs around them; and particularly for their concern to renew
ecumenical vision and leadership in each new generation of young people

Seek the good of the city

*We pray to you, O Lord, our God and Father,
because we are encouraged by Jesus Christ,
your Son and our Brother to do so.
You have said through the mouth of the prophet:
"Seek the good of the city and pray for it to the Lord":
we therefore pray you today for our cities and villages
and for the whole land,
for justice and righteousness, for peace and good order there.
— Have mercy, Lord, we pray*

*We pray for those who govern.
Teach them that you are the ruler of all
and that they are only your instruments.
Grant them wisdom for their difficult decisions,
a sharp eye for what is essential,
and courage to obey your commandment.
— Have mercy, Lord, we pray*

*We pray for all who, by your ordaining,
are responsible for justice and peace.
Hold back members of the police and armed forces
from practising torture.
Help them not to regard every suspect as a criminal
and not to treat every criminal as an object.
— Have mercy, Lord, we pray*

We pray for all who continue to seek salvation in violence.
Show terrorists that no blessing rests in violence.
Take the young among them especially into your care
and bring order into their confused thoughts.
Bring murder and kidnapping to an end.
— Have mercy, Lord, we pray

We pray for all who are no longer able to sleep in peace
because they fear for their own life
and for that of those near and dear to them;
we pray for all who no longer hope in your kingdom;
for all who are tormented by anxiety or despair.
Grant that they may be blessed
with faithful friends and counsellors alongside them
to comfort them with your strengthening gospel and sacrament.
— Have mercy, Lord, we pray

Lord, you have the whole wide world in your hands;
You are able to turn human hearts as seems best to you;
grant your grace therefore to the bonds of peace and love,
and in all lands join together whatever has been torn asunder.

From an intercessory prayer composed for use on Rogation Sunday
by the Evangelical Church of the River Plate, Argentina

Week 19

Bolivia • Chile • Peru

Why on earth had the Spaniards dragged enormous mirrors
and pipe organs from Europe across the Atlantic
through Panama and over the Andes to this valley?
And at what human cost to the peasants?

With such a history
is it any wonder South American Christians
now speak of God
who frees the oppressed
and loves the poor.
Not in the next life
But now.

Like a Mighty River, Lois Wilson

Common to these three countries are the great range of Andes mountains, and conquest by Spain in the 16th century. As a result of war, disease, and expropriation of land the indigenous Indian population was drastically reduced during the early years of Spanish rule.

American Indians are a profoundly religious and mystical people, and accepted the Roman Catholic faith brought by the conquistadores without too much difficulty, although many traditional Indian practices also persisted.

Bolivia

Population: 6.5 million.

Languages: Spanish, Quechua, Aymara.

Government: Multi-party republic.

Religion: Christians 94.5% (Roman Catholics 92%, Protestants 2.5%), Bahais 2.6%.

In spite of many revolts against Spanish rule, Bolivia did not gain independence until 1825. Since then political instability with innumerable coups and changes of government has seriously impeded progress. Badly hit by the collapse of the tin market, and lacking investment to develop other natural resources, Bolivia is the poorest of the South American countries. Over half the population today are Indian, and about a quarter of mixed race. The remainder are mostly of Spanish descent. About two-thirds of the people live on the high plateau. At 15,000 feet La Paz is the highest capital in the world. In recent years the cultivation of coca (from which cocain is obtained) has increased alarmingly, and it has been estimated that 75% of cultivated land is used for this purpose. Illicit drug-trafficking is a major problem.

Although the Roman Catholic Church has not experienced vigorous renewal to the same extent as in neighbouring countries, and suffers from a shortage of priests, its recent support of the rights of land-workers and small farmers has brought it into conflict with vested interests and led to harassment. Christian education, the righting of social injustices and discovering ways and means of using indigenous Indian elements crea-tively in worship are major concerns. The first Protestants to come to Bolivia, in 1827, were itinerant Bible Society colporteurs who preceded resident missionaries by about 70 years. Methodists and Baptists placed considerable emphasis on schools and agricultural projects, and the Methodists opened medical centres. Evangelical Protestant churches are both growing and multiplying; and all churches and religions are required to register with the state. Many sects and cults are entering the country which is facing what one bishop calls "a barbarous syncretism" bearing little relation to the real needs of the people.

Chile

Population: 12.3 million.

Language: Spanish.

Government: Republic. Military junta since 1973.

Religions: Christians 90% (Roman Catholics 75%, Protestants 15%).

Gaining independence in 1818, Chile was relatively quick to develop a sense of nationhood in spite of tremendous regional differences. In spite of the present long-running military regime, democracy is deep-rooted, and for most of its life since independence Chile has been ruled by elected parliaments. Long-standing economic problems have dogged the country, and attempts to reform the social order and meet the basic needs of the people have met with resistance from privileged landowners and industrialists. Since the present "National Security" regime, dedicated to the elimination of Marxism, gained power, innumerable people have been the victims of political execution, have disappeared, been tortured, or forced to leave the country.

The first Protestant missionary, a Bible Society agent, came in 1821 at the invitation of the president, and established schools. Later, Presbyterians, Lutherans, Methodists and others came. Anglicans engaged in evangelistic work with the Araucanian Indians. In 1909 the Pentecostal movement arose, initially within the Methodist church, but soon split from this and subsequently divided again within itself. These two Pentecostal churches have grown rapidly, and are now the largest non-Roman Catholic churches in the country.

Renewal in the Roman Catholic Church in Chile began before Vatican II, and this was the first country in the world to hold synods after that event. Liturgical reform, priority for evangelism, and concern and involvement in social problems are hallmarks of that renewal. Since the coup, concern for human rights and criticism of the regime have resulted for some priests in torture and death, and many foreign priests have been expelled. In response to the human emergency, the churches (Methodist, Lutheran, Orthodox, Pentecostal, Roman Catholic) as well as the Jews, united to set up an ecumenical Peace Committee, which was the only place to which victims of repression could turn for help. The committee provided legal and humanitarian aid on a large scale throughout the country. In 1975 it was closed by the government, its German Lutheran director refused entry, and personnel arrested. Much of the work has continued in other ways. However, within the churches themselves there is a polarization between those who have aligned themselves with the poor and exploited, and those who continue to opt for the status quo. The Christian Confraternity of Churches, formed in 1985, with member churches from a wide spectrum, plays a prophetic role in keeping the goal of unity before its members.

Peru

A land of stark contrasts, Peru's cultural history goes back at least 20,000 years, the last indigenous civilization, the Inca empire, which

extended beyond the bounds of present-day Peru, ending with the Spanish conquest. Independence was gained in 1826.

Population: 20.3 million.

Languages: Spanish, Quechua, Aymara and other Indian languages.

Government: Multi-party republic.

Religion: Christians 98% (Roman Catholics 95%, Protestants 3%).

The major changes which have taken place in the Roman Catholic Church in Latin America did not leave Peru aside. In response to the call to a new commitment to the poor, the church has spoken out against social injustices. A network of basic Christian communities developed in the 1970s, and remains a strong force today especially in rural areas and shanty towns. Protestants, who were forced to worship in private until 1915, came with a wave of immigrants from northern Europe. Denominations from North America came later, and a number of independent churches have sprung up. Pentecostal and Adventist groups together comprise the majority of the Protestant population, the traditional confessions remaining small. Protestants have become increasingly involved in social action programmes and several missions are working among Indians in the jungle areas.

The vast majority of people are extremely poor. Many from the rural areas have migrated to the cities where they live in sprawling shanty towns. Since 1980 a Maoist guerilla organization, Sendero Luminoso (Shining Path), has drawn considerable support. The violence of the organization has been matched by the response from government and military, and both sides are implicated in the massacres which have taken place. Of six Peruvian bishops who have eloquently championed the poor, four have been "mysteriously" killed in recent years — it is not known by whom. The present government, elected in 1985, faces a daunting task in attempting to tackle the country's many problems.

Intercessions and Prayers

A recent visitor to Latin America tells of how he learnt to say "gracias", "thanks", and how the familiar expression "demos gracias" became something more than a prayer said before eating, but a whole way of life lifted to God in an all-pervading atmosphere of gratitude.

For the deep sense of gratitude that pervades the life of Christian churches in South America — Demos gracias

For every sign of the church's identification with the poor and marginalized — Demos gracias

For the incredible courage and faithfulness of so many fellow Christians in these countries — Demos gracias

That for many in Latin America, hardships, suspicion, vilification, attacks, imprisonment, torture and exile are signs that they are in line with the gospel — Demos gracias

For the witnesses of hope, and the sense of communion and solidarity felt by Christians with martyrs of all lands, past and present — Demos gracias

Marking the frontier between Argentina and Chile, the monument, Christ of the Andes, pledges peace between the two countries.

The Christ of the Andes is no longer a statue, but is taking flesh and blood in the tormented struggles of the peoples of Latin America. He comes striding out of the Gulag Archipelagos...

I believe in the Great Commission, Max Warren

Amen, even so, come Lord Jesus.

The following meditation is from ten people while detained in the central police station, Santiago.

Our Father... here and now.
Our Father who art in heaven
    (and here in the police headquarters, amongst us, the detained.
    We who meet in your name day by day)
Hallowed be your Name
    (despite all the jeers and roughness with which they treat us
    when we name you)
Your kingdom come
    (where there is no degrading treatment, nor privations of liberty,
    nor roving salesmen dressed in rags, nor humiliated prostitutes,
    nor police obeying unjust laws)
Your will be done on earth
    (and on this part of the earth in particular)
As it is in heaven

Give us this day our daily bread
(the bread which takes away hunger, and the bread which
maintains within us the hunger and thirst for justice)
And forgive us our sins
(those that we have done to the police when we refuse to treat
them as brothers, or when we refuse to accept that they live
under great tensions and contradictions)
As we forgive those that sin against us
(or rather, as we try with all our being to forgive those that
sin against us, even the commissioner of police)
Don't allow us to fall into temptation
(by responding to a curse with a curse
to hatred with hatred, to maltreatment with maltreatment)
Free us from evil
(from grovelling and fawning, from humiliation, from despair and
desperation, and from our sense of loneliness and isolation)
Amen.

By your presence, Lord

transcend the limitations of our solidarity with your suffering children in
Latin America

calm and comfort those who live in any kind of fear

deal compassionately with families suffering from unemployment and
hunger

touch the consciences of all who hope to gain by the growth, trade and use
of cocain

strengthen the true faith; and grant that men and women may put their
confidence in that which is enduring

draw Christians together around one table and in one service of the poor
and needy

> *Lord of mystery, let us feel your presence at the very heart of life, and*
> *seek and find you in the depths of everyday things.*
>
> Prayer of Louis Espinal, Jesuit priest murdered in Bolivia

> *O Lord, in times of weariness and discouragement continue, we pray,*
> *to nudge people along in the ways of justice and peace.*
>
> *L'Amérique latine en prière*, compiled by Charles Antoine

Drawn up specially for use at the Faith and Order Commission meeting in Lima, Peru, in January 1982, the so-called Lima liturgy provides an opportunity for Christians of different traditions to go as far as possible together in a eucharistic liturgy:

Lord God, gracious and merciful,
you anointed your beloved Son with the Holy Spirit
at his baptism in the Jordan,
and you consecrated him prophet, priest and king:
pour out your Spirit on us again
that we may be faithful to our baptismal calling,
ardently desire the communion of Christ's body and blood,
and serve the poor of your people and all who need your love,
through Jesus Christ, your Son, our Lord,
who lives and reigns with you in the unity of the Holy Spirit,
ever one God, world without end. Amen.

Atlantic Ocean

Gulf of Mexico

Caribbean Sea

Pacific Ocean

1. Argentina
2. Chile
3. Uruguay
4. Paraguay
5. Bolivia
6. Peru
7. Brazil
8. Ecuador
9. Colombia
10. Venezuela
11. Panama
12. Costa Rica
13. Nicaragua
14. Honduras
15. El Salvador
16. Guatemala
17. Belize
18. Mexico

Latin American Council of Churches (CLAI)

Established as recently as 1982 and therefore one of the newest ecumenical organizations, the *Consejo Latinoamericano de Iglesias* represents a vigorous attempt to forge a unity of witness and service among Christians in Latin America. With its officers drawn from a number of different Latin American countries, its headquarters are presently based in Quito, Ecuador. The Council relates to more than a hundred Protestant churches and organizations throughout Latin America.

Functioning as "an attentive, objective and prophetic voice in enabling divine truths to be expressed in a timely way", the attention of CLAI is currently directed to a wide range of very practical issues including the widespread unrest felt on account of the burden of foreign debts; peace; the defence of human rights and the return of exiles; the unequal distribution of land, and the welfare of indigenous peoples.

CLAI publishes a newsletter, *Rapidas*, and a broadsheet, *Pastoral Solidaria*, designed to promote solidarity with the poor and to help churches in their pastoral work. In addition to its concern to promote ecumenical leadership, the Council of Churches also seeks to respond to requests from member churches for help with new patterns of worship more related to today's needs.

They speak of the unchanging need to make use of "the rhythms which our people love" and of "the simple and direct words of the psalms and gospel" in expressing their solidarity with one another, and their assurance of the Lord's presence in what they describe as "a time of pain, but also a time of song for Latin American believers".

Almighty God, we come to your presence with the awareness of your gracious love. You have given us a continent full of the glory of your creation. You have blessed us with people who have developed cultural beauties that even today enrich our lives. You have given us the glory of your gospel — promise and reality of our liberation. We thank you, Lord!

We confess that we have not been faithful stewards of so many blessings. The brutal conquest, the division of classes, the dictatorial oppression, the premature death of so many, are realities of yesterday and today which cause us pain and of which we are ashamed. Have mercy, Lord!

For the indigenous people of Latin America we give thanks to you and ask for the manifestation of your liberating power.

For the marginal inhabitants of our big cities, for the abandoned children on the streets, we ask your blessing.

Open our eyes to the reality of the resurrection of Jesus Christ as an anticipation and promise of a new day of love and justice which you are preparing for your people. Send your Holy Spirit, the power which gives testimony of your liberating action in our life and the life of our people.

We pray for the coming of justice and the realization of peace. We pray for your church so that she may live and announce freedom in Jesus Christ.

O Lord, we give thanks to you and ask forgiveness. Come to liberate your people, in Jesus' name.

Emilio Castro

Solidarity is another name for love

Solidarity is another name for the kind of love
that moves feet, hands, hearts,
material goods, assistance, and sacrifice
towards the pain, danger, misfortune, disaster,
repression, or death
of other persons or a whole people.
The aim is to share with them
and help them rise up, become free,
claim justice, rebuild.

In the pain, misfortune, oppression,
and death of the people,
God is silent.
God is silent on the cross,
in the crucified.
And this silence is God's word,
God's cry.

In solidarity God speaks the language of love.
God makes a statement,

utters a self-revelation,
and takes up a presence in solidarity.

God is love,
God stands in solidarity,
God is solidarity.
Where there is solidarity,
there is God, making an efficacious statement.

And everything God says —
in speech, in silence, in stridency —
is to seek solidarity, greater solidarity.

Jon Sobrino, Salvadorian Jesuit

Week 20

Czechoslovakia • Poland

To you, Creator of nature and humanity,
of truth and beauty, I pray:
Hear my voice, for it is the voice of the victims of all wars
and violence among individuals and nations.
Hear my voice, for it is the voice of all children who suffer
and will suffer when people put their faith in weapons and war.
Hear my voice when I beg you to instil into the hearts of all
human beings the wisdom of peace, the strength of justice,
and the joy of fellowship.
O God, hear my voice, and grant unto the world your everlasting peace.

From a prayer of Pope John Paul II

Czechoslovakia

Population: 15.5 million.

Languages: Czech, Slovak. Hungarian, Polish and Ukranian are also spoken.

Government: Federal socialist republic.

Religion: Christians 80%, Jews about 0.1%. Almost a quarter of the population are atheists or non-religious.

Situated in Central Europe, Czechoslovakia has been exposed to Franco-Teutonic influences from one direction, and Magyar and Slavic influences from the other. Early German missionaries brought the Roman Catholic faith into the area, Bohemia (northern Czechoslovakia) becoming Roman Catholic under King Wenceslas in the 10th century. In the 9th century, in response to a request from the king of Moravia (central Czechoslovakia) for missionaries who would teach his people in their own language, the Byzantine patriarch sent the brothers Cyril and

Methodius. They encountered opposition as a result of the growing rift between Rome and Constantinople, but nevertheless received support from the Pope. Reformation influences were strong in the 15th and 16th centuries, with the movement begun by the Protestant martyr Jan Hus, the founding of the Moravian Brethren, and the influence of Luther. In 1621 the Catholic Hapsburgs gained control, and although counter-Reformation pressures eased with the Edict of Tolerance, it was not until 1848 that Protestants gained equal rights with Roman Catholics. The dissolution of the Austro-Hungarian empire had political implications for the area, and since 1948 communist control has affected all the churches.

Although the constitution guarantees freedom of religion, all churches and religious communities require official recognition by the government. The majority Roman Catholic Church has experienced considerable restriction, and tension continues. There have been particular difficulties regarding ecclesiastical appointments, and many positions have remained vacant for years. The Czechoslovak Hussite Church, born out of a Roman Catholic modernist movement, influenced by the spiritual tradition of Hus, and incorporating a strong biblical theology, is the second largest confessional body. The Evangelical Church of Czech Brethren is a union of the Brethren and the fruits of the Hussite movement in which women played a prominent role. Various Lutheran and Reformed bodies are present. The Orthodox Church, autocephalous since 1951 is strongest in eastern Slovakia. All Christians face the problems of maintaining a faithful witness in a socialist state, and are concerned about issues of human rights and of peace.

Poland

Population: 37.4 million.

Language: Polish.

Government: Socialist republic.

Religion: Christians 90%. There are very small Muslim and Jewish communities, and a proportion of atheists and non-religious.

Poland became officially Christian in 966 with the baptism of the ruler who was converted to Christianity through his Roman Catholic wife. Over the centuries the faith spread and deepened under the influence of Christian rulers, and German missionaries and settlers, and Poland produced many saints and scholars. Protestant influences spread in the 16th century, but the Roman Catholic Church was given official recognition and the Protestant faith restricted. The 18th century political partition of Poland played an essential part in reinforcing the religious and cultural sense of identity that led to the founding in 1918 of an independent republic. During the second world war something like 6 million Polish citizens, half of whom were Jews, were killed. A further 1.7 million were deported to Russia. The Jewish pediatrician Janusz Korczak, the Roman Catholic priest Maximilian Kolbe, and the Lutheran bishop Juliusz Bursche are representative of the countless martyrs.

The Roman Catholic Church in Poland has traditionally served as a national and social focus, and the election of a Polish pope and his subsequent visits to his homeland have inspired and encouraged the people. Tolerated by the communist regime, the church continues to hold great significance in the daily lives of most people, and the proportion of Roman Catholics practising their faith is much higher than in Western European countries. The Solidarity movement, both in terms of the now banned trade union, and the wider movement towards democratization, has been both tempered and supported by the church. The younger Freedom and Peace movement seeks to hold together issues of international peace, individual freedom and justice, and ecology, as well as to increase understanding across the East-West line. The Orthodox Church, autocephalous since 1924, was greatly reduced in numbers when a large area of land with a considerable Orthodox population became Russian territory in 1945. Of the various Protestant bodies, only about a third are recognized by the government as churches. Although tensions remain, the Roman Catholic Church is slowly drawing closer to the other churches in Poland. One of the main tasks of all the churches is the education of children and young people in a communist society.

Intercessions and Prayers

When I'm down and helpless
When lies are reigning
When fear and indifference are growing
— May your kingdom come.

When joy is missing
When love is missing

and unbelief is growing
— May your kingdom come.

To the sick and lonely
To the imprisoned and tortured
— May your kingdom come.

Into the churches
Into our praying, into our singing
— May your kingdom come.

Into our hearts
Into our hands, into our eyes
— May your kingdom come. Soon!

A Czech litany

Let us thank God

for all such affirmations of faith and hope arising out of situations of restraint and hostility

for the early missionary activity of Cyril and Methodius, apostles to the Slavs

for a history of martyrdom, and solidarity between church and suffering people which has characterized life in Poland through the centuries

In the words of the Sunday eucharist prayer of the Czechoslovak Hussite Church, *let us pray* for the continuing everyday needs of the people of Czechoslovakia:

Bless, O God, the diligent work of all people who try to earn their daily bread for themselves and their families. Good Lord, help the miserable, comfort the sad, give rest to the tired and weary; give courage to those who suffer, freedom to the depressed, protection and shelter to orphans, and strength to the weak in their struggle against all temptations of violence and danger...

Let us also pray

for Poland; for the movements of Solidarity, and Freedom and Peace; and for a recognition of the dignity and the right to self-determination of the Polish people

for the Christian education of children and young people; for increased practice of Bible reading and prayer in homes; for perseverance in confessing the faith in a socialist environment for those things which concern women in Poland: "There are so many social problems which bother women as mothers, wives and sisters, and lead to a breakdown of family life — problems of alcoholism, drugs, and lack of means to live"

that the churches may grow together in a deeper ecumenical fellowship; that minority churches be saved from becoming inward looking; and majority churches look to the needs of their brothers and sisters

that in the uncertain circumstances of life in communist countries Christians may be conscious of the prayers of others

> *We are two hands: but belong to one body.*
> *We differ: we are right hand and left,*
>
> *one stretched joyfully to heaven, one rejoicing in victory,*
> *and one hanging sadly down incapable of grasping anything again;*
>
> *one hand full of strength and power,*
> *clenched in the desire for freedom,*
> *and the other tight with desperation;*
>
> *one hand that can throttle and beat and wound*
> *and one that bleeds —*
> *We differ; but belong to one body.*
>
> *Help us, O Lord, we who are your hands,*
> *that we may not be raised against each other,*
> *but together repeatedly show that we are one in prayer for your rule,*
> *and that we may remain united,*
> *because to you we pray together:*
> *May your kingdom come!*

From Poland

The concentration camp number of Blessed Father Maximilian Kolbe of Poland focuses attention and prayer on all victims of conscience, past and present, including those many persons without a "number" who have "disappeared" in so many countries.

16670

> *May the Lord accept our prayers*
> *and grant that we may see substantial progress*
> *in ecumenical understanding and in the will of God.*

Karol Wojtyla — Pope John Paul II

Week 21

Albania • Bulgaria • Yugoslavia

As the bread which we break
was scattered over the mountains
and when brought together became one,
so let your church be brought together
from the ends of the earth into your kingdom;
for yours is the glory and the power
through Jesus Christ for evermore.

Didache, 2nd century

Small Christian communities reportedly existed at least in the coastal areas of this region at about the time of the end of St Paul's ministry. They may have been largely composed of converted Jews of the diaspora. Later, organized Christianity came from both Rome and Constantinople; the Byzantine influence being considerable in the 9th century. By 927 Bulgaria was an independent Christian nation with its own autonomous church ranking as a patriarchate. The Serbian Orthodox Church first became independent in the 13th century. The whole area, however, was subjected to endless waves of invasion, and changes of rulers. Independence was gained and lost; patriarchates were suppressed and re-established. Protestant influences penetrated Yugoslavia in the 16th century, and newer Protestant denominations arrived in the 19th. Following centuries of control by the Ottoman Turks and consequent suffering of Christians, the area again experienced turbulence in this century, until the emergence of socialist republics after the second world war.

Albania

Population: 3 million.
Language: Albanian.
Government: Single-party socialist republic.

Before the Peoples' Republic was established in 1946, two-thirds of the population was Muslim and the remaining third Christian (20% Greek Orthodox, 10% Roman Catholic, and very small Protestant groups). Anti-religious pressure soon began to build up in this atheistic state, and in 1967 all religious institutions were closed. Churches and mosques alike were either destroyed or converted to secular use; a very few being preserved as "cultural monuments". Officially religion does not exist, and Albanians have been denied contact with the rest of the world. Recently, however, the country has begun to emerge a little from this isolation. Although the poorest country in Europe it is self-sufficient in fuel and grain, and people are well clothed and apparently well nourished. All agriculture and industry is state-run — efficiently enough to provide for free education and a social welfare system without the necessity of income tax.

You, O God, have made us human beings for yourself, and our hearts are restless until they find their rest in you. Grant unto your sons and daughters in Albania a renewed awareness of their creation at your hands, and an irrepressible longing to find their rest in you.

After the words of St Augustine

Bulgaria

Population: 9 million.

Languages: Bulgarian. Turkish and Macedonian spoken in some areas.

Government: Republic.

Religion: Christians approximately 80%, Muslims about 10%.

Formerly a monarchy, Bulgaria became a socialist republic in 1946. Approximately 80% of people belong to the Bulgarian Orthodox Church which "is the traditional faith of the Bulgarian people. It is bound up with their history and as such, by its structure, its nature and its spirit can be considered a church of the popular democracy" (Article 3 of the Law concerning Religious Faiths). This church, recognized again as auto-cephalous in 1945 and a patriarchate in 1953, was separated from the state in 1947. Armenians have been in this area since the 5th century, and today there is a small community (less than 0.25%) belonging to the Armenian Apostolic Church. Roman Catholics (about 0.7%) are mostly of the Western Rite, but some are of the Byzantine. There are about 16,000 Protestants — Congregationalists, Methodists, Baptists, Pentecostals and Adventists.

Legally there is freedom to practise religious rites — and also to engage in anti-religious propaganda. Although the churches operate within certain restrictions their witness is bearing encouraging fruit. Recently there have been some indications of a greater degree of tolerance towards the Christian church by the state. They find common ground in loyalty to the country and in contributing to the building of a new society, and participating in the movement for peace, unity and mutual understanding.

Yugoslavia

O Lord, in you have I trusted:
let me never be confounded.

From Te Deum Laudamus: 5th century, Yugoslavia

Population: 23.2 million.

Languages: Serbo-Croat, Macedonian, Slovenian.

Government: Single-party federal republic.

Religion: Christians 73%, Muslims 11%, a small Jewish community.

Born of the movement to unite the southern Slav peoples, the country of Yugoslavia was formed on the dissolution of the Austro-Hungarian empire at the end of the first world war. Invaded by German and Italian forces in 1941, and torn by civil war between rival resistance movements, it emerged as a communist republic in 1945. It practises a decentralized form of communism, and travel in both directions is freely permitted across its frontiers. Economic difficulties, with rising unemployment and inflation, have led to some unrest.

Considerable religious liberty is allowed in Yugoslavia, and it is possible to hold dialogue between Christians and Marxists. Senior jobs, however, tend to go to party members who are not allowed to belong to any religious body. Many churches are full, and young people, not necessarily from Christian families, form a significant part of the congregations.

Orthodox Christians number about 40% of the population, and are to be found especially in the east and centre of the country. Over the centuries the Patriarchate of the Serbian Orthodox Church has twice been suppressed. When the new nation emerged, the patriarchate was re-established and recognized by the Ecumenical Patriarchate of Constantinople. Although not a state church, it is the traditional church of the people, and exerts considerable influence. It produces a large variety of Christian newspapers and journals. There are sizeable communities of other churches of the Orthodox family, notably Albanian and Bulgarian. The Roman Catholic community, concentrated in the republics of Slovenia and Croatia to the west, accounts for about a third of the population. A proportion are Albanians, and there are a number of Byzantine Rite Catholics. Old Catholic communities also exist. Members of the Lutheran and Reformed churches are largely of German and Hungarian background, and there are congregations of newer Protestant denominations.

Intercessions and Prayers

"And a vision appeared to Paul in the night: a man of Macedonia was standing beseeching him and saying, 'Come over to Macedonia and help us.'"

In company with the people of those lands which gave rise to that plea let us thank God

for those who from the earliest times to the present day have sought to share the Christian faith in the Balkans

for Cyril and Methodius, the apostles to the Slavs, who spread Christianity in south-eastern Europe

for the endurance of the church in its witness to the faith throughout the ages, and especially at the time of the Ottoman domination and in this century

that God is not only where religion is permitted, but has a way of infiltrating even the most restrictive circumstances

Let us seek the forgiveness of God and of each other for the divisions that have hindered Christian witness:

> Lord, we have sinned against you and against each other.
> — Lord have mercy.

O Christ, our divisions are contrary to your will, and have impeded our common witness to you.
— *Christ have mercy.*

Lord, we have not loved you enough in our sisters and brothers, created in your image, but different from us.
— *Lord have mercy.*

Creator God, stop us wandering in alienation from one another. Satisfy the longings of our hearts, grant our rightful requests, and unite us soon in one holy church through your Son Jesus Christ who with you in the communion of the Holy Spirit lives and reigns eternally.

Prayer of an ecumenical group consisting of members
of the Roman Catholic, Lutheran, Orthodox and Pentecostal churches in Yugoslavia

Let us pray

for the churches and monasteries of **Bulgaria**, their metropolitans, bishops, priests, monks and people

that icons honoured by the people may continue to speak to them of a divine realm and the communion of saints

for all in these countries who humbly and quietly seek to be obedient to their Christian vocation while maintaining the vision of a wider whole

Grant, O Lord, that with your love, I may be big enough to reach the world; and small enough to be one with you.

Mother Teresa of Skopje and Calcutta

for hidden Christians in **Albania**, that God will continually strengthen their faith, and give them an awareness of belonging with us to a worldwide family

for growing harmony between various population groups; and for God's blessing on all efforts to facilitate local ecumenical cooperation and goodwill

Lord, you sent your Son Jesus Christ into the world to reconcile us to yourself and to one another. Help us to know how to work together with Christ towards the achievement of universal reconciliation. Amen.

Prepared by an ecumenical group from Slovenia, Yugoslavia,
for the Week of Prayer for Christian Unity, 1986

Remember, Lord, the city in which we dwell,
and every city and region, and the faithful that inhabit it.

Remember, Lord, them that voyage, that travel, that are sick,
that are labouring, that are in prison, and their safety.

Remember Lord, them that bear fruit, and do good deeds
in your holy churches, and that remember the poor.

And send forth on us all the riches of your compassion,
and grant us with one mouth and one heart to glorify and celebrate
your glorious and majestic name, Father, Son, and Holy Spirit,
now and ever, and to ages of ages.

And the mercies of the great God and our Saviour Jesus Christ
shall be with us all.

The Divine Liturgy of St Chrysostom,
commemoration of the diptychs of the living

Week 22

Hungary • Romania

O Heavenly King, Comforter, Spirit of truth,
present in all places and filling all things;
Treasury of blessings and Giver of life:
Come and dwell in us, cleanse us from every impurity,
and of your goodness save our souls.

Orthodox invocation of the Holy Spirit

Hungary

Population: 10.7 million.

Language: Hungarian.

Government: Single-party socialist republic.

Religion: Christians 84% (Roman Catholics 55-60%, Protestants 25%, Orthodox 0.5%), Jews 1%, atheists and non-religious 15%.

Christianity can be traced from the 3rd century in this land where at first both Roman and Orthodox missionaries were active. The Magyars (Hungarians), coming into the area from the east, had strong ties with the Byzantine church, but the Western tradition was adopted in 1001. The Reformation brought Lutheran and Calvinistic influences, and by the end of the 16th century Protestants were in a majority, most belonging to the Reformed church. This situation was reversed when the Austrian Hapsburgs expelled the Ottoman Turks, Roman Catholic settlers moved into the region, and a harsh counter-Reformation began. Hungary did not really gain independence from the Hapsburgs until after the first world war, and then only at the expense of much loss of life and a large area of territory. Becoming a republic after the second world war Hungary is now a socialist state. From the pattern of a feudal agricultural society it has become an industrialized nation — with an efficient agricultural sector also — in which all can participate.

Contacts between the churches and the state are dealt with through the state office for ecclesiastical affairs, which also gives some financial support. The Roman Catholic Church, which had previously enjoyed special preference, found it harder than some Protestants to adapt to life in a communist country. At first resisting the changes, it has felt threatened by increasing secularization and the official atheism of the government. But religious life remains active, and peace is a major concern. Of the Protestant denominations, the Hungarian Reformed Church is by far the largest, with smaller Lutheran, Baptist and Methodist churches. The theology of service, developed after the war, has given added impetus to the church's ministry among children with disability, old people and the sick. A unique venture in Eastern Europe is Christian-Marxist dialogue, in which the Reformed Church is active. The churches are particularly concerned by the effect of increasing secularism — alcoholism, divorce, and the break-up of family life. In this context Christian education is especially important. Most churches belong to the Ecumenical Council of Churches, and mission is an ecumenical priority.

Romania

Population: 22.9 million.

Languages: Romanian, Hungarian, German, and others.

Government: Single-party socialist republic.

Religion: Christians 86% (Orthodox 75%, Protestants 6%, Roman Catholics 5%); Muslims 1.2%, mostly ethnic Turks; Jews 0.5%; atheists 7%.

Its people an amalgam of the local Dacian population and their rulers, Romania emerged out of one of the Roman provinces. For a long time it remained a wedge of Latin culture between Slavs and Mongols. After being an autonomous national unit within the Ottoman empire for three and a half centuries, its people were buffeted between the armies of Austria, Hungary and Russia. Transylvania, formerly part of the Austrian Hapsburg empire, was incorporated into Romania in 1918.

Traditionally Christianity was brought by the apostle Andrew, and by the 3rd century existed in strength on the shores of the Black Sea. There were many local martyrs under the emperor Diocletian. Orthodoxy has been the main tradition for centuries and remains so today. Hungarian and Polish immigrants spread the Roman Catholic faith in Transylvania. Reformation influences reached the Hungarian and German people living in Transylvania early in the 16th century, and Reformed and Lutheran churches were established. The first Baptist community emerged among Germans in 1856. Following independence from Ottoman rule, the Romanian Orthodox Church became autocephalous. It became a patriarchate in 1925.

Services of worship in most churches are lively and well attended. Industrialization and rural depopulation, together with spreading secularism, pose new pastoral and missionary problems and opportunities. Ecumenical witness in the country depends very much on efforts to bring all churches, historical or new, together with all cultures and nationalities into a community serving and struggling with all people. In this connection the "social apostolate", a summons to pastoral care and service towards the whole of society, initiated by the late Patriarch Justinian (1948-77), is a major influence. Peace and disarmament are vital concerns. The Romanian Orthodox Church has launched three appeals for peace in recent years.

Intercessions and Prayers

O Christ, our God, who for us and for our salvation came down from heaven, and stretched out your loving arms upon the cross that all might be gathered into one body: deliver us from all forms of separation and disunity.

O Lord, who gives unto each nation its place and time and mission: grant us the gift of unity of the Spirit in the bond of peace, that the ancient church, and all Christians of this land each loyal to their confession, culture and nationality, may discover new forms of common Christian witness, and stand before the divided world as a united and humble fellowship.

O Lord, who commanded your disciples to pray both for their neighbours and their enemies: give us such love for one another, that with one voice and one heart we may glorify your name, the Father, the Son and the Holy Spirit. Amen.

Prayer for unity: Ion Bria

We give thanks

for the centuries of Orthodox tradition which gave Christianity its roots in Romania

for the renewal of Christian faith and life prompted by the Reformation, especially in Hungary and Transylvania

for the faithfulness with which many held to their Christian faith through centuries of suffering, persecution and oppression

for the spiritual strength which radiates from the Romanian monasteries

for the witness of service offered by the church in Hungary

We pray to God

for the members of different confessions, that they may grow together into a deeper ecumenical fellowship, sharing the richness of their Christian heritage, and strengthening one another in faith, hope and love

for the Christian education of young people

for the training of future generations of theologians

for a fruitful outcome of dialogue between Christians and Marxists

for the churches as God's instruments, that they may contribute to peaceful development in the process of reconciliation between neighbouring countries, and in the world

> *Almighty God, in your majesty and nearness I look into my soul and examine myself with regard to this great profession to which you have called me. I want to teach children and young people in a manner worthy of our homeland, of humanity, and of your heavenly kingdom. I sense the importance of the task and I feel my own weakness. God of strength, support me by your grace. Help me so to do my work that I am worthy of my calling. Grant me respect and love for young people, joy in my work, enthusiasm and commitment, that I may be a worthy worker for the future of your kingdom. Amen.*
>
> A Hungarian teacher's prayer

O Lord our God,
we thank you for the peace of our country and our homes.
We pray that the fruits of work well done may give joy to every worker.
Give your blessing to our congregation and church.
May we truly praise you and serve all your people.

We pray for our homeland, for the leaders of our nation, and for all who have power and bear responsibility.

We pray for our loved ones, and for those who have lived and died in the faith.

May we follow their example, and with them have a share in your kingdom of peace and light,

through our Lord Jesus Christ. Amen.

Prayer from the Reformed Church of Hungary, adapted

Week 23

Mongolia
Union of Soviet Socialist Republics

Khristos voskress!	*Christ is risen!*
Voistinu voskrese	*He is risen indeed*

Christ is risen from the dead: trampling down death by death; and upon those in the tombs bestowing life. Though you descended into the grave, O Immortal One, yet you put down the power of hades, and rose as conqueror, O Christ our God: you spoke clearly to the myrrh-bearing women, Rejoice: you bestowed peace upon your apostles, and to the fallen you brought resurrection.

Russian Orthodox

Mongolia

The Mongols made their mark on world history when, in the 13th and 14th centuries under Genghis Khan, they conquered an empire which included the territories of present-day Turkey, Iran, Russia and the whole of China. Since 1924 Mongolia has been an independent communist state in the sphere of influence of the Soviet Union. It has a population of approximately two million people and a landscape of grasslands and desert. Its traditional religion is Shamanism, with Buddhist Lamaism as a later addition. Together they claim the allegiance of about a third of the population. Although there was some Nestorian activity in this area in the 6th and 7th centuries, and later missionary effort on the part of Roman Catholic religious orders, and eventually in the 19th century by Protestants, there were also many persecutions and setbacks, and Christianity made little lasting progress in this area. To the extent that anything is known about religious life in Mongolia today, it seems likely that there are no more than a few thousand Orthodox Christians in the state. Expatriate diplomats and technicians, and possibly some Orthodox and Evangelical believers among Soviet troops stationed in Mongolia, constitute a constantly changing Christian presence.

O God,
that we may receive your blessing
touch our brows, touch our heads,
and do not look upon us in anger.

In a hard year be thou mercy;
in a year of affliction, be thou kindness;
dark spirits banish from us,
bright spirits bring close to us;
grey spirits put away from us,
good spirits draw near to us.

When I am afraid, be thou my courage;
When I am ashamed, be thou my true face;
Be thou over me like a blanket,
Be thou under me like a bed of furs.

Prayer from Mongolia

USSR

Population: 278.8 million.

Languages: Russian. Each republic also has its own language.

Government: Single-party federal republic.

Religion: Christians number over 96 million, or 36% of the population, of whom 60 million are Orthodox, 4 million Protestant, 3 million Roman Catholic. There are some 30 million Muslims, and 3 million Jews. A quarter of the population are active and militant atheists, and a third are agnostic or non religious.

Christianity began in the very early centuries slowly to penetrate in the southern parts of this territory, and gave birth to the Georgian Apostolic Church, believed to be one of the most ancient churches of Christendom. In more recent centuries Georgian Christians have experienced many vicissitudes under Arab, Mongol and Russian rule. Today the Georgian church, with its main centre in Tiflis, and an official membership of 5 million, is said to be enjoying a period of renewed church attendance with many young people in the congregations.

Also ancient is the Armenian Apostolic Church, Christianity becoming the state religion in Armenia in the 4th century. Armenians suffered severely under Turkish rule, and as recently as 1915-16 approximately 1.5 million Armenians were victims of genocide. Today more than 3 million Armenians live in the Soviet Republic of Armenia, 1.5 million in other parts of the Soviet Union, and the remaining 2 million are scattered around the world. The monastery of Etchmiadzin near Yerevan is the present administrative centre of the Armenian Apostolic Church, increasingly noted for the fervour of its Christian spirituality and practice.

Lord, through the shedding of the blood of your saints,
gather in joy all the scattered children of your church,
and all who weep bitterly at the sadness of disunity,
you who give grace for our salvation.

Armenian Orthodox

It is the baptism in 988 of Vladimar, Grand Prince of Kievan Russia which is accepted as the beginning of the Russian Orthodox Church as an organized, recognized and historical church of all tribes and nations of Early Russia. The year 1988 therefore marks the millenium of the life of this church, an event celebrated by the whole of Christendom. The centre of church and political life shifted from Kiev to Moscow in the 13th century, and in 1589 the Russian church became a patriarchate. Attempts by the patriarch to implement reforms in the 17th century resulted in schism and various groups of Old Believers broke away. After having been abolished in the 17th century, the See was restored again following the Revolution, thus laying the foundation for the renewal of the order and inner life of the church. A difficult transitional period followed as the church adjusted itself to the radically changed conditions of church-state relationships in the new socialist society. The second world war was a decisive period, during which the church gained the respect of the government and of society by the patriotism shown by its members. Emerging from the war united and inwardly consolidated, the church through its members became actively involved in the process of post-war restoration and the building of a new socialist society. The Russian Orthodox Church has been a member of the WCC since 1961 and participates fully in the life of the ecumenical movement. With a membership of at least 50 million it is by far the largest church in Russia, and is widely involved in peace-making activities.

The 4.5 million Catholics in Russia are concentrated primarily in Lithuania, western Ukraine and Byelorussia. They face considerable anti-

religious pressure, many bishops and priests have been imprisoned and some executed, and the church is subjected to severe restrictions. They include members of various Uniate churches, which makes relationships between Catholic and Orthodox more difficult. There is no central leadership and virtually no contact with the Vatican. In this and in other areas of Russia there are many un-registered, illegal and clandestine denominations — some estimates put their membership as high as 10% of the population — known to the Western world as the "underground" church. They are of all confessional backgrounds, and are mostly highly critical of the Soviet regime.

When my soul sheds its tears,
When my heart languishes in longing,
When my whole being shivers in fatigue,
Come, O Jesus, I beg you to come.
Draw near, Reviver and Consoler!
What is it you wish to tell me
by means of these people,
by these circumstances,
by this span of time?
Jesus, I implore you to shorten
the time of trial for us
for my dear ones, for my exhausted nation.
Jesus, I ask you — help those
who laid down their lives for our welfare;
assist them for whom you wish me to pray.

Prayer of Lithuanian prisoners

Fruit of the Reformation, Lutheran churches exist today in Esthonia and Latvia; and there are congregations in Siberia and Kazakhstan which maintain ecumenical connections through the Lutheran World Federation. Baptists came in the 18th century, and the Pentecostal movement spread during the 1920s. In 1944 Baptists, Mennonites, Adventists and Pentecostals joined to form the Union of Evangelical Christian Baptists of the USSR. There are about 80 other Protestant denominations, humbly and quietly maintaining faith in difficult days, and in this sense a challenge to us all. "Russian believers", it has been said, "can resist without stridency, persevere without the image of world victory that sometimes tempts we Christian activists in our political and religious struggle. In their long-suffering they can humble and teach us."

Good Jesus, patient as a lamb in the presence of your captors, keep us silent and still with love for you.

In peace let us pray to the Lord
for the peace of the whole world, *let us pray to the Lord*

Orthodox liturgy, USSR

Ky - ri - e e - lei - son, Ky - ri - e e - lei - son,

Ky - ri - e e - le - i - son.

for those who hold power and carry responsibility that they may consistently pursue policies that lead to peace, understanding and justice, *let us pray to the Lord — Kyrie eleison*

for the people of Mongolia about whom we know so little, *let us pray to the Lord — Kyrie eleison*

for the ordinary people of the Soviet Union, going about their daily tasks and experiencing the joys and sorrows common to all humanity, *let us pray to the Lord — Kyrie eleison*

for all who suffer for their faith, *let us pray to the Lord — Kyrie eleison*

for Armenians in the Soviet Union, *let us pray to the Lord — Kyrie eleison*

for greater mutual understanding between Christians, *let us pray to the Lord — Kyrie eleison*

for the celebration of a thousand years of Christianity in the Russian Orthodox Church; for the Armenian Church's thanksgiving for the gift of the holy chrism, and for God's blessing on all the meeting together which these events will bring, *let us pray to the Lord — Kyrie eleison*

Help us, save us, have mercy on us and keep us, O God, by your grace.

O Lord, I do not know what to ask of you. You alone know my true needs. You love me more than I myself know how to love. Help me to see my real needs which are concealed from me. I dare not ask either a cross or consolation. I can only wait on you. My heart is open to you. Visit and help me, for your great mercy's sake. Strike me and heal me, cast me down and raise me up. I worship in silence your holy will and your inscrutable ways. I offer myself as a sacrifice to you. I put all my trust in you. I have no other desire than to fulfill your will. Teach me how to pray. Pray yourself in me.

Prayer of the well-known hierarch and theologian,
Metropolitan Philaret of Moscow (1553-1633), and described as
"a prayer which has been used by millions of believers for many centuries"

Introduction
to Weeks 24, 25, 26 and 27

More than anything else I shall remember the visit to the old English fort at Cape Coast where the African slaves were kept chained in a dark dungeon at water-level till the boats took them to the slave ships, while in the chapel immediately above, the English garrison conducted worship, keeping watch through a hole in the floor on the inmates of the dungeon below. I am always amazed that these crimes can be so easily forgotten. Ever since that visit I have wished that some representative Englishman — an archbishop or a prime minister — might come to Ghana and go down in that dungeon, kneel down on the floor, and offer a prayer of contrition. I still hope it may happen.

Lesslie Newbigin, writing of his visit to Ghana, Unfinished Agenda

Not only Ghana, but all the countries to be prayed for in these next four weeks are situated on what used to be known as the Slave Coast, from which millions of Africans were transported by traders of many nationalities to work as slave labour on the plantations of the New World. There are a great many places where such acts of penitence are appropriate, but few as poignant as here on the coast of West Africa.

Lord, have mercy upon us.
Christ, have mercy upon us.
Lord, have mercy upon us.

Today with the exception of Nigeria, and to a lesser extent Ivory Coast, these countries are all poor. Most are sparsely populated, and predominantly agricultural, often at subsistence level. Their principal means of livelihood make them very vulnerable to weather conditions and to the fluctuations of world market prices, and many remain in debt. However, many countries are developing a tourist industry. Good beaches, fine scenery up-country, game reserves and fishing are tourist attractions.

Present-day boundary lines stem from the countries' colonial history; but of course the area in general has a history extending back for very many centuries before that, when ancient African kingdoms traded across the Sahara. A good deal of the quest for African authenticity looks back to those earlier days.

Christianity first reached these West African countries in the 15th century when Portuguese mariners and traders came to the coastal areas. Roman Catholic priests came with them, but contact tended to be intermittent, and in many places the church slowly died out. There was no Christian activity in the hinterland; and on the whole, the gospel message was received more readily on the offshore islands than on the mainland. The missionary movement of the 19th century led to the establishment of more permanent churches.

Week 24

Liberia • Sierra Leone

Liberia

Population: 2.2 million.

Languages: English and many local languages.

Government: Republic.

Religion: Officially a Christian state, though about one quarter of the population is Muslim, and many hold traditional beliefs. Most Christians are Protestant; 2% of the population is Roman Catholic.

Founded by the American Colonization Society for liberated slaves repatriated from the Southern USA, Liberia became an independent republic in 1847. Widely regarded as one of the more stable African independent states, the country has experienced a period of military rule. It was freed slaves who welcomed the arrival of both Protestant and Roman Catholic missionaries in the 19th century, and also set up churches including the oldest indigenous Baptist church in Africa. Educational work was begun at this time.

Although the Christian church in Liberia has remained small, it has made a significant contribution to national life, and its influence is out of all proportion to its numbers. In response to the social upheavals following from the 1980 coup, the churches have been active in championing the peoples' rights, and forthright in speaking out on matters of social justice.

There are literally two Liberias. In one Liberia, children have clothing and shelter for their bodies, education for their minds, and freedom and human dignity for their spirits. In the other Liberia, life is so drastically different that its daily ugliness transforms the buoyancy of hope into the fatigue of despair. *Come Lord Jesus, and rescue the perishing. Amen.*

Anglican bishop of Liberia

Sierra Leone

Population: 3.8 million.

Languages: English, Krio (i.e. Creole) and numerous local languages.

Government: Unitary single party republic.

Religion: Most people are Muslims (40%) or follow traditional African beliefs (50%). The Christian community is small.

Freetown, the capital, was originally founded as a settlement for ex-slaves, many of whom had been introduced to Christianity during slavery and now brought their faith with them. The settlement became a British colony in 1808, and was used as a reception centre for the large numbers of Africans being freed from ships which continued to trade illicitly after the slave trade was abolished. Many of the descendants of these slaves, the Creoles, eventually rose to positions of relative wealth and influence. Independence was gained in 1961.

The country remains poor, with very little industrial development, 80% illiteracy, and one of the highest infant mortality rates in the world. The government is trying to tackle the economic crisis and deep-rooted problems of corruption, but "few people can afford the luxury of being incorruptible when their salaries are far too small to feed their families". Islam is actively promoting medical and educational work. Numerically speaking the Creoles of Freetown have continued to constitute the bulk of the church in Sierra Leone, and the vast majority of people living up-country remain untouched by Christianity, although some churches are now active in these areas. Christian leaders who maintain a vision for outreach are able to point to areas of growth and renewal. The United Christian Council, formed in 1924, has twelve member denominations and one of the independent churches is also affiliated to it.

Intercessions and Prayers

We give thanks

for Liberia's significant Christian community, and for those who despite hardships and temptations remain cheerful and retain faith

for the rich human resources of Sierra Leone, and for the generosity and ancient wisdom of her people that out of the adverse climatic, economic and historical circumstances of this part of Africa so many remarkable men and women of God have emerged. "We have seen God at work in the lives and homes of many people, who, under much suffering and in great need, have learned to accept with contentment the situation in which they find themselves, and still give thanks for the goodness of God. 'All things work together for good...' has come alive for us in Africa!"

We pray

for the recovery of the national economy in these countries, and for honest and responsible stewardship on the part of national leaders

for the poor and needy. "The approaching season July-September is the 'hungry season' for those in the country areas of Sierra Leone; when food is in short supply, grain stocks exhausted, and people do and sell whatever they can to make a little money."

for boldness to preach the gospel of peace in the face of political instability in Liberia

"If Mary and Joseph had arrived at an African village [almost any village in Sierra Leone] they would have found a place. Someone would have given Mary a mat by the cooking fire, and there would have been grannies and aunties to help her with the birth. The men would have made room around the rice bowl for Joseph to dip his hand in while he told his story. Angel visitations, dreams and signs in the sky would have called forth awe and wonder but no surprise, for here the spirit world is fully as real as the physical one." (Dorothy R. Gilbert)

We pray that the story of Jesus may be effectively told and find a welcome in the hearts of country people in this part of Africa.

> *Lord, we pray that in all the contacts*
> *and conversations between people*
> *your story may be enthusiastically told*
> *and your living presence acknowledged. Amen.*

> *May God give you a long life, a well body, and a cool heart (peace).*
> A Krio blessing

Week 25

Cape Verde • Guinea • Guinea Bissau
Senegal • The Gambia

*May the word of God
reach all nations
and may He be recognized
as the only one true God.*

A prayer from Guinea

Cape Verde

The Republic of Cape Verde is an archipelago of 15 islands lying about 300 miles west of Senegal. It was colonized by the Portuguese in the 15th century, and Roman Catholic missionary orders met with considerable response in the islands. The population today is Christian, although secularization is increasing. The majority are Roman Catholics, but there are also small Protestant churches on most of the islands. The official language is Portuguese, a local Creole form being widely spoken as well as a number of ethnic languages. The resident population is approximately 300,000.

The impetus for independence was originally linked with that of Portuguese Guinea (now Guinea Bissau), although Cape Verde pursued a slightly separate course. Independence was granted in 1975. The link with Guinea Bissau was severed in 1981, but diplomatic relations have since been restored.

The country has suffered greatly from recurrent drought and consequently needs to import a high proportion of food requirements, and foreign aid is essential. About one million Cape Verdeans live outside the country, and the money they send home helps to alleviate the economic problems. The government is actively grappling with these problems and seeking to improve health and educational facilities; but the difficulties are enormous.

Intercessions and Prayers

Give thanks

for the continuing receptivity of the islanders of Cape Verde to the Christian faith

for the efforts of the government to improve the economy and to develop health services and education in the country

Pray

for the many Cape Verdeans living and working abroad, and for those who face economic difficulties and the effects of drought at home

for all places, like Cape Verde, of which we know little; yet where the Lord's Prayer is prayed, the Creed is recited, the Gloria Patri is sung and the good news of the Annunciation to Mary is commemorated; that each of us in our own very different circumstances may be united with our fellow Christians in the use of such acts of faith and devotion

> *Glory be to the Father,*
> *and to the Son,*
> *and to the Holy Spirit. Amen.*

Guinea

The Republic of Guinea has a population of 6.1 million. French is the official language, but a number of African languages are widely spoken. The majority of people are Muslims (69%), although some (29.5%) adhere to tribal religions. Christians are a tiny minority (1.3%) of whom the majority are Roman Catholics. Guinea is one of the world's poorest countries.

In earlier times, Guinea was part of the great African kingdom of Ghana. Islam was introduced by the Fulani in the 18th century and gained a considerable following. The country became part of French West Africa in the 19th century, and declared independence in 1958. A difficult period followed, during which relationships with neighbouring states deteriorated, and the country became virtually isolated. Tensions have since eased, especially since the military coup in 1984.

Roman Catholic missionaries came to Guinea in 1877; Protestants in 1918. The total Protestant community including Anglicans numbers less than 3,000 and there are no African indigenous churches. Following independence, the government was very pro-Marxist, and at this stage the church was persecuted. In 1967 all foreign missionaries, including priests, were expelled as part of an indigenization programme. This ultimately resulted in a strengthening of the local church as it responded to increased responsibility. The churches are especially active on the offshore islands where there are signs of renewal. The present government, though Muslim, is sympathetic and welcomes their cooperation in the work of development.

Intercessions and Prayers

Let us give thanks

for the opportunity open to the church in Guinea to cooperate with the government in the development of the country

for all signs of renewed vigour in the Christian community

Let us pray

for the poor and hungry of Guinea

for all who, in whatever small way, can begin to bring about change in the national policies and international economic systems that reinforce their poverty

> *I saw a child today, Lord, who will not die tonight, harried into hunger's grave. He was bright and full of life because his father had a job and feeds him, but somewhere, everywhere, 10,000 life-lamps will go out, and not be lit again tomorrow. Lord, teach me my sin. Amen.*
>
> Prayer of an African Christian

> *Grant, O God, to your children in Guinea that in all their times of testing they may know your presence and obey your will, through the grace of Christ our Lord. Amen.*

Guinea Bissau

The Republic of Guinea Bissau has a population of approximately 850,000. Portuguese is the official language, but Crioulo and a number of dialects are widely spoken. About 60% of the people follow traditional beliefs, and 35% are Muslim. The Christian minority of 5% is predominantly Roman Catholic of whom a number are foreigners.

Guinea Bissau was settled by the Portuguese in the 15th century and the Roman Catholic Church here dates from then. Liberation movements began to develop in the 1950s and the Partido Africano da Independência da Guiné e Cabo Verde (PAIGC) was formed. Fighting broke out between the PAIGC and the Portuguese in 1962, and in 1973 the PAIGC proclaimed independence which was recognized by the Portuguese a year later. The link with Cape Verde was maintained until 1980 when the latter withdrew as a direct result of a coup in Guinea Bissau.

Protestants arrived in 1939. The Igreja Evangélica da Guiné (founded by an evangelical group) is the only sizeable Protestant church in the country. There is a tiny Anglican community.

Intercessions and Prayers

Let us thank God

that using whatever imperfect means — whether soldier, trader, traveller, colonialist, missionary, or the humblest of local Christians — he has allowed the gospel to be planted in many lands, and has provided for its reformation and renewal

Let us pray

for those people who find it hard to change and who continue to cling to old beliefs

that the churches today may be faithful to our Lord's command to preach the gospel and make disciples of all people

> *Bless, O Lord, the independent nations of Africa as they emerge into the modern world and come into contact with the secular materialism of the West. May they ever value the spiritual awareness of their ancestors, and find its fulfilment in the face of your Son, Jesus Christ.*

Senegal

Converted to Islam in 1040 the vast majority of Senegal's people remain firmly Muslim, owing strong allegiance to three Sufi brotherhoods. Most Christians (about 3.5% of the total population) are Roman Catholics, with a small Protestant community springing from the work of missionaries of the Lutheran church, Assemblies of God and the Evangelical Church of West Africa. Over the years Christians have made a significant contribution to the country through their institutions, particularly schools, even though the number of church members has remained small.

The population is 6.4 million. French is the official language, with Arabic widely spoken, along with many local languages. Senegal became independent from France in 1960, and in 1982 entered into a confederation with its close neighbour Gambia. In spite of some prolonged contact with Christianity, most of the people remain either untouched or unresponsive to the Christian faith. Local Christian leaders are few, and ways of sharing the Christian faith in a meaningful and compassionate way remain largely unexplored.

The Gambia

A narrow strip of country along the banks of the river, The Gambia extends like a finger into Senegal. Of necessity links between the two countries are close. An attempted coup in 1981 was quelled with the aid of Senegalese forces, and this led to the formation of the Senegambian Confederation which is already making progress in the integrating of common services and policies. Formerly a British colony, The Gambia gained its independence in 1965. English remains the official language. Like Senegal it is a parliamentary republic, with freedom of religion guaranteed to its people. Some 87% of the population (3/4 million) remain firmly Muslim. About 10% continue to adhere to African traditional religions, though many are being gradually Islamicized. Christians total about 3%, of whom the great majority are Roman Catholics, with Protestants numbering but a few thousand.

In 1821 the first Christian church south of the Sahara was established in The Gambia by the Rev. John Morgan, a Methodist minister among African repatriates in Georgetown, MacCarthy Island Division. The liberated Africans later became known as the Creoles/Akus of Banjul. The Methodists were followed by the Roman Catholics and Anglicans and work among the Akus and the Wollofs of Banjul seemed more successful than in the province.

This situation has changed since the second world war. There are today many Christian groups among the Manjargos and the Karoninkas, the

majority of whom are Roman Catholics and Methodists. The bulk of
Manjargos are in the Casamance and in Guinea Bissau. The Gambia
Methodists have pioneered among the Konyagies and have built the most
recent church in the MacCarthy Island Division at Bani for the once-
migrant group, the Konyagies. The Anglicans have now a full-time pastor
at Basse and so have the Roman Catholics. Work continues to develop in
the provinces with priests, pastors and evangelists stationed in the main
centres at Georgetown, Basse and Farafenni. The Roman Catholics form
the majority among the Christian population.

Intercessions and Prayers

*We thank you Lord for the Senegambian Confederation and its
progress in the sharing of resources and services and for signs of
cooperation between the churches of the region. Amen.*

We pray with the people of Senegambia and other countries in the area
that their lands may be spared the effects of drought.

*O God, in whom we live and move and have our being,
grant us the rain we need,
so that your answer to our present earthly needs
may give us greater confidence to ask for eternal benefits.*

Prayer from the Roman liturgy

*O God our Heavenly Father,
you will that all should be saved
and come to the knowledge of the truth;
We pray for the children of Islam in Senegal and The Gambia.
Grant that they unto whom your unity is made known
may learn the richness of your love,
as it is revealed in your Son, our Prophet, Priest and King,
even Jesus Christ our Lord.*

Prayer for use in the Muslim world

*Lord, you want everybody to live in your Truth,
increase our faith in your Son Jesus Christ.*

Prayer of a Senegalese Christian

Week 26

Benin • Ghana • Ivory Coast • Togo

Years ago our Elders said,
"It is God who drives away flies from the tail-less animal."
The same God touches each of us with the Spirit of power
to cope and overcome,
to drive away fears and anxieties,
to help us to walk through life in the fire of faith.

Moderator of the Evangelical Presbyterian Church in Ghana

Benin

Benin's population of almost 4 million is almost entirely African. French is the official language, but each ethnic group has its own language. The country is a single-party republic and the present Marxist-oriented government has established stability after a very unstable period following independence. The majority of people (approximately 64%) follow traditional beliefs. About 14% are Muslims, and 21% Christians of whom the majority are Roman Catholics. The Methodist Church is the largest Protestant body. There are a number of African Independent churches.

Benin is constitutionally a secular state with equal rights given to all religions, but since 1975 religious and spiritual cults have been discouraged. Just over a decade ago all schools were nationalized, and the Roman Catholic Church in particular suffered pressure from the government, but this has eased in recent years. Although many ethnic groups remain untouched by the Christian faith there have recently been some migrations to coastal cities, and a number of small congregations have been established. In 1965 the Methodist Church initiated Action apostolique commune, an evangelistic thrust among the Fon people serviced by an international, inter-racial and inter-ecclesial team, in which Roman Catholics assist in the production of the scriptures in Fon. The Methodist

Church plays an active role in the socio-economic life of the country, and is involved in dialogue with Muslims, as is the Roman Catholic Church.

Lord our God,
we pray for the holy church.
That it be deeply rooted
in faith and in your love.

Prayer from Benin

Ghana

Population: 14 million.

Languages: English, four national languages recognized among others.

Government: Republic. Currently under military rule.

Religion: Christians 54%, Muslims 12%. The rest follow traditional beliefs.

Formerly a British colony known as the Gold Coast, Ghana was joined by the British-administered part of Togoland to become an independent nation in 1957. Since then its search for an appropriate form of government has been painful, frustrating and elusive, with alternating civilian and military rule. The search for an authentic and effective form of self-government, reflecting indigenous values and statesmanship, is rooted in a crisis of identity being experienced throughout Africa.

The first Christian preaching was undertaken by early chaplains in the fort settlements on the Slave Coast. Later, various missions began more sustained work outside the fort areas moving gradually up country. The growth of this work was largely due to ordinary church members moving about the country as traders and government officials. The church made a very significant impact on the community in the sphere of Christian education.

Today schools and colleges continue to serve the people of Ghana, offering education based on the Christian faith. Nowadays the management of such institutions is community-based, and the influence of the church is experienced more through individuals whose faith is held as an integral part of their professional lives. In recent years Ghana has been facing problems in the economic, political, cultural and social spheres, some resulting from external factors, e.g. the arrival of some one million homeless and unemployed Ghanaians expelled from Nigeria. "Whatever the external and internal factors acting on individuals as well as on the nation," says a representative of the Christian Council, "none of them can mould or determine the future more than the attitudinal response of the peoples to these pressures."

Intercessions and Prayers

In the midst of many shortages and much religious tension, human dignity, hope and faith abound in Ghana — *Thanks be to God.*

Our heavenly Father, we in Ghana heartily thank you for the manner in which you have been helping us in our struggle for survival and our fight against ignorance, disease and sorrow. We acknowledge your loving kindness to us in our efforts to establish your kingdom here, where we hope to rule ourselves in truth, love and justice. Let our land prosper in your might, as we pray in Jesus' name.

General secretary of the Christian Council of Ghana

Let us pray

for a stable and efficient government and administration, that armed interventions may give way to peaceful transition through the ballot box

for the responsible use of ecology; for honest financial management and appropriate economic policies

for the guidance of the Holy Spirit in the search for genuine expressions of life and living as well as the promotion of growth and responsibility

O God, we implore you,
bless the people of this land,
this beautiful land,
this green land,
this yellow land
under your wonderful sun.
You know what we need:
food for body, soul and spirit...

Prayer of a young Ghanaian

"Hold Ghana in your minds for just one second", comes the plea from Christians in Ghana. "Whatever you would pray for yourselves on your

busiest or your most lethargic, your most joyous and even your saddest
day, pray for us. All prayers count."

God of all nations,
we thank you for creating us with love in your own image.
You are united with your Son in the Holy Spirit in perfect unity.
We ask you to unite also all peoples and churches
in order to bring about your kingdom in this world.

Prayer from Ghana

Hallelujah

in Ewe Ghana
as taught by Alexander Gondo

Hal-le - lu-jah, Hal - le - lu - jah. Hal-le-lu - jah.

Hal-le - lu-jah, Hal - le - lu - jah. Hal-le-lu - jah.

Ivory Coast

With an economy based on an astute development of its agricultural
potential, and with a record of stable government (single-party republic)
since independence from France in 1960, the Ivory Coast is today the
most prosperous state in Francophone Africa. Until recently there was a
large foreign population (over 1 million) mostly French and Levantine,
and employed in state enterprises. The Ivorean population is growing
rapidly and now stands at around 10 million.

Although about 50% of the population still adhere to traditional African
religions, and some 24% are Muslims, there is also a sizeable (32%)
Christian community, mostly Roman Catholic, but including significant
African indigenous and Protestant communities. The first Roman
Catholic mission arrived in 1687, and over the years the church has made
a deep impact through education. The years 1913-15 were marked by the
presence of Prophet William Wade Harris of Liberia whose preaching led

to a remarkable mass movement of coastal people to Christianity. Many subsequently joined the Roman Catholic and Methodist churches; others founded an independent church of their own. The Methodists arrived in 1924 and remain the largest Protestant denomination.

Today there are a number of concerns common to other countries with a similar background of prosperity: the growth of materialism, a lack of concern for outreach on the part of Christians, and an easy-going lapse into syncretistic ways. More local worries revolve around the uncertain political future of the country, growing tribalism, rising unemployment and unfulfilled expectations among educated young people. Most Protestant bodies belong to the Evangelical Federation of the Ivory Coast. The Taizé community is attempting to promote conversations between Protestants and Roman Catholics.

We pray

for all African Independent Churches

for young people unemployed, and for the support and understanding of church and nation

for new initiatives to share the good news of Jesus with others

for Christ's gifts of unity and love among Christians in the Ivory Coast

O God, most mighty among the heavens, forgive us our sins — Amen
For private and secret sins, O God forgive us — Amen
For not walking uprightly, O God forgive us — Amen
Forgive our young people — Amen
Forgive our adults — Amen
Forgive our men — Amen
Forgive our women — Amen
Visit not the sins of our fathers on us — Amen
If you should visit their iniquities on us who worship thee,
we shall be hurt — Yes Lord
Therefore blot out all their sins this day, O Lord — Amen
Forgive us individually — Amen
Forgive us corporately — Amen
Grant forgiveness to all who worship you and do your will on earth —
Amen

An excerpt from a prayer of confession
recorded in an African Independent Church

Let us pray for those who foster violence,
those who do not forgive others.
May the Lord change their hearts
that they seek peace and love their brothers and sisters.

Prayer from the Ivory Coast

Togo

The Togolese Republic was formerly a part of Togoland, at one time a German colony and subsequently divided between the British and French. French Togoland (Togo) became independent in 1960. A period of political instability followed. The present government however has become a focus of national unity and stability, with equal participation between different ethnic groups in the country's sole political party.

It is estimated that about 60% of the population of almost 3 million follow traditional beliefs, some 25% are Christians, and about 7.5% Muslims. The majority of Christians are Roman Catholics. The first Protestants to enter the country were those (either immigrant or local) trained in Christian schools of the Gold Coast. The educational role of religious institutions today is recognized, and almost half the large school-age population is educated in Christian schools. The expulsion of all German missionaries at the beginning of the first world war resulted in greater self-reliance among indigenous Christians, and the Eglise évangélique du Togo is now an autonomous body. This, the Methodist Church, and Assemblies of God are the major Protestant denominations; and there are some African indigenous churches. A number of Protestant churches have been participating together in a Christian council since 1983; and Roman Catholics and Protestants cooperate in the South Togo cultural and religious research group which is currently engaged in cultural and ecumenical research.

Let us pray

for the many people in Togo who suffer desperate poverty, and for all attempts to alleviate it consistent with the peoples' dignity

for the large young population; for schools and for job opportunities

for the emergence of a strong Togolese Christian leadership

for the development of forms of evangelism appropriate to the country

for tourists, that they may be enriched by contact with local Christians

We pray

that in the bond of prayer and worship Christians in Togo may feel their solidarity with Christians elsewhere

> *Lord, you told the apostles that they should all be one.*
> *Let all Christians show and bear witness to this unity*
> *through their loving kindness.*

Prayer for unity from Togo

Bite not one another

Adinkra symbol of unity

Week 27

Nigeria

O Almighty God, we humbly ask you
to make us like trees planted by the waterside,
that we may bear fruits of good living in due season.
Forgive our past offences,
sanctify us now,
and direct all that we should be in the future;
for Christ's sake. Amen.

Prayer from Nigeria

The area now known as Nigeria is home to over 500 ethnic groups of which the Yoruba, Hausa, Fulani and Ibo are the largest. It is the richest and most populous country in Black Africa. The oil boom affected Nigeria, and cities, roads, population and the church have all expanded rapidly in recent years.

Population: 95.2 million.

Languages: English, Hausa, Ibo, Yoruba, and over 500 other ethnic languages.

Government: Military administration.

Religion: Overall numbers of Christians and Muslims are believed to be approximately even. Of the many denominations the Roman Catholic, Anglican, and Fellowship of Churches in Christ in Nigeria are the largest. Muslims predominate in the north and are numerous in the west. Traditional religions have their main strength in the central plateau.

The unity of Nigeria as a nation was imposed upon it by colonization, but the region itself has a long and rich cultural history. The main trade routes were to the north and east across the Sahara; and from this direction came Islam, which was established in the north by the 11th century, and spread more widely through the populace in the 19th, at the same time as

Christianity was being introduced in the south. The slave trade brought Europeans to the coastal area and a gradual process of exploration and colonization followed. Independence was achieved in 1960. A period of turbulence followed which included a civil war, from which Nigeria has emerged as a much more united nation.

The first Christian missionaries came in response to requests from returning freed slaves who were themselves Christians. Methodists, Anglicans, Presbyterians and Baptists arrived in quick succession, followed by Roman Catholics and Lutherans. Some of the early missionaries were themselves African. Cooperation was well developed from an early date. In 1926 a Christian Council for Northern Nigeria was formed, and the NCC for the whole of Nigeria in 1950.

The resurgence of Islamic fundamentalism in other parts of the world, and the move to take Nigeria into the Organisation of Islamic Countries are sources of considerable disquiet among Christians; and Christian-Muslim relationships have become extremely sensitive and sometimes inflammatory. Fear and suspicion have grown. Some look back to the destruction of the church in North Africa in early centuries, and wonder if that could happen in Nigeria.

In the face of all this the churches are becoming increasingly united and are taking evangelism more seriously. They are expanding steadily. The indigenous African Independent Churches are not only growing but proliferating, and there are now over 900 different denominations, although many are linked in one association or another. One of the larger groups, the Nigerian Association of Aladura Churches, incorporates 95 member churches. There are three ecumenical institutes which work closely with each other, as well as several interdenominational organizations promoting medical work, Christian education and inter-religious dialogue.

Intercessions and Prayers

Creator of Heaven and earth accept out thanks and accept our praises — Amen

Messiah, accept our thanks and accept our praises — Amen

As young people and adults, accept our thanks and accept our praises — Amen

As male and female, accept our thanks and accept our praises — Amen

On this Holy day accept our thanks and accept our praises — Amen
On all days accept our thanks and accept our praises — Amen
Let not the mouths with which we thank thee become sour — Amen
Let us not give thanks in sorrow — Amen
Let us not give thanks in tears — Amen
Let us not give thanks in regret — Amen
Let us not be thankful half-heartedly — Amen
Accept our thanks and our praises O Lord,
Make us useful to thee — Amen
Hear O Ruler of Heaven, through Jesus Christ our Lord — Amen

Part of a prayer of thanksgiving
recorded in an African Independent Church

Musing with a Nigerian Christian

Lord, we were brought up together, we and our Muslim neighbours;
their mothers were our mothers, their children were our children.

If they resented our church going, our identification with Western
forms of religion, the privileges we enjoyed in mission structures, they
didn't show it.

But suddenly, suspicion has entered between us, solidarity with fellow
Muslims across the world, new ideas, new feelings, new stirrings, a
new self-consciousness and identity on their part has plunged our
easy-going and taken-for-granted relationships into disarray.

Now we imagine all sorts of things about each other, impute to each
other all sorts of unworthy motives, read all sorts of things into each
others' words and actions.

Lord, there is no way back.
In our bewilderment please show us the way forward.

A prayer for freedom from fear

O Lord, we beseech thee to deliver us from the fear of the unknown
future; from fear of failure; from fear of poverty; from fear of
bereavement; from fear of loneliness; from fear of sickness and pain;
from fear of age; and from fear of death.

Help us, O Father, by thy grace to love and fear thee only, fill our
hearts with cheerful courage and loving trust in thee; through our
Lord and Master Jesus Christ.

Francis Akanu Ibiam

A *chorus of farewell*

At the end of some special service or meeting it is customary for the usual silence after the blessing to be broken by someone quietly but clearly lilting the words of an Ibo chorus:

Ezigbo hwannem, nyem aka gi — Ezigbo hwannem, nyem obi gi,

a refrain taken up powerfully by all present:

My good brother/sister, give me your hand,
My good brother/sister, give me your heart.

And shaking hands with each other as they sing, all move leisurely and lovingly out of the church until the compound re-echoes with

My good brother/sister, give me your hand,
My good brother/sister, give me your heart.

Likewise let us offer our hands and hearts to our Christian brothers and sisters in Nigeria in gratitude and in solidarity.

Christian Conference of Asia (CCA)

Inaugurated in 1959 as the East Asia Christian Conference, and today known simply as CCA, the Christian Conference of Asia contains in its fellowship some 113 churches and national councils from 16 Asian countries including Australia and New Zealand, comprising over 40 million Christian people.

The CCA functions "as an organ of continuing cooperation among its member churches and national Christian bodies". Among other things, it sponsors development, justice and human rights programmes; encourages ecumenical leadership development and many other ecumenical ventures; focuses attention on the problems of tourism in the area; and promotes interest in Asian Christian hymns, art and architecture.

Leader: *We pray for the churches*
     where many suffer
     for the sake of freedom and justice
     (Silence)

People: *Servant Lord,*
     lead us to be the willing servants of all.

Leader: *We pray for the churches*
     where there is success
     in terms of wealth, prestige and influence
     (Silence)

People: *Servant Lord,*
     lead us to be the willing servants of all.

Leader: *We pray for the churches*
     working closely
     with peoples' movements for peace
     for the good of all
     (Silence)

People: *Servant Lord,*
     lead us to be willing servants of all.

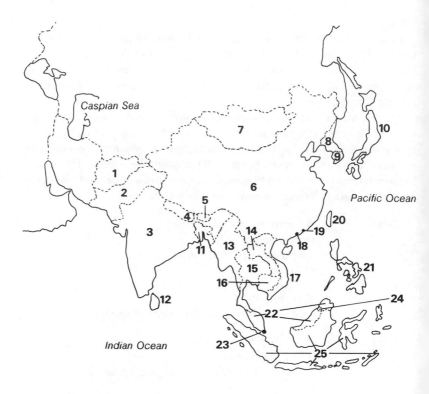

1. Afghanistan
2. Pakistan
3. India
4. Nepal
5. Bhutan
6. People's Republic of China
7. Mongolia
8. Democratic People's Republic of Korea
9. Republic of Korea
10. Japan
11. Bangladesh
12. Sri Lanka
13. Burma
14. Laos
15. Thailand
16. Kampuchea
17. Vietnam
18. Macao
19. Hong Kong
20. Taiwan
21. Philippines
22. Malaysia
23. Singapore
24. Brunei
25. Indonesia

O God, our Creator,
who gave us all that we are and have;
release us from self-love
to be able to share
   what we are
   what we know
   what we have
with one another
and in the world which you love.
In the name of Christ who makes this a possibility. Amen.

Sisters and brothers,
let us claim the freedom Christ gives.
May he empower us to serve together in faith, hope and love.
Go in peace to love and serve the Lord.

Prayers used at the 8th Assembly of the
Christian Conference of Asia, Seoul, Korea

Fellowship of the Least Coin

Conceived in 1956 as the brain child of the Asian Christian Women's Conference, the Fellowship of the Least Coin continues to catch the imagination and to draw a response from women all over the world. Whatever their backgrounds and circumstances, women are invited to set aside regularly the smallest coin of their country's currency, offering it with the prayer that women may become instrumental in bringing peace and reconciliation in the world.

God of peace,
help us to be committed as Christians to be peacemakers.
Give us the courage to speak up for truth and justice.
Empower us to be Christians not only in word but in action.
May your peace be achieved
by the power of love, tolerance and justice.
In the name of Jesus, the Prince of Peace. Amen.

Although the Fellowship retains a strong link with its countries of origin it is now organized on an international basis, with its fund handled by WCC, Geneva. In spite of the fact that gifts to its fund have increased greatly over the years and are now very widely applied, the main emphasis of the Fellowship continues to be on the prayer and solidarity of Christian women worldwide.

Our Father, we thank you that in Jesus Christ there are no rich or poor, but we are all one in you. As we present our "least coins", we remember the women of every land, rich and poor, educated and illiterate, in isolated villages and teeming cities, who share in this Fellowship. May we be rich in the things of the spirit by your grace and to your glory.

Prayers by two members of the Fellowship

Introduction to Weeks 28 and 29

The Theravada Buddhism of Kampuchea, Laos, Burma and Thailand, and the broader and more accommodating Mahayana Buddhism of Vietnam both trace their history back to the birth in approximately 560 BC of an Indian prince, Gautama, later to be universally known as the Buddha. At the age of 30 he renounced family life in order to seek after the truth, and after much rigorous searching came upon what he sought in an experience of a growing awareness of emancipation from self, known as his Enlightenment.

According to the teaching of the Buddha, those who desire enlightenment must follow the eight-fold path of right knowledge, resolve, speech, behaviour, livelihood, effort, mindfulness and meditation. This kind of self-discipline, with the very gentle life-style which accompanied it, moulded early Buddhist practice, and continues to make it a very attractive option to many people today.

Following the death of the Buddha the teaching of Buddhism developed in two main directions. Mahayana, or the Great Vehicle, broad enough to include all, spread to China, Tibet, Korea, Japan and Vietnam. The concept of the compassionate Buddha, who foregoes nirvana to devote himself to saving others, developed in Mahayana Buddhism. Theravada Buddhism, sometimes referred to as the Lesser Vehicle, emphasized that each person must work out his or her own salvation. "Make an island unto yourself" reads one of the sayings of the Buddha according to Theravada Buddhism. This rather rigorous and austere Buddhism experienced a revival in the 12th century AD. and, starting in Sri Lanka, spread through Burma into Thailand, Cambodia and Laos. With its well known Triple Gem:

I take refuge in the Buddha
I take refuge in the Dhamma (the teaching)
I take refuge in the Sangha (the community)

Theravada Buddhism has continued in recent years to experience renewal of its vitality and missionary impulse, not least in the countries prayed for during these weeks. In this connection some Christians engaged in dialogue with Buddhists have seen the possibility of an adaptation of the Triple Gem, but all would echo the words of another scholar to the effect that "the relationship between Jesus Christ, believed in as 'the light of the world', and the Buddha called 'the light of Asia' continues to be one of the persistent challenges to the Christian mission."

With all my heart I take refuge in God,
the Lord of all things, the Creator of the universe,
the merciful Father and Source of all good.

With all my heart I take refuge in Christ,
the Remover of all sin,
the One who re-establishes our pure nature within us,
the perfect revelation of the eternal Word of God.

With all my heart I take refuge in the One who embraces the whole
universe and has myriad ways and means of influencing souls,
the pure and tranquil Holy Spirit.

From the Norwegian of Karl Ludvig Reichelt,
Buddhist/Christian Centre, Tao Fong Shan, Hong Kong

Week 28

Kampuchea • Laos • Vietnam

God came down to us like the sun at morning
wounded to the heart by our helplessness.
Let us proceed in his strength
to love and serve one another.

Asia Youth Assembly

At one time, under the influence of early Buddhism, this area was one of the most peaceful in the world. These three countries are all still predominantly Buddhist but many other influences and forces have entered, and in recent years war and devastation have predominated. The first Christians to come to this area were members of the Roman Catholic missionary orders in the 16th and 17th centuries. The church became permanently established in what is now the southern part of Vietnam in 1666, later in Kampuchea, and not until 1885 in Laos. Protestant work did not begin until this century. Christians in the northern coastal region suffered greatly as a result of waves of persecution in the 17th and 18th centuries; and in the 19th century thousands were put to death in the south in a severe persecution motivated by religious and political considerations. Later in the 19th century the kingdoms and states of the area were colonized by France and became French Indo-China.

Kampuchea

Population: 7.3 million approximately.

Language: Khmer.

Government: Single-party republic.

Religion: Buddhists 85%, atheists 9%, adherants of tribal religions 3%, Muslims 3%, a tiny Christian minority.

Cambodia (Kampuchea) obtained independence in 1953 and enjoyed a period of relative stability, but was increasingly affected by the war in Vietnam and a communist insurgency movement (Khmer Rouge) within the country. A coup in 1970 ushered in a right-wing anti-Vietnamese government and thousands of resident Vietnamese were massacred. Others escaped across the border. The Roman Catholic Church, primarily a church of the Vietnamese and Europeans, suffered considerably. The ensuing civil war resulted in much loss of life and large-scale destruction.

In 1975 the Khmer Rouge gained control of the whole country, and put into operation a drastic programme of social change. Whole populations were moved out of the towns to work in the fields under forced labour conditions where many died. Professional and educated people were exterminated; 75% of all teaching staff and 96% of university students were killed. The Khmer Rouge attempted to eradicate all religion, and some 90% of Buddhist priests and an unknown number of Christians perished. It is estimated that at least 3 million people died during the four years of the regime.

In 1978 Vietnam, supported by a Kampuchean opposition group, invaded the country, and since January 1979 a Vietnamese-supported government has ruled in Kampuchea while the Khmer Rouge, in alliance with Prince Sihanouk, constitute a government in exile. As a result of the war and the social policies of the Khmer Rouge the country's economy, infrastructure and industry have been completely disrupted. As the then secretary general of the United Nations said: "The Kampuchean tragedy may have no parallel in history." Now, after years of relative stability and considerable outside aid, food shortages have been largely overcome, and recovery is beginning, but there is a serious lack of skilled and trained people. The government is not widely recognized internationally, a large Vietnamese force remains in the country, and war continues between the various factions.

Little is known about the present situation of the Christian church. The number of Christians is small, and they are scattered. Christian gatherings were made illegal in 1983.

Laos

Population: 3.6 million.
Languages: Lao, French, numerous tribal languages.

Government: Unitary single-party republic.

Religion: Buddhists 58%, adherents of tribal religions 33% mainly among non-Lao ethnic minorities, atheists 6%, small Muslim and Christian minorities.

Laos, then a constitutional monarchy, obtained independence in 1953, but communist opposition had already begun. By 1965 the Pathet Lao (communist forces) had gained control of the north-east of the country, and a de facto partition existed, with guerilla warfare continuing. Laos was closely involved with the war in Vietnam and the 1973 peace agreements provided for a cease-fire in Laos. A new government was set up involving both sides, but by 1975 the communists had won control.

In the year following all foreign missionaries were forced to leave the country. A number of Roman Catholic priests and Protestant pastors were imprisoned in forced labour or "re-education" camps. Most have since been released.

After the first wave of revolutionary enthusiasm socialist policies are being implemented gradually. "We cannot go post-haste. Socialization must be carried out slowly, according to the Lao population possibilities" (the deputy prime minister). The government allows religious freedom, and Christians collaborate with civil authorities in development programmes. The number of Christians is not known, but the small church, severely tried, "is being renewed and is growing". Christians "are now more convinced of their faith, more faithful and more courageous".

Vietnam

Population: 57.1 million.

Language: Vietnamese.

Government: Unitary single-party republic.

Religion: Buddhists 55%, atheists 22%, syncretistic new religions 11%, Christians 7.5% predominantly Roman Catholics. The main Protestant church is the Evangelical Church of Vietnam.

In Vietnam, nationalist groups operated from an early stage, and following Japan's surrender in 1945 proclaimed the Independent Democratic Republic without French agreement. Hostilities ensued eventually leading to division of the country into North and South. But trouble did not cease, and in 1961 USA entered the war which was to continue for another 12 years. Two years after the cease-fire the communist North Vietnamese gained control in the south. Since then, despite many difficulties, considerable progress has been made towards reconstruction.

After 1954 many Christians moved to the South to avoid living under a Marxist government. More people moved south to escape American bombing and since 1975 many, especially ethnic Chinese, have fled the country. However, a number of Christians elected to stay on in the North, and continued to relate to the communist government. It seems likely that arising out of continuous church activity during the long years of war, and after, a new interpretation of the Christian faith has been emerging in the North which may one day be shared with the rest of the world church.

The church in the South, both Catholic and Protestant, is now seeking to adjust to life under a Marxist government. The government has constituted a committee for Solidarity of Patriotic Vietnamese Catholics, and it is through this body that the Roman Catholic Church ordinarily relates to the government. All open evangelism ceased in 1975, seminaries were closed, and many priests were interned. About a hundred still remain in "re-education camps". The church is able to function, but with restrictions, and carefully watched by the government which nevertheless seems anxious to avoid confrontation.

Intercessions and Prayers

Look with mercy, O Lord, on the suffering people of Indo-China;
give respite and rest to those who have never known peace.
Protect the weak from oppression.
Grant that those who are enlightened by the Buddha
may see the light that is in Christ.

Dear God, we thank you for your love shown to us through Jesus Christ. Our hearts are heavy with sorrow for the people of Kampuchea who are suffering so much at this time. We pray that their load of suffering may be eased. We pray that you will give strength and courage to the people in that place, and help them to find their refuge in you. Amen.

Prayer of Cambodian Christian refugee woman

We pray

for the governments of these countries, and all who seek to help in the work of reconstruction

for all refugees from Kampuchea, Laos and Vietnam, especially those who are not accepted by any country

for those living in areas of continuing warfare, where life is very insecure and uncertain

for priests and pastors still held in prisons and re-education camps in Laos and Vietnam

We remember, O Lord,
those who suffer from any kind of discrimination;
your children, and our brothers and sisters,
who are humiliated and oppressed;
we pray for those who are denied fundamental human rights,
for those who are imprisoned,
and especially those who are tortured
Our thoughts rest a few moments with them...
and we pray that your love and compassion may sustain them always.

Week of Prayer for World Peace

for scattered Christian groups in Laos and Kampuchea, and the catechists, lay leaders and young people who minister to them

for those in the Golden Triangle, forced by economic circumstances to cultivate too much opium and for all efforts being made to control its growth and to substitute other means of livelihood

We pray for the peoples of Asia as they struggle for justice, peace and
an end to wars in face of situations of desperate poverty and yet with
great hopes for a new society in which human rights are carefully
respected, looking for adequate ways of development, seeking to
preserve their ancient and noble cultures as the context of human
existence, and as a gift to the whole human family...

Christian Prayer for Peace,
Pope John Paul II, Assisi, 1986

As we are together, praying for peace, let us be truly with each other
— Silence
Let us be aware of the source of being common to us all and to all
living things — Silence

Evoking the presence of the Great Compassion, let us fill our hearts with our own compassion — towards ourselves and towards all living beings — Silence
Let us pray that all living beings realize that they are all brothers and sisters, all nourished from the same source of life — Silence
Let us pray that we ourselves cease to be the cause of suffering to each other — Silence
Let us plead with ourselves to live in a way which will not deprive other living beings of air, water, food, shelter, or the chance to live — Silence
With humility, with awareness of the existence of life, and of the sufferings that are going on around us, let us pray for the establishment of peace in our hearts and on earth. Amen.

Thich Nhat Hanh: Vietnamese scholar, monk, poet and contemplative,
nominated by Martin Luther King Jr for the Nobel Peace Prize
in recognition of his work for reconciliation in Vietnam.
This litany was led by him at an interfaith gathering in Canterbury in 1976

May the grace of our Lord Jesus Christ
protect us from killing one another;
and may God's love fill our lives
with a peace that extends its hand to others
in true reconciliation and friendship.

Benediction, Christian Conference of Asia

Week 29

Burma • Thailand

Dear Lord, you wanted all people to live in unity and to love each other. Help us to break down the walls of separation. Break down the walls of race, colour, creed and languages. Make us one so that our unity and love for each other may win many to your fold. Amen.

Prayer of Burmese Christian woman

Burma

Population: 38 million.

Languages: Burmese, 125 other languages and dialects.

Government: Single-party republic.

Religion: Buddhists 87%, Christians 6% (of which the Baptists are the largest single denomination), Muslims 4%, and adherents of tribal religions.

Sometimes described as a country "shaped like a kite with a long tail", and with an early history of numerous small kingdoms struggling for ascendancy, Burma was annexed by the British in 1886, occupied by the Japanese during the second world war, and became independent in 1948. Considerable turmoil followed, but a coup in 1962 led to the eventual emergence of a socialist state. In an attempt to unite the nation Burma broke off its ties with the outside world in 1966. It resumed contact in 1978.

The earliest Christians in Burma were the Nestorians in the 10th century. Roman Catholics came in 1544, and Protestant missions may be said to have begun with the coming of Adoniram and Ann Judson, America's first missionaries to Asia, in 1813. Others followed, and the church became firmly established, particularly among the tribal peoples.

The extensive programme of lay training, undertaken prior to 1966, stood the church in good stead for the period of isolation, which many Christians regarded as an opportunity for the church to become indigenized.

Today there is a reality, a resourcefulness and a vitality about the church in Burma which is catching to those who visit. Considerable freedom is allowed and relationships with the state are good. Holding the view that "Christian unity and national unity cannot be separated" the churches work together to a high degree, and support national unity through their activities. Lay theological education continues to be an important ecumenical activity. They live daily with the question of what it means to be a Christian "in the land of the strongest, most true-to-the-original type of Buddhism".

One of Adoniram Judson's most famous sayings, "the future is as bright as the promises of God", still characterizes the church in Burma.

Intercessions and Prayers

Give thanks

for the Burmese peoples' determination to achieve selfhood, resist foreign influence and to work for unity and equality

for the church's presence and growth in some of the remotest parts of the country

Pray

that the "Burmese way of socialism" may lead to the unity and development of the nation

for an end to ethnic conflict, and for greater understanding and fellow feeling between those of different ethnic groups

for those who, in a situation of restricted freedom, are dedicated to the task of discovering and implementing ways of authentic Christian witness to the gospel of the kingdom of God in this land

for pastoral care and sensitive evangelism among the tribal people of Burma

> *Good Shepherd, we ask that you will seek the lost, heal the sick, bring back those that wander off, and let your people graze in safety in the mountains and valleys of Burma today.*

Council for World Mission

Thailand

Population: 52.7 million.

Languages: Thai, English, Chinese.

Government: Constitutional monarchy.

Religion: Buddhists 92%, Muslims 4%, adherents of Chinese folk religions 2%, Christians 1%. The king is protector of religions, and there is a high degree of religious liberty.

Staying in Bangkok briefly it was of course obligatory to visit the fabulous palaces built by the king made famous in the book and film "The King and I". Pillars and roofs covered in gold-leaf, a huge statue of the Buddha in solid gold, and another of jade. But the place that remains in the memory is a whole roomful of figures showing the Buddha in different acts of meditating, blessing and peace-making. But one of them was different. It showed the Buddha before his enlightenment, as an ascetic, emaciated, with his ribs sticking out and a look of intense suffering on his face. Only in front of this statue did I see a small heap of flowers. The calm faces of the other figures had drawn no such oblation. I even wonder whether people in their own agony and suffering do not sometimes want to hit out at that serene passivity. Sublimely inspiring at times, it could also infuriate. Especially in times of flood, famine and the ever-present possibility of war, the belief that God has shared our suffering makes a deep appeal, and draws out love.

A tourist

O God, our Father,
the fountain of love, power and justice,
the God who cares,
particularly for the least,
the most suffering and the poorest among us.

O God, Lord of creation,
grant us today your guidance and wisdom
so that we may see the human predicament for what it is.

Give us courage and obedience
so that we may follow you completely.
Help us, Lord, to bear witness

to the cross of your son, our Lord Jesus Christ,
who alone is the reason for hope,
and in whose name we pray. Amen.

Koson Srisang, Thailand

With ethnic roots traceable back 2000 years to China, Thailand emerged as a nation in the 13th century. Formerly known as Siam, the country took its present name in 1939. Thailand today recognizes the Kampuchean government in exile; a situation which breeds antagonism with Vietnam, and unrest and uncertainty in the refugee communities along its borders. Refugees from Burma, Kampuchea, Laos and Vietnam continue to seek entrance.

As in the case of Burma, the Christian presence in Thailand can be traced to the arrival of the Nestorians in the 10th century. French Roman Catholic priests arrived in 1662, but from 1688 onwards they were persecuted. Today however, the Roman Catholic Church is the largest in the country. The Church of Christ in Thailand owes its origins to the arrival of Baptist, Congregational and Presbyterian missions in the mid-19th century, and to their eventual demise in 1934 in order that an indigenous united Protestant church may come to birth. According to its department of ecumenical relations, this continues to be "a body struggling to be an indigenous church, with strong influences from the charismatic and pentecostal movements". These influences are strongest in Bangkok, whereas the church's membership is predominantly in the rural areas, where "the fundamental social reality of patron-peasant relationship is not challenged by the gospel". Human rights, and other community action groups, are however emerging. Members of this and other churches, along with Buddhists, Muslims and Sikhs are involved in a programme of continuing dialogue.

In addition to being an important centre of Theravada Buddhism, Thailand is noted for its temples, palaces and pagodas. Tourism is the country's largest source of foreign exchange. The Christian Conference of Asia, together with sub-units of the WCC, has for some time been much concerned with the problem of prostitution linked with tourism in south-east Asia — sometimes called sex tourism — and has been active in promoting a Christian response to this problem.

Pray

for the members of the small minority Christian community in Thailand for compassion and integrity for the rulers of the country, that resources and opportunities for improvement may be more equitably shared

for all who are abused and debased by prostitution tourism, and for those who exploit them

for refugees in Thailand, that the pain and agony of warfare and exile may be overcome

O God, be with us in this new day. Heal the wounds made by war. Ease the suspicions that lurk in the back of the mind about people we cannot see and do not know. Prepare us for a life as full of unexpected joys as it is of unexpected sorrows. All this we ask in Jesus' name — who is always the same — yesterday, today and tomorrow.

Prayer of Thai Christian woman

Lord, we take refuge in your compassionate name,
we take refuge in your gospel of forgiveness,
we take refuge in the fellowship of your universal Church
on behalf of all Christians in Buddhist lands. Amen.

Week 30

Indonesia

Bhinneka Tunggal Ika – Diversity in Unity
Motto of the Republic of Indonesia

Referred to by its people as "water land", Indonesia is an archipelago of 13,677 islands of which 6,044 are inhabited. A chain of active volcanoes increases soil fertility even as it causes destruction.

Population: 165.2 million and growing rapidly. The fifth most populous country in the world.

Languages: Bahasa Indonesia, over 200 other languages and dialects.

Government: Unitary republic.

Religion: Muslims 82%, Christians 14%, Hindus 2%, Buddhists 2%.

Most Indonesians are of Malayan racial origin. Their forebears probably came to the archipelago in two waves, the first arriving about 3000 BC and the second about 300-200 BC. Because of the geographical features of the islands, they developed in isolated groups, and now there are over 300 distinct ethnic communities. Indian influences penetrated from about 100 AD bringing Hinduism and Buddhism, and Bali is predominantly Hindu today. Islam came first in the 13th century and its spread continued. There are now more Muslims in Indonesia than in any other country.

The Portuguese came in the 1520s bringing Roman Catholic Christianity, and Francis Xavier laid the foundations of a church which suffered heavy losses through anti-Portuguese reaction. Dutch occupation, begun in 1605, brought Protestant pastors, and Roman Catholic missionaries were expelled. Church growth among Indonesians was slow until the 19th century when missionary activity increased and Roman Catholic work was again permitted. Christians suffered during the Japanese occupation (1942-45), but at the same time the churches began to experience independence. The country itself had been striving for independence for some time, and proclaimed it three days after the Japanese surrender. The Netherlands granted legal independence in 1949.

In view of the religious diversity of the people, it was decided to create neither a religious nor a secular state. Instead it is based on the Pancasila (Five Pillars): belief in One Supreme God; just and civilized humanity; national unity; democracy; social justice. Five religious groups, Islam, Catholic Christianity, Protestant Christianity, Hinduism and Buddhism are recognized, and all have equal rights and status. Recently all organizations, including religious groups, have adopted the Pancasila as their only foundation in the life of society, nation and state. The church, although strongly committed to the Pancasila, affirms that Jesus Christ is its Lord and Head.

The distribution of Indonesia's population is extremely uneven, with nearly two-thirds living on the islands of Java, Bali and Lombok. This has led the government to embark on an extensive transmigration policy involving moving millions of people. One effect of this is to spread the influence of Islam more widely, although others are also moving.

Whilst Christianity is represented throughout the country, some areas are predominantly Christian, and the church continues to grow. About a quarter of Christians are Roman Catholic. Some of the numerous Protestant bodies are regional and some indigenous; by far the largest tradition is the Reformed. The churches have an extensive ministry in education, somewhat less in health and a little in social work. Internally, many have a range of programmes for women which reflect a widening of the status and activities of women in society generally. Youth organizations are considered important both on account of the large percentage of young people in the churches, and the rapid social changes taking place in society.

The Communion of Churches in Indonesia was founded in 1950 and now has 58 member churches, some of them Pentecostal. It is unique in that its stated purpose is to become one Christian church in Indonesia. Relationships with the Roman Catholic Church have steadily improved since Vatican II, and there are now many areas of cooperation.

Intercessions and Prayers

I believe in God, who is love and who has given the earth to all people.
I believe in Jesus Christ, who came to heal us, and to free us from all
forms of oppression.

I believe in the Spirit of God who works in and through all who have turned towards the truth.
I believe in the community of faith which is called to be at the service of all people.
I believe in God's promise to finally destroy the power of sin in us all, and to establish the kingdom of justice and peace to all humankind.

An Indonesian creed, Christian Conference of Asia

Give thanks

for the richness of diverse races, cultures, and religious communities of the Indonesian archipelago

for the faith and witness of the church in Indonesia; and for the contribution of Christians to nation-building and national unity

for the ministry of the church among the poor and under-privileged

Give us strength, give us courage
in joyful willingness and humble readiness
to be thrown into the struggle of humanity
to be with the people,
those crawling in the gully of misery
moaning, stabbed by sorrow, squirming in agony,
isolated from everything that could alleviate their distress;
that they may see the brightness of solidarity
and feel the never-ceasing love of fellowship in Christ.

Fridolin Ukur

Pray

for all efforts to live together in harmony, and to promote justice and wellbeing for the whole people of Indonesia

that Christians may continue to uphold integrity and truth, and help the nation succeed in its struggle against corruption

that Christians may truly be a community for the people, faithful and imaginative in their ministries, and sensitive and generous in their relations with people of other faiths and persuasions

for the many people who continue to live in poverty, who are unemployed, or who live in overcrowded circumstances

for a just and humane implementation of the transmigration scheme; for all families who are moving, and for those already living in the area, that the necessary adjustments may be made peacefully for young people growing up in a rapidly changing social environment

for the Communion of Churches in Indonesia, that its efforts to foster Christian education and renewal, and to promote greater union among the churches may become a blessing to all

O God, who sent the Holy Spirit on the first disciples of Jesus
who were waiting in Jerusalem for this promised gift,
we beseech you to pour this same inspiration
on Christians in Indonesia and all over the world.

Prayer of an Indonesian Christian woman

Week 31

United States of America

O God, who has bound us together in this bundle of life, give us grace to understand how our lives depend upon the courage, the industry, the honesty and the integrity of our fellow human beings; that we may be mindful of their needs, grateful for their faithfulness, and faithful in our responsibilities to them; through Jesus Christ our Lord.

Reinhold Niebuhr

It is no accident that one of the first modern devotional acknowledgments of our human interdependence should come out of a nation rich in human potential, material resources and political significance. This theme of interdependence was later reinforced by Martin Luther King in his now famous speech pleading with the American people for "a revolution of values", in which loyalties might become ecumenical rather than sectional. "Every nation", he urged, "must now develop an over-riding loyalty to humankind as a whole in order to preserve the best in their individual societies."

Population: 238.8 million.

Languages: English, Spanish, indigenous Indian and immigrant languages.

Government: Federal republic.

Religion: Christians 88% (Protestants 59%, Roman Catholics 27%, Orthodox 2%, Episcopalians 2%), Jews 3.2%, Muslims 1%. Small communities of other faiths.

Prior to the arrival of settlers in the "new world", the country was inhabited by Indian tribes who lived by farming and hunting. Their tribal culture included a deeply spiritual faith that rooted itself in the integrity of God's creation. Through the years the land that was first theirs has been taken away and much of the population forced to live on reservations or required to become acculturated into society at large. Although the American Indian population has decreased dramatically, Indian spirituality, tribal identity and culture have been kept alive, and today there are strong movements to restore land rights and to preserve the rich Indian heritage.

Grandfather, Great Spirit,
you have always been, and before you nothing has been.
There is no one to pray to but you.
The star nations all over the heaven are yours,
and yours are the grasses of the earth.
You are older than all need, older than all pain and prayer.

Grandfather, Great Spirit,
fill us with light.
Give us strength to understand and eyes to see.
Teach us to walk the soft earth
as relatives to all that live.
Help us, for without you we are nothing.

From an American Indian prayer, Dakota

The Spanish conquistadores first brought Christianity to the country in the early 16th century. Waves of immigrant settlers followed, mostly from Europe, but there were also sizeable immigrations from Asia and Latin America. Many of the European settlers came because of religious persecution at home, so from early days freedom of religion has been a hallmark of the country, although there was a time of intense discrimination against Roman Catholics. Though in the earliest years of settlement most states recognized a state church, that pattern was abolished by the constitution of 1789 which legally separated church and state. This has meant that each church depends on its own religious vitality and faithfulness for growth, and has made it possible for each entity to preserve its own tradition and style of life. The preservation of religious freedom continues to be a challenge in an increasingly diverse society.

God of our weary years, God of our silent tears,
Thou who hast brought us thus far on the way;
Thou who hast by thy might, led us into the light,
Keep us forever in the path, we pray.

James Weldon Johnson

This prayer, taken from what is called the Negro national anthem, lifts up the unique pain and suffering of Black people in the USA. For more than two centuries Africans were brought over to work as slaves. Although the Civil War (1861-65) ended slavery, the nation was left with a deep scar on its vision of equality — a scar which remains even today. Discrimination against Black people in both church and society led to the birth, in 1787, of the first historic Black church, the African Methodist Episcopal Church. Today there are seven large historic Black churches. They are a strong force in the Black community, and wield considerable political influence in society at large. All but one are members of the World Council of Churches and the NCC, and their relationship to these bodies remains one of challenge to the ecumenical movement.

The complexity of the religious landscape in the USA can hardly be overstated, the plethora of denominations being largely a result of earlier patterns of immigration. However, within the major confessions a number of mergers have taken place in recent decades, and others are in process. Ecumenical life has been enriched since Vatican II with increased cooperation with the Roman Catholic Church. The strong presence of the Jewish community (which, although small in proportion to the total population, represents the largest number of Jews in any country of the world), and growing numbers of Muslims, Baha'is, Buddhists, Hindus and others have created an increased awareness of the need for interfaith dialogue and action.

Today the National Council of the Churches of Christ in the USA has 32 member communions. In addition there are approximately 400 regional and local councils of churches. Of these, many have Roman Catholic members, and some are interfaith. Church Women United brings together women from Roman Catholic, Protestant and Orthodox traditions. Many conservative Protestant denominations are joined together in the National Association of Evangelicals which gives ecumenical expression to the concerns of many not engaged in the National Council. The issues however are common, and include matters like economic justice in a world of limited resources, ecology, nuclear disarmament, peace, women's rights, racial justice and renewal of congregational life.

The richness and diversity, the size and complexity, the power and the promise of the USA make it a major influence in the world. Let us pray with Christians and those of all living faiths who fast and work and pray in this nation, that its people might live up to their vision of equality and justice and peace.

Intercessions and Prayers

We pray that our neighbourhoods, cities and nation
become places where justice and peace are honoured and celebrated
and humanity revered and dignified.
And show us how and where to make a start.

Bishop Lyman Ogilby

O God, you are like a weaver-woman in our lives. Out of the energy of
the universe you have spun each one of us into a unique, colourful
strand with our own special hue and texture, and have woven us
together into your human family that blankets the globe. We admit that
our own choices have severed us from your loom of life and created
rents in the whole of our human fabric.

We have allowed ourselves to be bound by the narrow contexts into
which we were born and now live our daily lives. To insulate ourselves
from fatigue and isolation and to insure our own survival, we have
often refused to ask the hard questions that need to be asked for the
sake of the wellbeing of all people.

O weaver-woman God, open our eyes to the mystery and power of
your Spirit. Refresh us with the light of your vision so that we may
once again recognize the beauty and wonder of the specially spun
thread that we are and the splendour of the one colourful cloth of
humanity. Re-attach us to your loom so that your vision may be made
plain through us.

In the name of the Christ, the One who was at one with all of life.
Amen.

Prayer from the USA, exact source unknown

We pray

for God's grace to heal the festering divisions between peoples and histories

for ecumenical encouragement for Black church leaders concerned about family breakdown, growing illiteracy, drug abuse, violence, and all other social ills traceable to the fundamental problem of deprivation

for the 40 million poverty-stricken people living on the edges of US society, and for those who work to alleviate their situation

for all immigrants, and those who serve God's fugitive people through the Sanctuary Movement that the measure of freedom given to the churches may inspire them to seek a new unity, as bold and radical now as was the notion of religious liberty two hundred years ago

Almighty God, we offer our prayers
for the National Council of the Churches of Christ in the USA,
earthen vessel, fragile, flawed, incomplete...
yet with a vision of unity.

We struggle to become all we could be.

We pray for the gift of love
that we may trust and care for one another.

We pray for the gift of patience
that we may hear and respond to each other.

We pray for the gift of courage
that we may be bold in our work and witness.

We pray for the gift of humility
that we may accept what cannot be changed.

We pray for the gift of grace
that we may rejoice in our shared humanity.

We pray for the gift of faith
that we might believe we will be one.

We pray that you will hold the ecumenical movement in your care,
and make us wholly yours. Amen.

Joan Campbell

Short prayers for big needs

Adolescents

Lord, I could use some help.

AIDS

God, help everyone living with AIDS
Guard their lives and their loved ones
Guide their healers and their helpers
Give us all new wholeness and new hope.

Homelessness

Let those who have no home to go to in the evening,
Impartial Provider, who have no place to rest their bones, no place to

lay their head, no place but the street, an alley, a niche, have the best of your company.

The urban poor

Lord, we know that you'll be coming through the line today, so, Lord, help us to treat you well, help us to treat you well.

Prayer of a poor Black helping woman before the weekly foodline
a mile and a half from the White House

Statistics in this book

Thank you, Lord, for counting me one of your sheep. Teach me, Lord, to count better, like you. Amen.

A personal God

Lord, one of the problems I have with praying is that you always get too personal. I keep praying because your being so personal is one of the joys. Amen.

Jesus

You are the healing, the loving, the touching. You are the laughing, you are the dancing, Jesus, Verb of God — you are the moving — move in me.

Prayers by: Grant M. Gallup, John Fandel,
Mary Glover, Albert S. Newton, Marilee Zdenek

Prayer for peace

Let us pray for the world that is immeasurable, a society of millions of people and newspapers full of news.

Let us pray for the smaller world around us: for the people who belong to us, for the members of our families, our friends and those who share our worries, and those who depend on us.

Let us pray for the leaders of governments and those whose words and actions will influence the situation in the world — that they may not tolerate injustice, seek refuge in violence

*or make rash and ill-considered decisions
about the future of other people.*

*Let us also pray for all who live in the shadow of world events,
for those who are seldom noticed:
the hungry, the poor, the broken and unloved.*

*We beseech you, O God, send your Holy Spirit
to help us give a new face to this earth that is dear to us.
May we help create peace wherever people live.*

*Give us the wisdom to see where we can make a difference
in the great nuclear debate that goes on around us,
and grant us the courage to form our conscience
in the image of Christ.*

*Let your Spirit have power over us
and put us on the path that leads to peace. Amen.*

Pax Christi, USA

Week 32

Canada

Lord, in your creation you have revealed your awesome power,
and in redemption you reveal your relentless love.
Through your vigilance by night and by day,
teach us more intimately of your power and your love. Amen.

From Ecumenical Prayers,
compiled by churches in Canada and the USA

Population: 25.4 million.

Languages: English, French, various indigenous, European and Asian languages.

Government: Federal parliamentary state.

Religion: Christians 90% (Roman Catholics 47.3%, Protestants 41.2%, Orthodox 1.5%), Jews 1.2%. Members of other faiths increasing in number largely due to immigration.

Undefended since it was first drawn, the border between Canada and the USA is the longest in the world, and today three quarters of the population of Canada live within 200 miles of it, in irregularly spaced areas separated from each other by vast distances. Many nations of native peoples had inhabited this continent for thousands of years by the time Europeans began to arrive in the early 16th century. In what is now Canada, they were scattered throughout the whole country, and were very much prepared to share with the newcomers the resources the Creator had given them. It was they who taught the settlers how to "live the land". As Europeans discovered the natural resources, and Britain assumed government in the early 19th century, treaties were drawn up under which the Indians lost their land rights, and eventually also their culture and traditions. The Christian church participated in the process of assimilating the native peoples into the European way of life; and it was not until 1986 that an apology was made, by the United Church of Canada, for this denigration of dignity, culture and spirituality.

The Roman Catholic Church is the longest established and most widespread confession in the country, owing its origins to 16th- and 17th-century French immigrants. It is strongest in Quebec, the predominantly French-speaking province to the east. In the 18th century British Anglican, Methodist, Presbyterian and other immigrants introduced their denominations into the Atlantic provinces and Ontario. Later, other European immigrants established Orthodox, Lutheran, Reformed, Baptist and Mennonite congregations. In 1925 Congregationalists, Methodists, and the majority of Presbyterians joined to form the United Church of Canada which is now the largest Protestant denomination in the country. The Canadian Conference of Catholic Bishops is an associate member of the Canadian Council of Churches, established in 1944.

Ethnic and religious pluralism contribute to the rich variety of life in Canada, as well as to some tensions. Difficulties between French- and English-speaking Canadians are now gradually decreasing. Most of the churches, separately and together, are strongly committed to the struggles for justice of the native peoples of Canada. Ecumenical concerns include worldwide peace initiatives, the status of refugees, human rights and pressure for disinvestment in South Africa. Theological and ethical questions are acquiring increasing importance in relation to ecumenical growth. Future programmes will take account of the country's wide variety of churches and other faiths.

Intercessions and Prayers

Welcome

You have come from afar
and waited long and are wearied:
Let us sit side by side
sharing the same bread drawn from the same source
to quiet the same hunger that makes us weak.
Then standing together
let us share the same spirit, the same thoughts
that once again draw us together in friendship and unity and peace.

Prières d'Ozawamick, Canadian Indian liturgical text

Thanksgiving

For human contact, for courage and vision that bring people together
for loving embrace — we give thanks.

For those around the world who stand together and work together for justice and peace — we give thanks.

In the knowledge that death and terror, bombs and hunger, do not have the last word — we give thanks.

For the promise that justice and peace will embrace, that love and fidelity will come together — we give thanks.

For Justice and Peace, Alyson Huntly, United Church, Toronto

We pray

that ecumenical initiatives within and outside Canada towards disarmament, justice and peace may be strengthened

that there may be respect for the heritage, culture and rights of the native peoples of Canada

for a better understanding between English- and French-speaking people

for a more responsible stewardship of natural and mineral resources

for all who by force of circumstances must live very isolated lives

for all recent immigrants as they settle down and seek to make a new life for themselves and their families; and for harmony between the various racial and ethnic groups

You, O God, have spoken to us through the story of Ruth the sojourner and were yourself present among us in Jesus to gather and welcome all those who were cast out or adrift from their societies; stir us and speak to us afresh through the migrant people of our time.

United Church of Canada, adapted

Linked with the words of 1 Peter 2:24, "By his wounds you have been healed", the figure in a Toronto church of a woman, arms outstretched as if crucified, provides the inspiration for the following prayer:

O God,
through the image of a woman crucified on the cross
I understand at last.

For over half of my life I have been ashamed of the scars I bear.
These scars tell an ugly story, a common story,
about a girl who is the victim when a man acts out his fantasies.

In the warmth, peace and sunlight of your presence
I was able to uncurl the tightly clenched fists.

For the first time
I felt your suffering presence with me in that event.
I have known you as a vulnerable baby,
as a brother, and as a father.
Now I know you as a woman.
You were there with me
as the violated girl caught in helpless suffering.

The chains of shame and fear no longer bind my heart and body.
A slow fire of compassion and forgiveness is kindled.
My tears fall now for man as well as woman...

You were not ashamed of your wounds.
You showed them to Thomas as marks of your ordeal and death.
I will no longer hide these wounds of mine.
I will bear them gracefully.
They tell a resurrection story.

Anonymous

Jesus, make our hearts ever gentler and more humble,
so that we may be present to those you have confided to our care,
and in this way make us instruments of your love
which gives life and joy and real freedom.

Jean Vanier, Canadian founder of L'Arche Community
for people with mental handicaps and their families

The blessing of the God of Sarah and Hagar, as of Abraham,
the blessing of the Son, born of Mary,
the blessing of the Holy Spirit who broods over us
as a mother over her children,
be with you all. Amen.

Lois Wilson, Toronto

Week 33

Australia • New Zealand

O God, you are my God: early will I seek you,
My soul thirsts for you, my flesh longs for you.
As the eagle belongs to the air,
and the dolphin belongs to the sea,
so we belong to you, O God, my God.

Australian Prayers, Bruce D. Prewer

Australia

Population: 15.8 million.

Languages: English and many others.

Government: Federal parliamentary state.

Religion: Christians 85%. Small minorities of Muslims, Jews and Buddhists, and some of no religion at all.

Australia has been home to its Aboriginal people for more than 40,000 years. British occupation began in 1778, using the country at first as a penal colony. More recent immigrants have come from many countries. The Aborigines were gradually crushed as their land was taken, and by the end of the 19th century their numbers had been greatly reduced to perhaps one hundred thousand people. Chaplains accompanied the first convicts and until 1936 the Church of England enjoyed privileges not granted to others. The foundations of many Protestant churches were laid by early pioneers. More recent immigration has increased the number of Roman Catholics and strengthened the various Orthodox churches.

At present the largest denominations are Roman Catholic, Anglican, and Uniting Church in Australia. This church, formed in 1977 by a union of Congregationalists, Methodists and Presbyterians, uses liturgies drawn from many traditions, and seeks to affirm and practise diversity in unity. In the Orthodox family the Greek Orthodox is the largest body. The

Christian church is increasingly multi-cultural, concerned to care for new immigrants. Support for the Aborigines, now increasing in number again, in their plea for justice with particular reference to land rights, is a major concern. Another aspect of the church's life is ministry to those in remote areas, at the mercy of climatic extremes, and separated by vast distances. In this generally affluent country the Australian Council of Churches is involved in issues of justice for the poor and for women.

Intercessions and Prayers

You must think me silly, God.
I just wanted to take your hand and walk with you
and show you things you'd seen a million times before.

Australian Images, Aubrey Podlich, a Queensland pastor

and thank you

for the awesome beauty of this wide red land

for the rich diversity of its peoples

for your Aboriginal sons and daughters, and their ancient longing for you

and ask you

for inspiration and administrative skills for the churches hosting the WCC Seventh Assembly in Canberra in February 1991

that interchurch relationships at local level may be deepened, and cooperation extended to neglected sections of the community

that the rights and identity of Aboriginal peoples may be respected:

God of our ancient people, Lord of all tribes, show those of us who are
more recent arrivals in this great south land how best we can
acknowledge the dignity of Aborigines and allow them to make their
rich contribution to the well-being of our growing nation.

Australian Prayers: from a prayer by Bruce D. Prewer

for forgiveness and reconciliation between different ethnic groups

Dear God, you have forgiven us our sins;
please enable us to forgive each other.
Lord Jesus, bring healing and reconciliation to this nation,
and make us a people who will walk and live together

in lasting acceptance and respect for each other.
In Jesus' name and for his sake. Amen.

Prayer offered in St Andrew's Cathedral, Sydney, by Bishop Arthur Malcolm,
himself an Aboriginal, in response to an apology made by the
Anglican Church for its part in the suffering inflicted on the Aboriginal peoples.

Give wisdom to those in authority in this and every land,
and guide all peoples in the way of righteousness and peace,
so that they may share with justice the resources of the earth,
work together in trust, and seek the common good.
Father, hear our prayer, through Jesus Christ our Lord.

From the Service of Holy Communion, Second Order
An Australian Prayer Book, 1978

New Zealand

Population: 3.3 million, of which 12% is of Maori descent.

Languages: English, Maori.

Government: Parliamentary state.

Religion: Predominantly Christian, the largest denominations being Anglican (25% of the population), Roman Catholic (15%) and Presbyterian (12%).

The Maori, of Polynesian origin, are the indigenous people of Aotearoa New Zealand. Christian missionaries from Britain successfully urged the British Queen to enter into the Treaty of Waitangi (1840), which guaranteed to the Maori the full enjoyment in perpetuity of their possessions. The Treaty's promises were broken in the rush of pakeha (white) settlement. A period of forced "assimilation" failed to integrate the Maori who have never ceased the struggle to preserve what they hold dear. A number of different denominations accompanied the rapidly increasing number of settlers.

New Zealand-Aotearoa is conspicuous for its humane social welfare legislation, opposition to apartheid, and its anti-nuclear commitment. In all these areas the churches are active as single denominations and together through the Conference of Churches in Aotearoa-New Zealand, which has replaced the NCC with a wider membership including the Roman Catholic Church. The NCC Maori section had previously reconstituted itself as Te Runanga Whakawhanaunga i Nga Hahi o Aotearoa, the Maori Ecumenical Council, which also includes Roman Catholics. "We have grasped Christianity with an unshakable grip," claimed a Maori elder recently, "because it makes sense to everything that is noble and good in being Maori." Many churches have been suffering a decline in numbers and commitment, but with the emergence of indigenous demands arising out of the Maori membership, the church may now be experiencing a renewal in depth as a century and a half of history is reviewed, redressed, and redirected in paths closer to the gospel of justice and peace.

Intercessions and Prayers

Lord God of all Peoples,
We have settled in this land, Aotearoa.
We bring to you an offering from our abundance.

Here we acknowledge that many of our ancestors
came from other lands,
to escape tyranny and oppression
to discover freedom and space
and to appreciate your good earth.

We praise you for clear unpolluted skies and comet-filled heavens,
for tree-filled suburb, and flowers of street and garden.
We acknowledge that for all of this land's beauty of people and places,
there are also shadows where we have spoilt or broken your world.

We pray that this offering may be used here in Aotearoa
to mend the brokenness,
challenge destructive attitudes,
and build trusting relationships.

Hear our prayer in the name of Jesus. Amen.

From an offertory prayer, New Zealand

Gracious God,
we pray for the peoples of
New Zealand-Aotearoa.

Help them to discover what allegiance
to Christ means in their land.

Free them from the colonial mentality
to shape a church which challenges the forces of death
and celebrates the promise of their present reality.

May there be an authentic encounter
between the people of the land, the Maori,
and those who have come from afar.

By your Spirit, keep the churches open
to listen and respond to the yearnings for justice
of Maori and women, youth and unemployed.

Through repentance and conversion
guide your church into a unity
that serves Christ's vision for your new creation,
through Jesus Christ, Amen.

T.W., a prayer from the Conference of Churches
in Aotearoa-New Zealand

Using this symbol we pray with Christians
in Aotearoa-New Zealand

for the government, in its firm stand
for peace, and efforts to maintain
freedom from nuclear pollution;

for young people tempted by
materialism, alcohol and drugs;

for the unemployed;

for the Conference of Churches
in Aotearoa New Zealand, and
the Maori
Ecumenical Council Te Runanga
Whakawhanaunga i Nga Hahi o
Aotearoa;

for growing unity and understanding
between all the churches;

that the partnership within
the churches of women with men,
Maori with Pakeha, may mirror the
unity sought for the whole nation

ONE IN CHRIST

The heart at the centre represents the love of God. The two
curls surrounding the heart are
the two peoples, Maori and
Pakeha (whites), joined together under the umbrella of
Christ (the large curl at the top).

The two sets of curls of
waves at either side of the base
represent the troubles we have
to face in the world, but as long
as we have faith in Christ we
can overcome these troubles.

Pacific Conference of Churches (PCC)

O Jesus,
Be the canoe that holds me up in the sea of life;
Be the rudder that keeps me in the straight road;
Be the outrigger that supports me in times of temptation.
Let your Spirit be my sail that carries me through each day.
Keep my body strong, so I can paddle steadfastly on
in the voyage of life. Amen.

An islander's prayer from Melanesia

"Much water has gone under the canoes since 1961," says the long-time chairman of the National Council of Churches in Tonga, himself involved in the very first regional gathering of churches held in 1961, which led to the inauguration of the Pacific Conference of Churches in 1966.

In the face of the vast distances, the isolation, and the enormous cultural and linguistic disparities of the Pacific, the Christian church has acted as a powerful centre and uniting force in Pacific society, though it has itself been greatly hampered by its own denominational insularity. Embracing many national councils of churches, some thirty different Protestant denominations, and the Roman Catholic Episcopal Conference of the Pacific (including ten Roman Catholic dioceses) the Pacific Conference of Churches has gone a long way towards overcoming that insularity.

Promoting ecumenism, and a theology of the Pacific sometimes called "coconut palm theology", the Conference's emphasis on the riches which those of different cultures and traditions have to share with each other has been facilitated by the holding of workshops, and the promotion of Pacific research and scholarship. Unhappily, not only fertile coconut seeds in the shape of good ideas and experiences have circulated in the Pacific, but other less welcome elements. All kinds of sects have proliferated in recent years, secularism threatens to erode the traditional values of the island people, while the testing of nuclear devices and the dumping of nuclear waste by foreign powers continue to be matters of grave concern.

Other concerns include cooperation between the island nations, and the question of self-determination for those still under colonial rule; dialogue with other faiths; unemployment; the creative involvement of women and young people; and the search for a Pacific identity.

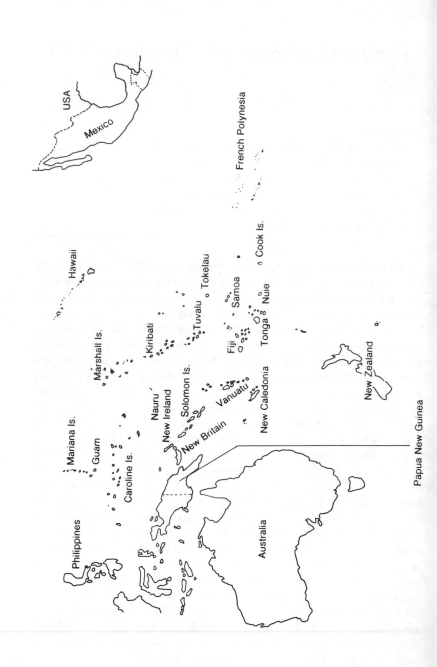

Week 34

The Pacific Islands

Almighty God, your word of creation caused the water to be filled with many kinds of living beings and the air to be filled with birds. With those who live in this world's small islands we rejoice in the richness of your creation, and we pray for your wisdom for all who live on this earth, that we may wisely manage and not destroy what you have made for us and for our descendants. In Jesus' name we pray. Amen.

Prayer from Samoa

This area, sometimes known as Oceania, includes over 2000 islands in more than 30 major groupings. They fall culturally and geographically into three main areas, although there is some overlap. In general terms *Polynesia* lies to the east. Extending from Hawaii to New Zealand, it includes Tonga, Samoa, the Cook Islands, Niue, Tuvalu, Tokelau and others. *Melanesia*, the largest of the areas, is also the most diverse, with small social groupings and very many languages. It lies to the west and includes New Guinea, the Solomon Islands, Vanuatu, New Caledonia and Fiji. *Micronesia* lies on and north of the Equator, and includes the Marshall Islands, Kiribati, Nauru, the Caroline Islands, Guam, the Mariana Islands and others.

Political groupings are more complex, and although in many cases a small group of islands comprises one nation, this is not always so because of the way in which they have been colonized and sometimes changed hands. Many are now independent, but France, USA, and Indonesia remain colonial powers. However the small size of the independent nations often renders them economically and technically dependent on some foreign power.

Until about 50,000 years ago these islands were uninhabited. People then began to arrive in small numbers from Asia, and over thousands of years groups of diverse people spread eastwards, gradually establishing new human communities. The first Europeans to penetrate the region were Spanish explorers and missionaries in the 16th century. Sustained

Christian missionary activity began in 1797 when members of the London Missionary Society landed in Tahiti. From then on, many denominations and nationalities were involved, and soon islanders themselves began to spread the good news to other island groups.

Early missionaries faced many difficulties. Warfare was endemic; and cannibalism and infanticide were practised as part of traditional belief systems. Many Europeans lost their lives, and there were many martyrs among the islanders. However, the faith spread from Tahiti to Papua New Guinea. In the 1939-45 war some islands became battlegrounds, and some were occupied; and most remaining missionaries either perished or were interned. The churches themselves not only survived but became more independent, and local grassroots forms of worship and spirituality emerged.

Today the population of these islands is about 6 million of whom about 80% are Christians. Roman Catholics are strong in Papua and New Caledonia, Methodists in Tonga and Fiji, Congregationalists in Samoa and the Cook Islands, Anglicans in the Solomon Islands, Presbyterians in the New Hebrides, and Lutherans in Papua. As in other respects diversity is a keynote of the region. A gradual lessening of tensions between the denominations has been evident throughout this century, and ecumenical cooperation has developed much more rapidly in recent decades.

In the coconut palm — the tree of life which provides food and drink, clothing and shelter — people see many aspects of God's provision and the workings of the spirit in their lives. "Coconut palm theology" instances the way seeds are carried from island to island, and take root; likening this to their own growing awareness of their interdependence across denominational boundaries and island allegiances.

There has always been, and continues to be, movement of people in all directions in the Pacific. Current trends are towards the larger cities, larger islands, border countries and greater employment possibilities. Many find a higher material standard of living, but at some cost to their dignity and traditional way of life. Tourism is a growing industry in some parts of the region, and some islands have rich mineral deposits. Others are used by foreign powers for strategic and military purposes. Since the first testing of a nuclear weapon at Bikini Atoll in 1946, the area has continued to be used for this purpose, as well as for the dumping of nuclear waste. Often precautions for the local population, and arrangements for their rehabilitation have been grossly inadequate, and many continue to suffer the effects of radiation.

Keep the ocean clean
Keep Palau clean
Keep the air clean
Keep your hair.
Leave us alone so we can stay alive and happy.
Leave the ocean so the fish can survive and we people can survive.
Keep the nuclear waste out of the ocean.

From the West Caroline island of Palau,
a fifth-grader's cry of protest

The environment of the small but vivacious communities of the islands is the nourishing, at times threatening, sea. Pacific Islander Christians have a special way of comprehending the world. Most human beings look outward on solid earth. Islanders live on small pieces of earth surrounded by the wealth — and menace — of the sea. Travel and arrival, life and death, the Good News ... have distinctive meanings for church and people. Christ is the Pacific Prince, chief of chiefs come from afar.

To Live Among The Stars, John Garrett

Intercessions and Prayers

We believe that Creation is a gift of God, an expression of our Creator's goodness.

We believe that as human beings we are part of this creation and that we share in a special way in the creative power of God.

We believe that the resources of our lands and waters and air are precious gifts from our Creator, to be used and looked after with loving care.

We believe that there is a rhythm to God's creation, like a drum beat; when we lose the beat, or the drum is damaged, the music is out of tune.

We believe that in order to be good stewards of creation, we have the responsibility to seek information on important concerns of our people and our region, and to share information in our communities.

We believe that like flowers we can bloom fully only when we are planted in God's love.

We believe that as Christians we are called to be peace-makers, in the true peace which God promises us.

We believe that this may sometimes mean "disturbing the peace" as Jesus did, for a purpose — to restore the purpose of God.

We believe that our Pacific ways are also a gift from God; we are invited to use the values of our Pacific culture to build societies of justice and peace.

We express these beliefs, reminded of the love of God, the grace of Christ, and the fellowship of the Holy Spirit. Amen.

Taken from a creed. Women of the Pacific: Worship Workshop

Together with the people of the Pacific we give thanks

for the coming of the Christian faith

for those many Islanders who hazarded their lives in spreading the good news; and in keeping the faith through the years of war and occupation

for community and celebration, and the wholeness of life lived in the region

We pray

for the national councils of churches, and the Pacific Conference of Churches with its many regional concerns

for theological education, carried out on an ecumenical basis

for those who are suffering the effects of radio-active fallout, and those who fear for the future

for schools (47% of the population is under 15), trying to provide a modern education whilst preserving a rich cultural heritage

for young people leaving the rural areas in search of "better" jobs, experiencing difficulties and frustrations, and sometimes resorting to drink or drugs which often lead to violence

for families bewildered by the changes and pressures brought by the tourist industry and an increasing consumer economy

We ask you, dear God,
that just as the great Southern Cross
guides our people as they sail over the Pacific at night,
so may the cross of Jesus Christ
be our sure and certain guide to lead us day by day.

The Bible Society of Papua New Guinea

Lord, in your mercy
help all the peoples of the vast Pacific Ocean
to be good stewards of the sea and its resources.
Help all people everywhere
to acknowledge that you alone have spread out the heavens
and rule over the seas,
and that the waters are a gift from you.

Lord, in your mercy — Hear our prayer.

Lord in your mercy,
help the scientists and technicians of the world
to use their knowledge and skills for the good of all,
and not for destructive purposes.
May the countries which produce nuclear energy
channel such bounty for the good of humankind.

Lord, in your mercy — Hear our prayer.

From a litany by Jabez L. Bryce, Anglican bishop in Polynesia

We pray for the peoples of Oceania in their concern to preserve their
cultures, and to keep their lands and their seas free from war and the
effects of war technology; may they be strengthened as they strive to
keep true values alive, and as they seek in a happy and peaceful spirit,
opportunities and justice for all.

Christian prayer for peace, Pope John Paul II, Assisi 1986

O God our Father,
save our shores from the weapons of death,
our lands from what may deny our young ones love and freedom.
Let the seas of the Pacific Ocean
carry messages of peace and goodwill.
Turn away from our midst any unkind and brutal practices.
Let each child swim, and breathe the fresh air
that is filled by the Holy Spirit.

O Lord Jesus,
bless all that are makers of that inner peace
that breaks down the barriers of hatred;
and unite us with the open arms of your cross,
that all the peoples of the world may live happily together. Amen.

Sione Amanaki Havea, Tonga

The coconut, marked with a cross, and kicked, rolled and finally hacked with a knife, is used as a moving commentary on Isaiah 53 and 55 in a service which concludes with the water and meat of the coconut being used to celebrate the Lord's supper. It is perhaps the incorporation of this rather more painful aspect in the symbolism of the coconut palm which is to the fore in the minds of Christians in the Pacific in these troubled days.

O Lord, our palm trees can no longer hide us from the world. Strengthen our hearts that we may look with confidence to the future.

Prayer of Tahitian pastor

Week 35

The Islands of the Indian Ocean

O God, we pray that you will give us enough wisdom and faith to realize the depth and richness of our human dignity; and the necessary courage to defend our own dignity and that of others, against all that would distort and devalue it.

Prayer from Seychelles

By far the largest islands in this vast ocean are Madagascar (Week 16) and Sri Lanka (Week 49). The other main groups are the Comoros, Maldives, Mauritius and Seychelles which all have a history of colonial rule. Various countries hold other island territories in the region.

The Comoros

The archipelago of the Comoros, situated between Madagascar and the coast of mainland Africa, consists of four volcanic islands and numerous small islets. The country declared independence in 1975, except for the island of Mayotte which elected to retain links with France. The islands are poor and severely under-developed, exporting perfume oils and vanilla. The population (about 400,000) of the Federal Islamic Republic of the Comoros is of mixed Arab, African and Malagasy descent. Arabic and French are the official languages, but most people speak Comoran. The vast majority are Muslims. There are very small Christian and Bahai communities, mostly made up of Malagasy and other expatriates, many of them seasonal workers. The country was totally unevangelized until 1973, and open evangelism continues to be unwelcome.

Maldives

The Republic of Maldives embraces over a thousand small islands south-west of Sri Lanka, of which only 202 are inhabited. The Maldivian

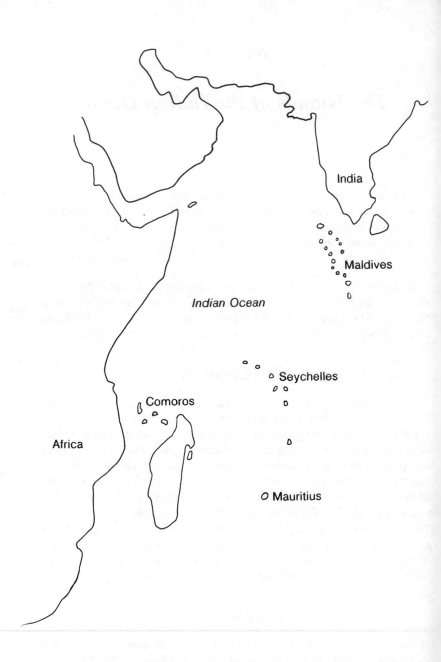

population of 181,500 are of Sinhalese origin, and speak Dhivehi, a language related to Sinhala. Their forebears were Buddhists but were converted to Islam in 1153. Living on the small coral islands most subsist by fishing and collecting coconuts. A tourist industry has been developed in recent years and contributes greatly to the economy. Islam is the only officially recognized religion. Christianity is represented by Sri Lankan and Indian workers, and visiting tourists.

Mauritius

Consisting of the larger island from which the country takes its name and several smaller ones, Mauritius has been independent within the British Commonwealth since 1968. The official language is English, but Creole and a number of Indian languages are widely spoken. With no indigenous inhabitants the islands were settled mainly from India and East Africa, and colonized by the French and then the British.

The present population of 1.1 million is composed of Indians (about two-thirds), Creoles (about a quarter), and small European and Chinese minorities. Reflecting the ethnic balance, Hindus make up 52% of the population. There are significant Christian (27% of whom the majority are Roman Catholics) and Muslim (18%) communities; and smaller numbers of Buddhists, Jews, Sikhs, Bahais and adherents of traditional religions. The main priority of the Roman Catholic Church is the transformation of institutional parishes into warm, caring basic Christian communities, sharing the good news of the gospel in villages and city wards. Drug abuse is an acute problem in Mauritius, and the church is expanding its work in the rehabilitation of addicts. Contact between members of the different faiths, and a recently held interfaith conference, have given an added dimension to the ecumenical scene.

Seychelles

A group of more than a hundred widely scattered islands, and originally uninhabited, Seychelles was annexed by France in the 18th century and later ceded to Britain. Independence as a republic was gained in 1976, and the country now has a socialist single-party system of government. Very few of the islands are inhabited, and 98% of the population (about 66,000) live on the three which are most developed. Tourism, agriculture and fishing are the major industries.

The people are of mixed African, European, Polynesian, Chinese and Indian origin; and Creole is the official language. Almost all are Christians, about 90% being Roman Catholics and 8% Anglicans. The creation of a peace zone in the Indian Ocean, with particular reference to the absence of nuclear weapons, and protection of the environment are special concerns of Seychelles.

Intercessions and Prayers

Let us give thanks

for the beauty of the islands of the Indian Ocean and the blending of different races and peoples

for the way in which Christianity has been faithfully practised and served by pastors and people over many years, and for the facility for renewal in the face of new needs and opportunities

for the growing cooperation of the different churches and for many enterprises undertaken together

for the warmth of welcome and hospitality experienced by Christian visitors to churches in the region

> *O God of all the people and all the nations of the earth,*
> *we praise you for the loveliness and diversity of your creatures.*
>
> *This day we thank you for Mauritius,*
> *where you have gathered the people of Africa and Asia and Europe*
> *into one island nation, surrounded them with great beauty, and*
> *blessed them with a spirit of tolerance and with growing prosperity.*
>
> *Defeat, O God, the forces of evil*
> *which exploit human weaknesses and prejudices*
> *for the selfish interests of the few.*
>
> *Confirm the Christian churches in their struggle to be faithful to the*
> *gospel, and also open and loving in their relations with the people*
> *and institutions of other faiths.*
>
> *Strengthen, O God, all those who work for true justice and peace*
> *among the people of Mauritius; that tolerance may grow into under-*
> *standing, and that prosperity may benefit all.*

Prayer from the Presbyterian community in Mauritius

Let us pray

for continuing peace in the region; and for all efforts to protect the environment

for small communities of people, eking out a basic living from the natural resources around them

for drug addicts and those who work for their rehabilitation

that those who visit the islands as tourists may do so with sensitivity, that local people may benefit, and the understanding of all be enhanced

for isolated Christians in the Comoros and Maldives, that their sense of belonging to the worldwide church may be strengthened

> *Lord Jesus, we claim your promise*
> *for all small groups of Christians;*
> *that where two or three are gathered together in your name*
> *you will be present in the midst of them;*
> *present to inspire, present to encourage, present to bless.*
> *Risen Lord, we claim your promise.*

for God's blessing on an ecumenical project to translate the Bible into Mauritian Creole; and for Roman Catholics, Anglicans and Presbyterians cooperating in theological education by extension

for God's gift of unity between people of different races and religions

> *Almighty God,*
> *always you have wished for the unity of all humanity.*
> *Distrust and division are none of your doing!*
>
> *Grant to all humanity, and especially the people here,*
> *unity in diversity, and peace in mutual respect.*
> *Grant us the joy of living together in your friendship,*
> *and of working for the good of our nation*
> *under your watchful care.*
>
> *This we ask of you through Jesus Christ our Lord,*
> *who lives and reigns with you and the Holy Spirit,*
> *in perfect unity for ever and ever. Amen.*

Part of a prayer, dear to Hindus and Buddhists as well as to Christians,
which is used on the feast day of blessed Fr Jacques-Désiré Laval,
a French missionary priest, revered in Mauritius
as an apostle of unity and a founder of the church

Week 36

The Caribbean Islands
French Guyana • Guyana • Suriname

Red eyes, batons,
red fire, red blood,
black oppressed, fearful white
uncertain and ambivalent mulatto — help us to serve thee, O God

Black power, racial harmony
socialism, democracy
law and order
subversion, oppression,
Imperialism, rule by the masses — help us to know thy will, O God

Which road to follow?
leave the country?
Vigilante protection?
Fight for the peasants?
arbitrary legislation? — help us to know thy will, O God

Help us to know thy will O God
How can we pray this?
Such a prayer
Cast against the background
of our unconcern, our apathy,
our denial of our heritage
of racial harmony
of our sufferers
such a prayer O God
shall be our judgment — help us to do thy will, O God.

Intercession on Caribbean Choices, E. Anthony Allen, Kingston, Jamaica

Throughout the immensely varied and bewildering collage of nations and races, creeds and cultures, political systems and languages of the Caribbean, one thing remains common: the history of colonial domination from which the present situation derives.

The region, which includes Guyana, Suriname and French Guyana on the South American mainland, and Belize (Week 37) as well as the islands, was originally inhabited by the peaceful Arawaks and rather less peaceful Caribs. The Amerindian population was largely decimated by the early colonizers and is now reduced to small minority groups living in Trinidad, St Vincent, Dominica, Belize, Guyana and Suriname. The first colonizers, the Spanish, were soon followed by the Dutch, British and French; and for more than 300 years the conflicts of Europe were partially played out in the Caribbean. By the end of the colonial era Spain had lost out to Britain and the USA.

"The region was historically not meant to be a society," says Dr Dale Bisnauth, associate general secretary of the Caribbean Conference of Churches, "it was meant to be a plantation, owned and operated by European capitalists. The colonies were perceived as sources of primary agricultural products which could be made into manufactured goods for the European market. Economically, then, the region's history has been one of metropolital plunder and exploitation from which it will take years to recover."

Plantations necessitate a sizeable labour force, and this had to be imported. Thousands of West African slaves were brought annually, so that the population became predominantly African. In addition Indians, Chinese, Indonesians and Europeans were brought as indentured labour.

Most Caribbean countries are now politically independent, but a number are still under British, French, Dutch and US sovereignty; and some, for example, Puerto Rico and the Netherlands' Antilles have varying degrees of associated status. Spanish, English, French or Dutch is the official language in most places; and more than one of these or a local patois is often the norm. In addition various Asian and Amerindian languages are widely spoken in some areas.

Economic domination, however, remains and the region "caught in a trade bind forged in colonial times" is a region of poverty. "The problem of the external debt hangs around the region's collective neck like an albatross, adding to the misery of its impoverishment and underdevelopment. The problems — unemployment, inadequate health and housing facilities, drug abuse etc — which derive from the economic deprivation of the region are many. Add to them the fact of cultural alienation and the picture is not encouraging." (Dale Bisnauth)

We are weary
of the years of sowing and reaping;

of planting the good, new seed with hope,
and harvesting nothing.
We are weary
of the days of fruitless toiling;
of lending our strength to an alien's gain
and profiting nothing.
We are weary
of hypocrisy, falsehood, corruption,
of the slogans fashioned to allay the fear of the disinherited.
We are weary
of the voices shrouded in shadows of war, crying out for peace,
yet knowing no peace.
We are weary
of the years of uncertain getting,
of the unfailing years of spending.
We are weary
of the bright voices speaking hope, of the dark voices telling doom,
of the moments of striving and the hours of failing.
Lord, we are weary.

From a litany of justice, hope and peace, Caribbean Conference of Churches

In the past, in addition to the loss of identity resulting from the conditions of slavery, European cultural and value systems were imposed on the Caribbean peoples; and the historic churches contributed to this process. Now there is a new identity problem. "Situated as it is between the poor South and the rich North, the region shares the poverty of the South, but its peoples aspire to lifestyles of the North whose consumer patterns bombard them from media programmes. The fracture in the psyche that this creates is not helped by the region's vulnerability to other pressures from the North..."(Dale Bisnauth)

O Lord, lead us not into imitation!

Prayer of the East Asia Youth Assembly

Cuba, the largest of the Caribbean islands, threw off cultural and economic domination in its Revolution of 1959, which toppled the previous repressive dictatorship. Since then the country has been developing its own brand of socialism, and restructuring its basically agricultural economy. An Ecumenical Council is active in developing a corporate Christian response to the new social and political realities of the Revolution.

We believe in you, O God,
for you have made the suffering of humanity your suffering.
You have come to establish a kingdom of the poor and humble.
Today we sing to you, because you are alive,
you have saved us, you have made us free.

Affirmation from Cuba

Christianity first came to the Caribbean with the colonizers, who brought all their own separate denominational churches with them. Some of the first slaves were also Christians. Roman Catholics or Protestants dominated according to who ruled, and the churches have sometimes been criticized for furthering the interests of their parent nations.

Today in most Caribbean territories over 90% of the people are Christians. This figure drops to about 50-75% in Trinidad and Tobago, Suriname and Guyana, where there are significant numbers of Hindus and Muslims; and to 42% in Cuba, where 55% of the population are either atheists or non-religious. There are small Bahai communities throughout the region. Traditional African and Amerindian religions are still followed, and Voodoo, a syncretism of Christianity and African rites, is strong in Haiti.

History has left the Caribbean with a very broad religious spectrum, complicated by loyalties to the country of origin and the practicalities of language. In recent years there has been an influx of new and largely fundamentalist sects from North America, aided and abetted by the tremendous influence of the electronic church. Current concerns are many, and individual churches vary in their emphases, but theological reflection related to the region, peace with justice, the problem of drug abuse, unemployment, the deepening of spiritual life and growing ecumenism are recurring themes. In many national councils of churches the Roman Catholic Church is a full member.

Intercessions and Prayers

Give thanks

for the growth of the Christian faith in the Caribbean

for the growing unity of churches as expressed in the Caribbean Conference of Churches and in the national councils of churches of the region

for growing tolerance between Christians and peoples of other faiths and beliefs

Thank you, O Lord our God, for all that you have done to sustain us.
Here in the Caribbean there are so many things that give us pleasure:
beaches, mountains, valleys, trees, fruits and flowers.
Indeed, all nature celebrates you in this part of your creation.
Thank you for the people who dwell in our territories,
that in them we see a reflection of all the races of the world.
Thank you for your beloved Son Jesus Christ;
for his life, his mission, his teaching, his sufferings,
his death and resurrection;
And that this Jesus who is our Saviour, lives today.

Caribbean Conference of Churches, 4th Assembly

Lord, how glad we are that we don't hold you,
but that you hold us.

Prayer from Haiti

Pray

for peace in the region, and particularly in strife-torn Haiti, and in Suriname now returned to parliamentary rule

for justice and the observance of human rights

for the poor and disadvantaged that they may have hope

for the eradication of poverty and a fairer distribution of resources in all countries

for the Caribbean Conference of Churches, and for individual churches that they may be instruments of peace, justice and development

for all Christian families in the region

O God, in baptism you have called us by name and made us members of your people, the church.

Raise up good and holy families, loving husbands, wives and parents.

Raise up from among our families and friends, dedicated and generous leaders who will serve as sisters, priests, brothers, deacons and lay ministers.

Give your Spirit to guide and strengthen us, that we may serve your people following the example of your Son, Jesus Christ, in whose name we offer this prayer.

A prayer for family life and for vocations suggested for use by members of congregations in the Roman Catholic Archdiocese of Kingston, Jamaica

We pray that thou wilt watch over us in St Lucia,
for there are so many things happening on this small island of ours.

Schoolgirl's prayer from St Lucia

For this and other areas of the world where life has been grossly disturbed
by the advent of tourists, we pray:

Loving Creator,
may those who visit the Caribbean
enjoy its natural beauty and the rich variety of its people
not as things to be paid for by money
but as your gifts to be loved and handled with care.

With those who, long after our prayers have ended, continue to serve the
church in the Caribbean we pray:

O God, we pray that you will keep together those you have united.
Look kindly on all who follow Jesus your Son,
and who are consecrated to you in a common baptism.
Make us one in the fullness of faith,
and keep us in the fellowship of justice, peace and love. Amen.

Caribbean Conference of Churches,
opening service of the Fourth Assembly

1. Belize
2. Cuba
3. Jamaica
4. Bahamas
5. Dominican Republic
6. Puerto Rico
7. Haiti
8. Leeward Is.
9. Windward Is.
10. Trinidad
11. Suriname
12. French Guyana
13. Guyana
14. Netherlands Antilles

Caribbean Conference of Churches (CCC)

"We, as Christian people in the Caribbean, separated from each other by barriers of history, language, culture, class and distance, desire because of our common calling in Christ to join together in a regional fellowship of churches for inspiration, consultation and cooperative action" — so read the opening words of the constitution of the Caribbean Conference of Churches.

Inaugurated in 1973, the CCC now has 33 member churches from a wide variety of traditions including the Roman Catholic Church and a number of evangelical bodies. With its headquarters in Barbados, and with area offices in Trinidad, Jamaica and Antigua, the CCC extends its regional ecumenical umbrella to such mainland countries as Belize, Panama, Costa Rica, Guyana and Suriname.

"Promoting ecumenism and social change in obedience to Jesus Christ and in solidarity with the poor" is the current mandate. Ongoing concerns include regional integration, Caribbean identity, third-world tourism, the region as a zone of peace, human rights, racism, the wellbeing of migrants and refugees, as well as concern about the avenues for self-destruction being made increasingly available especially to the young.

In this context "the thrust of the CCC is declaredly developmental". Working for the benefit of those at the bottom of the economic ladder, whether those in rural communities or the great number of unemployed or under-employed in the cities, it "is convinced that developmental pro-grammes must be integrative, participatory, community-based and oriented, facilitative of reflection, renewal, change and human liberation. Above all, they must be with the poor, by the poor and for the poor" (Dale Bisnauth).

Loving God, we are concerned about the spread of hatred in our time.
Some of it has led to crime, violence of all sorts, marital breakdown,
tribal conflicts and tensions among peoples and nations.
Strike out, O God, the root causes of all hatred,
that justice, peace and love might prevail.

Lord in your mercy
Hear our prayer

We commit to God the work of all who strive to create a more healthy society in these Caribbean lands: who work among the poor, the unemployed; who try to point our youth to a life away from drugs, alcohol, licentious behaviour, and to point them rather to the paths of true human dignity and responsibility. Grant them the encouragement to continue their noble aims.

Lord in your mercy
Hear our prayer

Caribbean Conference of Churches, 4th Assembly

Many Caribbean Christians would feel more at home *singing* the prayer cycle! This prayer by Patrick Prescod is best sung to the accompaniment of steel band, piano, flute and guitar, but any lively accompaniment will serve.

Patrick Prescod   Noel Dexter

The right hand of God is writ-ing in our land,

Writ - ing with pow-er and with love,   Our

con-flicts and   our fears, our tri-umphs   and   our tears Are re-

corded   by   the   right   hand   of   God.

The right hand of God is pointing in our land,
Pointing the way we must go.
So clouded is the way, so easily we stray,
But we're guided by the right hand of God.

The right hand of God is striking in our land,
Striking out at envy, hate, and greed.
Our selfishness and lust, our pride and deeds unjust
Are destroyed by the right hand of God.

The right hand of God is healing in our land,
Healing broken bodies, minds, and souls.
So wondrous is its touch with love that means so much,
When we're healed by the right hand of God.

The right hand of God is planting in our land,
Planting seeds of freedom, hope, and love.
In these Caribbean lands, let God's people all join hands,
And be one with the right hand of God.

Patrick Prescod

Week 37

Belize • Guatemala • Honduras • Mexico

Give us, Señor, a little sun, a little happiness and some work.
Give us a heart to comfort those in pain.
Give us the ability to be good, strong, wise and free
so that we may be generous with others as we are with ourselves.
Finally, Señor, let us all live in your own, one family.

Prayer on a church wall in Mexico

Belize

Formerly known as British Honduras, Belize was under Spanish sovereignty before it was under British. It became fully independent within the Commonwealth in 1981, and has a parliamentary form of government, and close links with the Caribbean. The official language is English, but Spanish and some American Indian languages are also spoken. Guatemala has laid claim to Belizean territory since the mid-19th century, and successive attempts at a settlement have so far failed. In spite of the fact that over half the population (166,300) lives in the capital, the economy depends mainly on agriculture. Floods and hurricanes are natural hazards. In recent years considerable immigration from neighbouring Latin American countries, especially El Salvador, has approximately balanced movement out of Belize to the USA from whence people send much-needed money home.

About 95% of people are Christians; approximately 60% being Roman Catholics and 40% Protestants of whom half are Anglicans. There are small Bahai and Jewish communities. The Belize Christian Council seeks to provide "a comprehensive service programme under ecumenical leadership for the benefit of the people of Belize". With a wide range of membership including the Roman Catholic Church and the Salvation Army as well as various associate bodies, it relates to the Caribbean Conference of Churches.

Let us pray

for Belize, that its people may live in harmony with each other and with those of neighbouring lands

that its young people may make the fullest use of their energies and opportunities; and their elders give them ground for hope in a worthwhile future for their country

for the Belize Christian Council and its social action programmes, particularly those among women and pre-school children

for the concern of the churches to encourage local leadership and for their involvement in education and primary health care

for the unemployed and the homeless; those caught up in the sale and use of drugs; for families split by migration

> *Grant, O Lord, that the people of Belize may have peace and prosperity and be a stabilizing influence in the turmoil of Central America. Prosper the educational work of the Christian church, and give unity where there is discord, for Jesus Christ's sake. Amen.*

Guatemala

Population: 8.5 million.
Languages: Spanish and more than 20 indigenous languages.
Government: Multi-party republic.
Religion: Christians 99% (Roman Catholics 94%, Protestants 5%).

The indigenous inhabitants of Central America, the Mayan Indians, were more than halved in number by the effects of the Spanish conquest in the 16th century. Most of those who survived lived in the highlands of what is now Guatemala. This country enjoyed a period of democratic government earlier this century, but fears of communist infiltration prompted the US government to support the military coup which ended it. Since then there has been considerable instability and increasing violence. The root causes — poverty and landlessness — remain unresolved. There have been reports of violations of human rights, and many deaths for political reasons. The country has been described as "a nation of widows and orphans", and many of these children now roam the streets. Up to 500,000 Indians have been displaced by the fighting, many of whom have sought refuge in camps in Mexico. At the same time Guatemala is host to many Salvadorean refugees. A new government has now been elected and faces a massive task.

Christianity was first brought by the Spanish, later by other Europeans, and then North Americans. The Roman Catholic Church, formerly closely allied with the ruling power, experienced a considerable reawakening in the 1950s, and many bishops, priests and lay people took up the option to identify with the poor. As a consequence they have been harassed and branded as communists, and some have been tortured or lost their lives. Protestant churches, which have grown steadily since 1940, have also been involved in human rights issues. The first Protestants to enter the country were the American Presbyterians in 1882. It was they who developed the system of theological education by extension which has been taken up worldwide. Education and health have been major concerns of the mainstream Protestant churches. In recent years numerous fundamentalist sects have entered the country and attracted many converts. Unfortunately their message of salvation often includes anti-communist propaganda, and they are regarded with suspicion by traditional Protestants and Roman Catholics alike. The experience of being poor and the struggle for justice have drawn together many Christians from both Roman Catholic and Protestant backgrounds.

But let justice roll down like waters,
and righteousness like an overflowing stream.

Amos 5

The message that the poor Christians from Latin America hear comes straight from the Bible. Isaiah 65, Amos 5, and Psalm 146 are, among many others, passages that Latin American Christians are reading as promises God holds out to them, both now and when Christ returns.

A testimony given before the US House of Representatives Subcommittee on Human Rights and International Organizations, Committee on Foreign Affairs

Captivate me, Lord.
Till the last of my days,
wring out my heart
with your hands
of a wise old Indian
so that I will not forget your justice
nor cease proclaiming
the urgent need
for humankind to live in harmony.

Prayer/poem of self-exiled Guatemalan resistance poet, Julia Esquivel

Pray for

all current Guatemalan initiatives for peace with neighbouring countries, and for a positive response

all who seek to bring about constructive land reform and a more just distribution of the country's resources

the thousands of families in unabated distress, still hoping for news of "disappeared" family members

the large numbers of Indian people who have fled, or been displaced by army activity

Guatemala's unemployed and poor people, and the many young children who have lost one or both parents in political violence

Christian communities and all other means by which the good news of the resurrection is mediated in Guatemala today

> *Jesus, we believe that you are living.*
> *The steps that you took before, we are taking now.*
> *Your resurrection is present in each sister and brother who rises up.*
> *Help us so that all people may be resurrected in a new Guatemala*
> *where peace, justice and equality will reign,*
> *so that nobody is hungry.*

Prayer of an Indian woman member
of the Guatemalan Committee for Justice and Peace

Honduras

Population: 3.9 million.

Language: Spanish.

Government: Multi-party republic.

Religion: Christians 98% (Roman Catholics 95%, Protestants 3%).

A major centre of ancient Mayan culture before the 10th century, Honduras today is one of the poorest countries of Latin America. Largely dependent on agriculture, and at the mercy of hurricanes, floods and drought, the country is reliant on economic aid. Landowners have never been as rich and powerful as in neighbouring countries, and perhaps for this reason, Honduras has not experienced the same degree of violence as its neighbours. Nevertheless, in recent years political unrest has been increasing. The presence of about 47,000 refugees from El Salvador and Nicaragua and some Contras, as well as heavy US military involvement in the country, add to the tensions.

In the 1960s the Roman Catholic Church pioneered the training of lay people from remote areas as rural "delegates of the word". This grassroots evangelism went hand in hand with concern for social issues, and the concrete problems affecting people. Rural education programmes and pressure for land reform provoked antagonism, and there were arrests, deaths and confiscation of property. A number of Protestant confessions are present. Although numerically small they have made significant contributions in areas of social concern, notably education and health, in addition to their evangelistic work.

We pray

for Honduras, one of the poorest nations in the hemisphere, with massive malnutrition among its rural population, and constantly threatened by floods, drought and crop failures

for the Christian church's response to the potentially volatile situation existing in the country

for church-run schools, clinics, nutrition centres and agricultural projects

for the massive influx of refugees from El Salvador, Guatemala and Nicaragua

> ### To Guatemalan refugees in Mexico, from Salvadoran refugees in Honduras:
>
> *We still pray, we still sing*
> *We still dream of the day*
> *when the birds will return*
> *and the flowers*
> *and our lost loved ones.*
>
> *We still live with the belief*
> *that love and gentleness and faith*
> *will blossom forth one day*
> *like roses in winter.*
>
> *We still believe that God*
> *will be born again in our land*
> *as we prepare the stable of our hearts*
> *for the birth of a new people.*

By his coming to the world in the form of a stranger seeking welcome,
and as an exile looking for the promise of refuge and hope,
may the God of Ruth and Moses bless the people of Honduras.

Mexico

Population: 79.6 million.

Languages: Spanish and indigenous Indian languages.

Government: Federal republic.

Religion: Christians 98% (Roman Catholics about 94%, Protestants 3.7%).

The revolution of 1910, which began largely as a movement to free the country from prolonged dictatorship, continued as a revolt against large landowners, and marked the beginning of social change in Mexico. Despite this there are still large numbers of landless people, and poverty and malnutrition in rural areas is extensive. A growing population, together with Mexico's remarkable industrial expansion, has encouraged migration to the cities, and Mexico City, on the site of the ancient Aztec capital, is now the largest urban concentration in the world. New cities have grown up along the border with USA, where foreign-owned factories employ large numbers of people. Poverty and lack of work encourage further migration, both legal and illegal, across the border into USA. There have been times when this source of cheap labour was more or less welcomed, but now the situation is different and these migrants are very vulnerable to both exploitation and deportation. In spite of its own population explosion — half the population is under 16 years — Mexico is host to some 46,000 refugees, mostly from Guatemala.

The 1910 revolution profoundly affected the Roman Catholic Church which was one of the largest landowners, and for a time the church was persecuted. Now there is a kind of *modus vivendi* between church and state, and although the ruling party is officially atheist, many of its leaders are Roman Catholics. Whilst the hierarchy tends to be conservative and the majority of people traditional Catholics, there are those who are attempting to relate their theology and liturgical practice to social issues and to local culture. Some prestigious Jesuit schools have closed, and transferred their resources to educational work in slum areas. Some bishops have protested publicly against violations of human rights, for although Mexico has the reputation of being one of the least oppressive countries in the region there have been reported violations. The first Protestants to come to Mexico came as individuals during Spanish rule, and faced the Inquisition. Protestant missionaries came later. Now there are a considerable number of Protestant groups and sects. The flourishing Pentecostal churches constitute about two-thirds of all Protestants in the country.

The violent earthquake of 1985 killed thousands of people and affected maybe 100,000 families. The work of reconstruction and rehabilitation will continue for years. In various church-sponsored organizations the people themselves have been mobilized to help build their own homes, thereby reducing costs as well as giving them a sense of purpose and community organization.

We pray

for the "damnificados" or earthquake victims of Mexico, and for the ecumenical committee offering help to them

for those many poor people who are nevertheless heirs to a rich life in Christ; and for all who seek to help them to enter into more of the material promises of the kingdom

for countless children on the streets, and for all who work to give them some kind of dignity and future

for young women tempted away from their own communities by the prospect of work in border factories, with all the problems inherent in such a situation

for all who furtively cross borders in search of work and refuge

for those who have to administer the law in border areas, that they may afford human dignity to all

for the work of the church on the border, offering hospitality, advice and practical help,

for Mexico City, with its population growing by at least a million a year

> *God of our daily lives*
> *we pray for the people of the cities of this world*
> *working and without work;*
> *homeless or well housed;*
> *fulfilled or frustrated;*
> *confused and cluttered with material goods*
> *or scraping a living from others' leavings;*

angrily scrawling on walls, or reading the writing on the wall;
lonely or living in community;
finding their own space and respecting the space of others.
We pray for our sisters and brothers,
mourning and celebrating —
may we share their sufferings and hope.

Jan Pickard, Methodist Church Overseas Division

Lord,
if this day you have to correct us
put us right not out of anger
but with a mother and father's love.
So may we your children
be kept free of falseness and foolishness.

Prayer from Mexico

Week 38

Costa Rica • El Salvador • Nicaragua Panama

Señor,
sálvanos de caer en el pecado
de creer que la esclavitud en Egipto
es mejor que la lucha aquí en el desierto.

Lord,
free us from falling into the sin
of believing that the slavery in Egypt
is better than the struggle here in the desert. Tómas Téllez, Nicaragua

Becoming part of the Federal Republic of Central America after achieving independence from Spain in 1821, Costa Rica, El Salvador and Nicaragua became separate independent republics in 1838. Panama was part of Gran Colombia until 1903. Its relative stability and diversified economy have given it a greater prosperity than its neighbours, but it nevertheless has a considerable foreign debt. The other countries are largely agricultural, although El Salvador is more industrialized; and all struggle with burdens of debt. The civil war in El Salvador and the troubles in Nicaragua are enormous drains on resources and destabilizing factors throughout the region. The political violence and upheaval of the area is matched by unruly natural forces.

The Contadora group of nations — Colombia, Mexico, Panama, Venezuela — together with its support group of Argentina, Brazil, Peru and Uruguay have proposed peace agreements for the region, and offered to provide an international force to protect sensitive borders. The most recent initiative has come from the president of Costa Rica. Costa Rica, a country of small farms rather than large land-holdings, has enjoyed almost unbroken constitutional government since independence.

Population, religion, government and language

Costa Rica: 2.4 million, Christians 98%.

El Salvador: 4.9 million, Christians 99.2%.

Nicaragua: 2.9 million, Christians 99.3%.

Panama: 2.2 million, Christians 92%.

Traditional Indian religions still exist, and in Panama there are adherents of many different world faiths.

All these countries are multi-party republics.

The official language is Spanish, but indigenous Indian languages are spoken throughout the region, as well as English in parts of Nicaragua.

Colombus reached this part of Central America in 1502, and the settlers who followed were accompanied by priests who were ardent evangelists towards the indigenous Indians. Many took up their cause, and opposed the harsh and repressive measures adopted by the authorities; but for the most part the Catholic Church, firmly allied to Spain, greatly increased its wealth and power. Some 90-95% of people are Roman Catholics except in Panama where the proportion is slightly lower. Following the second world war, and largely in response to a wave of anti-communism, the rural areas of Central America were singled out for attention by an influx of foreign clergy and religious orders. For the first time priests and nuns came face to face with the severe poverty and exploitation of rural people. Through this experience the church underwent a reawakening, and began to contribute to a slow process of building among its people an awareness of their rights and dignity as children of God.

Methodist immigrants from the Caribbean arrived in Panama in 1815. German Moravians began work in Nicaragua in 1849, and by involvement in agriculture and literacy, as well as wider educational and medical work, provided a social and pastoral ministry to various ethnic groups. In Costa Rica expatriate traders initiated Protestant services in private homes, and the first church to be built was non-denominational. The traditional Protestant churches, mostly founded by North American missionaries, have been active in the fields of education and health, notably the Baptists in Nicaragua who have established medical training programmes. Pentecostal churches have grown rapidly since the second world war. Today Protestants number between 3 and 8%, and there are also a number of indigenous groups. Some, but not all, Protestant Christians have increasingly spoken out against repression and identified with the poor, working closely with Roman Catholics at this grassroots level.

We live in a world of division, where over $1 million a minute is spent on military expenses, and the gifts that God gave to the human family are used for division and domination. Trusting in God's mercy, we say — Lord, have mercy.

We live in a world where half the members of the human family do not have safe drinking water, thus failing to complete the creation task which a loving God has left us. And so we pray — Christ, have mercy.

We live in a world whose land and wealth is so poorly divided that while many are obese and go on diets, 700 million people are malnourished. And so we pray — Lord, have mercy.

Lord God, we ask you to forgive us our sins, to enlighten our imagination, so that we can share more equally the gifts you have left for all of your children, so that creation may join us in praising your name. Amen.

Oscar Romero, Archbishop of San Salvador, martyred in 1980

In *Costa Rica*, which has one of the most advanced social welfare systems in the world, the church has had an important role in implementing social reform. The Roman Catholic diocesan centre concerned with social teaching, besides offering courses for clergy, provides them also for community workers and trade union officials. A Protestant centre for the region is engaged in pastoral and ecumenical training programmes.

Torn by strife, *El Salvador* has been the scene of political murders and human rights violations; and suffering continues. Exactly who — government, armed forces, or the death squads of the landed aristocracy — carries out the atrocities has varied from time to time. "I have frequently been threatened with death," said Archbishop Oscar Romero shortly before his death. "I should tell you that as a Christian I do not believe in death without resurrection... My death will be for the liberation of my people and as a testimony of hope for the future." Christian people, gathering together in small basic communities to celebrate the eucharist, study the Bible, share their sorrows and strengthen each other, draw inspiration from those who have died in the struggle, and live in that same spirit of resurrection hope.

I believe in you, companion,
human Christ, worker Christ,
who conquered death.

With your immense sacrifice
you begat the new person for liberation.
You are resurrecting
each time we raise an arm
to defend the people from the dominating exploiter:
because you are alive in the ranch,
in the factory, in the school,
I believe in your struggle without truce
I believe in the resurrection.

From the Creed, Nicaraguan Campesino Mass

According to one description, *"Nicaragua* is as weak and fragile as a new-born. It desires peace and the freedom to live and grow as it chooses. The Herods of the world have a disproportionate fear of this tiny country..." Initially embarking on wide-ranging reforms, the Sandinista government at first had the support of many Christian leaders, who have, however, been critical of more recent government restrictiveness. Baptists and Moravians — both active ecumenically — were initiating members of the Evangelical Committee for Development Aid which has played a vital part in social development work.

Panama's geographical situation brings it the benefits derived from the canal and its international banking system, but also the problems and external pressures which accompany these. The Christian church has been challenged and inspired by the example and witness of Latin American Christians. A member of one denomination speaks of a "spring of the church" which is blowing across the continent, crossing denominational and geographical boundaries, issuing in a fluorescence of faith and theology unknown perhaps since the early days of the church.

Intercessions and Prayers

Blessed be God,
who is always renewing the church by his Holy Spirit,
making young again what had grown old.

Act of praise following Vatican II

Loving Lord, you will the health and wholeness of all your people,
we pray for all those who suffer in Central America
those who suffer anxiety and terror
those who suffer deprivation of food and shelter
Lord, please hear us — Mercifully hear us.

We pray for refugees, for the homeless and those who are fleeing from violence
for the sick, the unsettled, and for widows and orphans
for those who identify with the poor and oppressed, and as a consequence suffer
Lord, please hear us — Mercifully hear us.

We pray for those who are working for peace, and for the healing of human bodies and communities
for doctors and nurses and teachers
for members of basic Christian communities
for those who strive for the peaceful and fruitful use of the earth
for all in the region who seek to bring about justice and a lasting peace
Lord, please hear us — Mercifully hear us.

Christian Aid: adapted

With Christians in Central America let us recall that great company of Christian martyrs, known and unknown, who have stood firmly by their faith in the time of testing.

In their company let us pray

for peace in Central America; for the efforts of the Contadora group of nations, and all peace initiatives

for the displaced people of El Salvador, and all who are helping them to settle in new places

for ecumenical cooperation in Nicaragua on all matters concerning the welfare of the wider human family

for congregations in Panama and Costa Rica; for their work and worship together, and their joint concern for the community, particularly the young and unemployed, the destitute and the elderly

for perseverance and an awareness of Christ's living presence for all Christians in Central America

And now
when I fall down
under the burden of my cross
Lord Jesus
be my Cyreneo.

Jerjes Ruiz, Nicaragua

Our Father, who are in this our land,
may your name be blessed
in our incessant search for justice and peace.
May your kingdom come
for those who have for centuries awaited a life with dignity.
May your will be done on earth and in heaven
and in the church of Central America,
a church on the side of the poor.
Give us today our daily bread to build a new society.
Forgive us our trespasses,
do not let us fall into the temptation
of believing ourselves already new men and women.
And deliver us from the evil of war
and from the evil of forgetting that our lives
and the life of this country are in your hands.

The Lord's Prayer as used by Christian communities in Nicaragua

Week 39

Colombia • Ecuador • Venezuela

Blessed be God.
Blessed be our Father in heaven.
Blessed be the God and Father of our Lord Jesus Christ.
Blessed be his holy name.
Blessed be Jesus Christ, true God and true man,
the Saviour of the world.
Blessed be the life-giving, the liberating Spirit, the Holy Ghost,
the Counsellor, the Comforter.
Blessed be God in the splendour of his angels,
in the glories of his saints.

The Divine Praises: traditional act of devotion in the Roman Catholic Church
and therefore appropriately said with the majority of Christians
in the countries prayed for this week

The coast of this area, originally inhabited by American Indians, was sighted by Columbus in 1498. The Spanish conquest quickly followed, and African slaves were subsequently brought in to work on the plantations. The area of what is now Columbia was liberated in 1819 and the remainder of the territory soon after. Initially the whole of this area, together with Panama, constituted Gran Columbia. Ecuador and Venezuela seceded as independent republics in 1830, and Panama separated in 1903. The area is subject to natural disasters: earthquakes, floods, landslides and the eruption of volcanoes.

Roman Catholic missionaries came with the Spanish, and as in other parts of the continent the Roman Catholic Church became the state religion, closely aligned with the ruling power. However, diversity of language, difficult terrain, and in some areas the hostility of the Indians made for difficulties in evangelization, and the acceptance of Christianity was of varying depth and completeness. Independence created difficulties for the church, and the number of priests fell drastically. Although Roman Catholicism is the religion of the vast majority of people — more than 95% — there is no state religion in any of these countries. The first Protestant witness was that of Bible Society agents travelling in the region shortly after independence. Sustained work began in Colombia in 1856 when Presbyterian missionaries from the USA established schools and medical centres. Christian Brethren organized a permanent congregation in Venezuela in 1883, and the Gospel Missionary Union began work in Ecuador in 1896. Other groups followed, and work often expanded from one country to the next.

Population, language and government

Colombia: 27.9 million and rising rapidly.

Ecuador: 9.7 million (excluding nomadic Indian tribes). Increasing rapidly.

Venezuela: 17.8 million (excluding Indian jungle inhabitants).

The language is Spanish, but Quechua and other indigenous languages are widely spoken.

Colombia and Ecuador are unitary multi-party republics. Venezuela is a federal republic.

Colombia

Potentially a rich country, and in some respects relatively well developed, Colombia has suffered an extraordinary amount of politically motivated violence since independence. As if that was not enough, thousands lost their lives in a volcanic eruption in 1985. Successive governments have faced the problems of violence, illicit drug cultivation and trafficking, and severe poverty among the people. The gap between the "haves" and the "have-nots" remains wide, and Colombia has one of the highest infant mortality rates in the world.

It was at Medellín in Colombia that the Conference of Latin American bishops took place, which was to have such a profound effect on the life of the Roman Catholic Church in the region. Recognizing the widespread social ills, and the church's apparent alliance with the rich and powerful, the bishops made a commitment to become "the church of the poor". The church became committed to "liberación" — liberation from oppression of all kinds. Despite this, the church in Colombia remains one of the most conservative in Latin America, and small, more radical groups arising within it have often faced opposition from the bishops. Some priests and lay people (notably Camilo Torres, killed in 1966), frustrated in their efforts to bring about social change by peaceful and political means, joined revolutionary groups. At grassroots level there has been a resurgence of traditional Catholic practice in spite of a severe shortage of priests.

Given government recognition in 1930, Protestants are a small minority, and at times have been regarded with suspicion. On the whole, the Protestant churches are conservative. A number of independent churches, mostly Pentecostal, have developed. Protestants in Colombia now enjoy considerable freedom.

Ecuador

In days gone by the Spaniards solemnly dedicated Ecuador to the Sacred Heart of Jesus. With or without such dedication, Christians believe all people and places to be firmly held in the heart of God, even though today's Christians in Ecuador have widely differing understandings of its implications for them.

O Christ,
as the spear opened a passage to your heart
we pray that you would ever keep a way open
to the hearts of your people everywhere...

With a long history of oppression of the people generally at the hands of wealthy landowners, Ecuador continues to suffer under a massive debt, and an ever widening disparity between rich and poor. Cuts in social services, wage freezes and unemployment have led to unrest, and precipitated displays of force by those in authority. Normally a peaceful people, current outbreaks of violence are a new and disturbing feature of Ecuadorian life.

The Roman Catholic Church, while offering the traditional comforts and consolations of religion, has by and large been content to maintain the status quo. Protestant churches, invited into the country during a more liberal period of government, contributed educational facilities. The many later Protestant arrivals have been very conservative, emphasizing personal evangelism, and wary of social involvement. There have, however, been significant exceptions in both Catholic and Protestant communities. Inspired by Vatican II and the Medellín conference, some Roman Catholic bishops, priests and lay people have dedicated themselves to the service of the poor, and to agitation for land reform and the observance of human rights, attempting to develop forms of piety more related to the real circumstances in which people live. They have been regarded with suspicion by the authorities of church and state. In the Protestant churches — a small community of some 20,000 persons — an early lead in ecumenical and social work was given by the United Evangelical Church of Ecuador. Much of its work was later taken on by the United Andean Christian Foundation, involving a number of different confessions in the running of schools and clinics, in agricultural work and the giving of scholarships. Individual members of a number of Protestant churches have been influenced by the wider ecumenical movement, and the Christian Council of Latin America seeks to build bridges of under-standing between different religious communities. An earthquake in 1987 affecting some 90,000 people, prompted the reactivation of a seven-organization Ecumenical Committee for Earthquakes. By and large, however, Christians in Ecuador, like people the world over, pray about domestic matters like forthcoming elections, jobs, youth, and for peace of mind and peace of life. It is along these lines that they would have us pray with them.

Venezuela

Until recently oil exports made Venezuela relatively wealthy, and with the wealth came increasing materialism. Recently however, the economic situation has deteriorated, and Venezuela now faces a large foreign debt. Stringent economy measures, always unpopular, have resulted in unrest, with strikes, riots and guerrilla activities. The country has become a major trade route for illicit drugs, grown and processed elsewhere; and it is feared that illegal cultivation in the country is increasing.

The Roman Catholic Church faces a shortage of priests, of whom a small proportion are indigenous, whereas a much higher proportion of sisters are Venezuelan. A system of "parish curates" (sisters with special training who carry out pastoral work in cooperation with priests and directly under the bishop) was tried as an experiment in the slum areas of Caracas. It subsequently spread and is especially appropriate in rural areas. The largest of the Protestant confessions is the Assemblies of God who among other things are engaged in evangelistic work among the Guajiro Indians. Other Pentecostal groups are also present, and there is a significant number of indigenous churches. An evangelical newspaper, published in Venezuela, circulates in every Latin American country. A number of Orthodox churches are present, all related to bodies in the USA. The Venezuela Council of Churches unites most Protestant churches and missions, but has no outside affiliations.

Intercessions and Prayers

O God, we bring before you the people of Latin America whose suffering seems to have no end, tearing our hearts apart and challenging our faith in the God of justice. In spite of the suffering, we want to be instruments of reconciliation, not allowing hate to be the motivation behind our struggles to eradicate injustice. Listen to the pleas of your people. Amen.

Felipe Adolf, general secretary, Latin American Council of Churches

We believe in a loving God,
whose Word sustains our lives
and the work of our hands in the universe — God is Life.

We believe in his Son among us
who brought the seed of life's renewal.
He lived with the poor to show the meaning of love — He is the Lord.

We believe in the Spirit of Life,
who makes us one with God;
whose strength and energy renews our fight — The Spirit is Love.

We believe in the church of God
at the service of all the people
so that we may see the truth on earth — She bears God's word.

We believe in this new life
which bread and wine give to us
to work for God in unity — this is our glory.

We believe in everlasting life and the future of a new world
where the word of God will be the truth to all
in Christ our Lord.

Creed of Camilo Torres, Colombia

We give thanks

for those who, drawing their strength and courage from the presence of lively Christian communities, speak out boldly against injustices

for common ecumenical action born of necessity, and yet going beyond it

for the mountain and forest scenery of this region; for tropical jungles, lakes and waterfalls, and beautiful beaches attracting many visitors and much-needed foreign currency

> *O Lord, I don't want to be a spectator*
> *A tour passenger looking out upon the real world,*
> *An audience to poverty and want and homelessness.*
>
> *Lord, involve me — call me —*
> *implicate me — commit me —*
> *And Lord – help me to step off the bus.*
>
> A tourist's prayer, Freda Rajotte

We pray

for those who live in places where law and order are difficult to maintain, and where life is insecure and uncertain

for family members disappeared; and for those without hope

for those caught up in the awful net of dependency, and for those who cultivate and trade in illicit drugs

for schools and health centres, and for those who do not have access to adequate health care or education

In Ecuador repayments on international loans cost millions of dollars a year while every half hour a child dies from malnutrition:

> *I hunger and I eat, three times a day — or more;*
> *They hunger and they do not eat,*
> *They hunger and they do not eat,*
> *They hunger and they do not eat;*
> *Help me to help them.*
>
> A North American prays for the hungry: John Fandel

With an estimated annual average of more than a hundred natural and human-caused disasters occurring each year, we pray for the emergency desks of United Nations, of CICARWS (the inter-church aid commission of the WCC), and all who seek to coordinate international aid in time of need.

> *O God, we find ourselves dealing in death and deprivation where we know your will is fullness of life for all. Forgive us and stir us to new*

life in the service of your kingdom of truth and justice, that the whole world may be made new and drawn into unity in him who is the life of the world, Jesus Christ, our Lord. Amen.

Week of Prayer for Christian Unity, 1983, John Poulton

Stop! ferocious animal
God was here first,
Then you.

Ecuador, prayer to stop a dog biting
Psalm 59:14, 15

Week 40

Burkina Faso • Chad
Mali • Mauritania • Niger

O Lord, grant us to love you.
May the love of you be dearer to us
than ourselves and our families;
than wealth, and even than cool water.

Prayer attributed to the prophet Muhammad

Together with Cape Verde, Senegal and The Gambia, these countries constitute the Sahel, which literally means "edge of the desert". Once, thousands of years ago, a lush fertile area, it is increasingly being invaded by the desert. From approximately the 8th to the 16th century great African kingdoms thrived in what was then a savannah region, and their cities were centres of trade for the caravan routes crossing the Sahara to the Mediterranean. Now these are some of the least developed and poorest countries in the world. Rainfall is erratic, and between 1968-74 the whole area suffered devastating drought. This has recurred in more recent years and is now extending into areas hitherto unaffected.

Formerly French colonies, all these countries obtained independence in 1960. All are republics, but Burkina Faso, Mauritania and Niger are currently under military rule, and the military play a significant part in the government of Mali. The people belong to a considerable number of ethno-linguistic groups, often culturally very different. French is the official language (plus Arabic in Mauritania), and numerous local languages are widely spoken. The multiple health problems are mostly those of poverty and lack of water. Only a small proportion of adults are literate.

We must have patience: patience with others; patience with thirst while travelling; patience with weariness; patience with children. We must accept everything in patience, both happiness and suffering.

A woman of the Peulhs, a Fulani nomadic group from Niger

Islam was first introduced into the area in about the 10th century. Today the majority of people overall are Muslims, although the proportion varies from country to country. Traditional African religions remain a significant force. Some Berber Christians, driven out of North Africa, were in what is now Niger in the 7th century, but they were isolated and disappeared. A sustained Christian presence dates from 1895 when the White Fathers entered Mali from Senegal. Gradually over this century work has proceeded throughout the area, but in general the church is not well established and many Christians are expatriate. Most are Roman Catholics. Protestants are few, mostly belonging to pentecostal or fundamentalist groups. The Assemblies of God is the largest Protestant group in the region.

Burkina Faso

Population: 8 million.

Religion: Adherents of traditional religions 42%, Muslims 41%, Christians 11.8% (Roman Catholics 7.6%, Protestants 4.2%).

Known as Upper Volta until 1984, Burkina Faso has the highest population density in the area and is exceptionally poor. More than 80% of the people are farmers or nomadic herders. Both groups have been severely affected by the drought, and loss of livestock has forced many nomads to attempt more settled farming. About a quarter of the population has left the area to seek work in the cities of Ivory Coast and elsewhere.

In such a setting the churches have previously been largely involved in work in rural areas; and today the Roman Catholic church and the Fédération des Eglises des missions évangéliques are actively engaged in simple practical schemes to help subsistence farmers to increase productivity. During the drought of the 1970s a joint Christian-Muslim lay organization was formed to work together for the provision of basic needs and education under the slogan "Where two people agree to walk along part of a road together, God is the third." Recent migration to the cities means that now there are new opportunities for the church there also. The Roman Catholic Church in Burkina Faso organizes and promotes the Week of Prayer for Christian Unity for the region.

Chad

Population: 5.1 million.

Religion: Muslims 44%, Christians 33% of whom the majority are Roman Catholics, adherents of traditional beliefs 23%.

With a great many ethno-linguistic groups, predominantly Arab and Muslim in the north, and Black African (mostly Christian or adherents of traditional beliefs) in the south, Chad has suffered intermittent but prolonged civil war. In recent years thousands have fled to neighbouring Sudan, Central African Republic and Cameroon to escape the fighting. Since 1980 the drought has been increasingly severe and widespread, and the cause of further refugee migration.

The Christian church grew relatively quickly in the 1960s and 70s, but 1973 brought a period of persecution when at least 130 African pastors were put to death because they refused to submit to initiation rites decreed by the president of the time. Since the coup of 1975, however, religious freedom has been officially upheld, although in a situation of war there have been local incidents. The Roman Catholic Church patiently continues its pastoral and evangelistic ministry in the villages, many of which have small Christian communities with a chapel or a place in the open air with benches made of branches where the congregation gathers on Sundays to pray. For all the churches the training, disrupted by the fighting, of priests, pastors and evangelists is a major concern.

Mali

Population: 8.3 million.

Religion: Muslims 80%, adherents of traditional beliefs 18%, Christians 2% of whom rather more than half are Roman Catholics.

A large part of Mali is in the Sahara, and most of the people live in the more fertile south. About 90% of them are engaged in subsistence farming and herding, but the extending drought continues to reduce the area of suitable land. In spite of food shortages, the desperately poor farmers sell some of their crops in the more lucrative markets of neighbouring countries, and crop smuggling is a long-standing problem.

The Roman Catholic Church and a number of Protestant groups are working in the country. The administration by Christians of famine relief supplies has strengthened relationships between Christians and Muslims.

Mauritania

Population: Approximately 2 million (no recent official estimates available.)
Religion: Muslims 99.4%, Christians 0.4%.

Mauritania is an Islamic republic with an Arab-speaking Moorish majority. Before the drought 80% of the population were nomadic pastoralists; by the 1980s 80% of their pasture land had become desert. The Negro population in the Senegal valley to the south is engaged in settled agriculture.

The ceding of the southern part of western Sahara to Mauritania in 1976 (see Week 4) and the subsequent fighting brought the country almost to bankruptcy. Fish and iron-ore are the main natural resources. The church is entirely expatriate and mostly Roman Catholic, with a handful of Protestants.

Niger

Population: 5.7 million and rising.

Religion: Muslims 88%, adherents of traditional beliefs 11.6%, Christians 0.4% of whom most are Roman Catholics.

In the years following independence the government of Niger seemed to be one of the most stable in Africa. But the effects of the drought, which affected Niger more than any other Sahel country, led to widespread civil disorder, and an army coup followed in 1974.

Some 95% of Roman Catholics in Niger are expatriates, but the church has recently renewed evangelistic effort in the villages and is meeting with some positive response. The Protestant evangelical churches make a significant contribution through educational and medical work which is much appreciated. Relationships between the church and the government and Muslim community are good.

Intercessions and Prayers

Life is made up of happiness and suffering. Do you know what happiness is like? Little drops of milk which splash up over your body while you are milking. And do you know what suffering is like? Sparks of fire that burn you as you sit round the fire. The suffering of fire and the happiness of milk. You know that they are nothing like each other. And in the life of each of us there is fire and milk.

A Fulani woman

O God, who comes to us in our great joys, our crushing sorrows, and in our day-to-day lives; be with us now as we share ourselves with our Sahelian sisters and brothers in this time of prayer. In Jesus' name. Amen.

Vancouver Worship Book, adapted

Joining our joys and sorrows with those of the people of the Sahel let us thank God

for their faith and fortitude

for every opportunity we have to share in the fire and milk of the human condition

for new cooperative ventures, enabling people to work together for a better and more secure life

Let us pray

for the governments and peoples of Burkina Faso, Chad, Mali, Mauritania and Niger

for all missionaries, expatriate technicians and relief workers, local pastors and religious, working in areas where conditions are very harsh

for refugees from war and drought

for the rural poor

for those many people who have moved into towns and cities in search of food and livelihood

for those affected by health problems linked with drought; eye diseases, intestinal and other infections; and all workers and agencies which bring relief

for the WCC Programme of Solidarity for Development in Sahel, and its many small-scale projects; irrigation schemes, market gardening, well-digging, village grain banks, tree-planting and women's education

for responsible and sensitive use of outside aid

for the traditional "naam" or "power" groups being rediscovered and adapted to today's needs

> *We pray, O Lord, for the nomads and peasants who strive to make a living on the edge of the Sahara Desert, and especially those driven by hunger into the refugee camps and city slums. Give wisdom to those who plan the long-term rehabilitation of these lands: this we ask in the name of Jesus who hungered in the wilderness. Amen.*

> *Lord God, spring of living water,*
> *give to those who live in dry and barren lands,*
> *the vision to see them as they might be,*
> *the skill and resources needed to make them fertile again,*
> *and more than these, the spiritual insight needed to recognize*
> *that in you alone the human spirit finds its true satisfaction.*
> *For Jesus' sake. Amen.*

Michael Saward, adapted

Let us pray also

for peace throughout the region

for all Christian congregations in town and countryside

for the healing of divisions in the Protestant communities, and the promotion of deeper understanding and sympathy between Catholics and Protestants

> *Lord, help us to accept the gift of peace*
> *that Jesus came to bring.*

In Chad and in other places we are invited to imagine small local Christian communities meeting together to pray on Sundays; while statistics in Mauritania and Niger present a picture of a small, largely expatriate Christian presence. With all of them we pray:

> *Almighty God, you have given us grace at this time with one accord to make our common supplications to you; and you have promised that when two or three are gathered together in your name you will grant their requests. Fulfil now, O Lord, the desires and petitions of your servants, as may be most expedient for them, granting us in this world knowledge of your truth, and in the world to come, life everlasting.*

Prayer of the Third Antiphon, Liturgy of St John Chrysostom, 5th century

Week 41

Cameroon • Central African Republic

Lord Jesus, print on us your likeness,
Your divine likeness,
For it is your face,
Your divine face that we long for.

At the Sixth Station of the Cross, Engelbert Mveng SJ., Cameroon

Cameroon

Population: 9.6 million.

Languages: French, English and many local languages.

Government: Single-party republic.

Religion: Christians about 50% (Roman Catholics 32%, Protestants 17%), adherents of traditional beliefs about 25%, Muslims 22%.

When I think of my mother, I see not only the woman who gave me birth, but all those rural African women, hardly visible to the modern eye, who wake up early each morning to produce, process and store 80% of the food we eat in Africa. I see those rural women who, unfortunately, are progressively being deprived of access to arable land and of control of modern agriculture. I see the effects and its consequential link with Africa's grave food shortage.

I continue to see this "invisible" African woman in her condition and potential. Although the most silent and unrecognized, she remains the hardest worker in the entire world; she is also among the finest and strongest Christians in any land. With less than US$25 as the only annual monetary income, she performs wonders; she builds churches, pays and feeds pastors, sends her children to good Christian schools and teaches them daily to pray and trust God.

Ruth Engi-Tjeca, Cameroon
Fellowship of the Least Coin

The impetus to bring the gospel to Cameroon came originally from Jamaica when slaves obtained their freedom, and some of the first missionaries were Jamaicans. The subsequent history of the country resulted in the work being taken over by different missions, thus sowing the seeds of separate churches. Today Baptists and Presbyterians make up the largest Protestant bodies. There are smaller Lutheran groups and a number of indigenous churches. Roman Catholics arrived in 1890 during the period of German occupation, and a mass movement began in 1934 particularly among young people. All the churches continue to make significant contributions to the country especially in the fields of health, education and agricultural development, which are major concerns of the government at the present time. The church is actively engaged in evangelism in rural areas, and is growing, whilst an ecumenical body is concerned with spiritual, social and economic issues in the capital.

Central African Republic

Population: 2.7 million.

Languages: French, Sango.

Government: Single-party republic.

Religion: Christians 84,5% (Protestants 50%, Roman Catholics 33%, African Indigenous 1.5 %), adherents of tribal beliefs 12%, Muslims 3%.

Situated in the heart of Africa, the Central African Republic had been ruled and administered by tribal chiefs, a Sultan, colonial traders and the French government before gaining independence in 1960. Since then it has experienced both civil and military government. In recent years thousands of refugees from Chad have entered the country, which has made land available for them. The refugees have built homes and begun to establish traditional patterns of village life while they wait to return.

The first Roman Catholic mission was established in 1984. Protestants came after the first world war. There have been some schisms from churches founded by North American and European missions to form independent indigenous churches. Numerically the Christian church grew dramatically after independence. There are now some ten Protestant denominations, predominantly Baptist and Brethren. Many were established largely on an ethnic basis, and today, sadly, there is little cooperation among them. According to a senior pastor the present authorities "are conscious that true peace and justice come from God". They recently set aside a fast day when all churches as well as those of other faiths prayed for peace and justice in the country. The need, at local level, is for pastors more suitably equipped to meet the needs of the more educated members of their congregations and, at the national level, to address the conscience of the government on matters of peace and justice.

Intercessions and Prayers

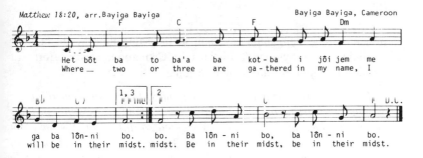

Matthew 18:20, arr.Bayiga Bayiga

Bayiga Bayiga, Cameroon

Het bōt ba to ba'a ba kot-ba i jōi jem me
Where _ two or three are ga-thered in my name, I

ga ba lōn-ni bo. bo. Ba lōn - ni bo, ba lōn - ni bo.
will be in their midst. midst. Be in their midst, be in their midst.

Christians in both these countries, accustomed largely to the practice of extempore prayer, welcome fellowship with Christians throughout the world, and invite us to *"engage in free prayers of intercession before Almighty God" for:*

In Cameroon

the peace and security of the country

efforts to promote the green belt through the training of men and women in appropriate methods of farming, tree-planting and conservation

the "Health for all by the year 2000" programme

young people in an increasingly secular and materialistic environment

women in their day-to-day life and work

the church's ministry among the poor and deprived, and all efforts to combat the underlying causes of alcoholism and juvenile delinquency

all programmes of evangelism and revival

In the Central African Republic

God's continuing blessing on every decision and action taken by the government for the wellbeing of the people

resolution of ethnic differences in the interests of the common good

the development of the country in such a way as will serve the best interests of local people

the refugees of Africa and of the world

resources to train church leaders

a new unity of spirit and action among members of different church bodies

Commemorating their autonomy, and at the same time aware of their shortcomings, Presbyterian Christians in Cameroon use this form of confession in which we are invited to join:

> *O Lord, with sorrow and dismay we confess before you our failure to live up to the trust committed to us. For so many years your word has been preached among us, but has yielded so little fruit. We have not given the example of redeemed lives. Because of our lack of love and joy and devotion there are still those, even among our friends and in our families, who have not yet accepted you as Saviour and Lord. The power of worship of ancestral spirits is yet unbroken in our country. Even many who were once baptized and have grown up in our midst have become cold and have turned away from you. O Lord, we humble ourselves before you in shame, and plead with you, through Jesus Christ, your Son, our Lord. Amen.*

> *Lord God,*
> *grant that we might sleep in peace in this hut;*
> *and that at the break of day we may find ourselves in safety*
>
> A night prayer from Cameroon

> *My God, I praise you, I thank you for my mother.*
> *For all that she could give me,*
> *for all that she gave of herself,*
> *a true, living school of love and humility.*
> *She reveals to me your mystery —*
> *thank you for her revelation of your truth.*

Now, O God, I pray for all the children
of Africa, of Asia,
of America and Europe.
For all the children of the world.
Give me a heart like that of a mother
the heart of a black woman for her children.

Le tronc béni de la prière, Mamia Woungly-Massaga

We pray you, Lord our God and Father,
remember all those who are deprived of their country;
who groan under the burden of anguish and sorrow
enduring the burning heat of the sun and the freezing cold of the sea,
or living in the humid heat of the forest,
searching for a place of refuge.
A refuge which they will find nowhere,
for you alone are our true refuge.

Lord, cause this storm to cease.
Move the hearts of those in power
that they may respect human beings
whom you have created in your own image;
That the grief of these refugees may be turned into joy,
as when you led your people Israel out of captivity.

From a prayer for refugees, Pedro Tunga

Almighty God, Lord of heaven and earth, we humbly pray that your
gracious care may give and preserve the seeds which we plant in our
farms that they may bring forth fruit in good measure; that we who
constantly receive from your goodness may always give thanks to you,
the giver of all good things; through Jesus Christ, your Son our Lord.

Prayer often used in the Cameroon
during the planting season, March/April

God of love, God of mercy, God of all power!
Why do you let your people die
— your people whom you have redeemed?
Why do you let the earth suffer
— the earth you have created in your sovereign power?
Lord, look and see the misery of the famine
that is ravaging your people;

*Look and see these children, these women and men, who are dying of
hunger and who cry to you in their need.*
*Give them, we pray, according to your grace and according to their
need, to the glory of your name.*
Lord God, our Father and God of all power,
you who hold the universe in your hand;
Give your people bread we pray;
Cause the rain to fall
and make the soil fertile in the fields of your people.
Give them an abundant harvest
and protect it from the ravages of climate and pests,
that your people may rejoice in the fruits of their labours,
according to your promise.

Grant the prayer of your people, Lord to the glory of your name.
May your name be magnified in Jesus Christ,
our Lord and Saviour. Amen.

From a prayer for harvest in a time of drought, Pedro Tunga

Week 42

Congo • Equatorial Guinea
Gabon • São Tomé and Príncipe

He comes to us as one unknown, without a name, as of old by the lakeside he came to those men who knew him not. He speaks to us the same word: "Follow thou me" and sets us to the tasks which he has to fulfil for our time. He commands. And to those who obey him, whether they be wise or simple, he will reveal himself in the toils, the conflicts, the sufferings which they shall pass through in his fellowship, and as an ineffable mystery they shall learn in their own experience who he is.

Albert Schweitzer, one-time missionary in Gabon

I will follow you, Jesus
And I will give you all
For by your strength
I will follow you in everything.

Congolese hymn, sung with mounting excitement
on the way to baptism

Congo

Once part of the African Kingdom of the Congo, and touched by early Portuguese explorers and missionaries, this area came under French influence in the 18th century and obtained independence in 1960. It is now a single-party socialist republic with a population of 2 million. Industrialization — it is one of the most industrialized countries in Africa — has resulted in migration to the cities where unemployment is rising.

Christians number about 93% (54% Roman Catholics, 25% Protestants, 14% African indigenous) of the population. Sustained Christian activity began in 1883 when Roman Catholic priests arrived at the coast, and subsequently sent missionaries inland along the Congo river. The Roman Catholic church has grown steadily since the beginning. Protestants arrived early in this century. The autonomous Evangelical Church of the Congo, with its charismatic life-style and emphasis on evangelism, is the largest Protestant body and is growing. Baptists began work in the sparcely populated north in 1921. Of the indigenous churches the Kimbanguist church (see Week 43) has the largest following. In 1978 the government banned over thirty religious bodies, not all of them Christian. Seven: the Roman Catholic Church, the Evangelical Church of the Congo, the Salvation Army, the Kimbanguist Church, the Church of Zepherin Lassy, Islam (0,5%) and Tenrikyo (one of the Japanese new religions), remain legally permitted. All church schools were nationalized in 1965, but the churches are allowed to maintain training institutions for evangelists, pastors and religious communities. They remain involved in medical and development projects.

Equatorial Guinea

Consisting of the mainland territory of Rio Muni, the island of Bioko (Fernando Póo) and three small groups of islands, this country experienced colonization, first Portuguese and then Spanish, from the 15th century onwards, before becoming independent as a republic in 1968. For almost eleven years it was ruled by a president who assumed dictatorial powers. There was much suffering and many fled. Since a coup in 1979, it has been under military rule. The economy was in ruins at that time, and the country continues to rely on international aid. The official language is Spanish, but Fang and others are widely spoken.

89% of the population of 300,000 are Christians, the vast majority Roman Catholics; and less than 5% adhere to traditional beliefs. The earlier regime was militantly atheistic, and atheists and non-religious account for about 6%. The Roman Catholic church came with the colonial powers. Baptist missionaries from the West Indies came to Fernando Póo in 1841, but were later expelled by the Spanish. In 1870 the British Methodist church responded to an appeal from local Protestants sent via a ship's captain, and a Methodist community grew on the island. Presbyterians came to Corisco in 1850 and thence to the mainland. The resulting Evangelical Church of Equatorial Guinea became the major Protestant body. This church, together with Methodist congregations and members of Crusade, recently joined together to form the Reformed Church of Equatorial Guinea. Sadly there is now strife within this body over issues of lay participation and responsibility.

Gabon

This single-party republic, formerly part of French Equatorial Africa, obtained independence in 1960. A relatively small population (1.2 million) together with abundant mineral resources and forests help to make it the richest country in sub-Saharan Africa in terms of average income. Nevertheless, more than half the population is engaged in subsistence agriculture, unaffected by modern economy. French is the official language. Fang and Bantu are widely spoken.

Christian missionaries, both Roman Catholic and Protestant, came in the 1840s. At first they faced considerable resistance and met with many difficulties; and only slowly did they penetrate inland from the coast. However, since the end of the 19th century the church has grown steadily. Now about 95% of people profess Christianity: 65% Roman Catholics, 19% Protestants and 12% members of African indigenous churches. There are three Protestant groups: the Evangelical Church of Gabon which is much the largest numerically, the Evangelical Church of South Gabon and the smaller Evangelical Pentecostal Church. Traditionally the churches have been involved in education and health services. Now increasingly urbanization and the associated secular tendencies of corruption and indifference present additional concerns and challenges.

São Tomé and Príncipe

Consisting of two main islands and four rocky islets the single-party republic of São Tomé and Príncipe has a population of 108,000. Almost all are Christians. The practice of traditional religions, very prevalent at the turn of the century, has now almost disappeared due largely to Roman Catholic evangelistic activity. The country has a long association with Portugal, and by the end of the 15th century was a supply centre for Portuguese exploration. More recently, São Tomé was for many years the penal colony for Angola. Independence was negotiated in 1975. The use of agricultural land for export crops, on which the country depends economically, means that 90% of food requirements have to be imported.

Of the Christian population the vast majority are Roman Catholics. Although administratively centred elsewhere, a diocese was established for the territory in 1534. Protestants and members of indigenous churches total about 5%. The Evangelical Church owes its existence entirely to indigenous efforts. It was planted by an Angolan Christian exiled to São Tomé for penal servitude, and originally the scriptures and hymn book were written down from memory.

Intercessions and Prayers

Leader:	*Jesus, we want to grow in knowledge.*
All:	*Help us to grow in body, mind and spirit.*
Leader:	*Jesus, we want to grow in faith,*
All:	*We thank you for the people of faith in Bible times and in our times whose lives are an example to us.*
Leader:	*Jesus, we want to grow in hope.*
All:	*We pray for all who are helping to bring freedom, peace and justice in our world.*
Leader:	*Jesus, we want to grow in love.*
All:	*Help us to love one another as you have loved us and given yourself for us. We pray for those who today are giving their lives for others.*

Children's prayer:
prepared by women of Africa

We thank God

for the power of the Bible to speak to the present-day needs of children and women and men everywhere

that God so often uses unlikely people and circumstances to serve the kingdom

for all local missionary movement and outreach

for the large Christian communities in these countries

The eucharist or Lord's supper plays a very important part in the lives of Congolese Christians. Having carefully prepared themselves, local Christians, Catholics and Protestants alike, including the old and the sick, travel long distances to attend such a service. As an act of imaginative solidarity let us join with Christians in all these lands in saying the Sanctus in their African setting:

Holy, holy, holy Lord, God of power and might,
heaven and earth are full of your glory.
Hosanna in the highest.

Blessed is he who comes in the name of the Lord.
Hosanna in the highest.

Let us pray

for the cities of these countries, their growing populations, and the response of Christian congregations to their needs and opportunities

for the work of the church in mining areas and in growing townships

for Christian witness against corruption and indifference

for new ways of sharing the good news with those who succumb to superstitition and sorcery

for vocations among young people to full time service in the church

for the Christian formation of pastors and priests, evangelists, teachers and youth workers

for the fluctuating economies of these countries, and for those most affected, the poor and lowest paid, including many pastors

for unity within and between the different churches

Lord Jesus Christ, you said to your apostles:
I leave you peace, my peace I give you.
Look not on our sins,
but on the faith of your Church,
and grant us the peace and unity of your kingdom
where you live for ever and ever. Amen.

The Roman Mass

O God:
Enlarge my heart
    that it may be big enough to receive the greatness of your love.
Stretch my heart
    that it may take into it all those who with me around the world
    believe in Jesus Christ.
Stretch it
    that it may take into it all those who do not know him,
    but who are my responsibility because I know him.
And stretch it
    that it may take in all those who are not lovely in my eyes,
    and whose hands I do not want to touch;
through Jesus Christ, my Saviour. Amen.

Prayer of an African Christian

Week 43

Burundi • Rwanda • Zaïre

*The cross is the hope of Christians
the cross is the resurrection of the dead
the cross is the way of the lost
the cross is the saviour of the lost
the cross is the staff of the lame
the cross is the guide of the blind
the cross is the strength of the weak
the cross is the doctor of the sick
the cross is the aim of the priests
the cross is the hope of the hopeless
the cross is the freedom of the slaves
the cross is the power of the kings
the cross is the water of the seeds
the cross is the consolation of the bondmen
the cross is the source of those who seek water
the cross is the cloth of the naked.
We thank you, Father, for the cross.*

A 10th century African hymn

The 15th century Kingdom of the Congo covered a wider area than present day Zaïre when Portuguese explorers and missionaries first made contact with its people. One of their kings, Afonso I, became a major Christian figure in African history. In his reign churches were built, and schools established to provide Christian education for children. His son Henrique became the first Black African bishop, serving in the region until his death in 1534. However, Portugal's primary interest was trade, and it failed to nurture the new Christian community in this kingdom which, together with its church, eventually disintegrated. When Roman Catholic priests and Baptist missionaries came to the area over three centuries later they found little remaining of that earlier church.

Of the three ethnic groups in Rwanda and Burundi the Twa pygmies, now by far the smallest numerically, were earliest here. Tutsis, the last to arrive, migrated from the north and established supremacy over the majority Hutu people. The Tutsi kingdoms continued, almost until independence in the case of Rwanda, and a little after in the case of Burundi. Tension between the Hutu and Tutsi has continued, and there has been a major episode of violence in each of these countries since independence.

In the 19th century European explorers opened the way for missionaries to come into the region; and also for colonization. Zaïre (Belgian Congo) was colonized by Belgium; Rwanda and Burundi by Germany. The latter was evicted in the first world war, and the area administered under mandate by Belgium. Zaïre became independent in 1960, Rwanda and Burundi in 1962.

Roman Catholic missionaries began to penetrate into these areas in the latter half of the 19th century, and this church enjoyed a privileged status under Belgian rule. In Rwanda and Burundi a mass movement began in the 1930s, and at its height there were a thousand baptisms a week in Burundi. Baptists and Presbyterians soon followed the Roman Catholics into the Congo region, and were themselves followed by many others. The first Protestants to enter Rwanda and Burundi were German Lutherans from Tanzania, but they were forced to leave during the first world war. Their work was subsequently taken over and expanded by various Protestant bodies. The Anglican church entered from Uganda, and it was in the mission stations of this church in Rwanda that the revival movement first began.

In 1921 Simon Kimbangu, a Baptist catechist in the Congo, began a ministry of preaching and healing, and rapidly gained a large following. The authorities became alarmed, and he was imprisoned as a dissident for the rest of his life. His followers were severely persecuted and many were exiled; but the movement continued to grow, and in 1959 the Church of Jesus Christ on Earth by the Prophet Simon Kimbangu was officially recognized. It is the largest indigenous church in Africa, and is active in a number of countries.

Burundi

Population: 4.8 million.

Languages: French, Kirundi, Swahili.

Government: Single-party republic. Under military rule since 1987.

Religion: Christians 85%, adherents of traditional beliefs 13.5%, Muslims 1%.

The vast majority of people in Burundi live in rural areas, where poverty and unemployment, though enormous problems, are not easy to quantify. A rapidly increasing population adds to the difficulties, but the extended family system ensures that all are cared for, and no one goes without food and shelter. The traditional sense of solidarity leads those who have resources to share with those who have not.

With 78% of the population Roman Catholic, this is one of the most Catholic countries in Africa. Protestants including Anglicans number about 7%, of whom the largest body is Pentecostal. The East African revival spread through Burundi in the 1950s and had its greatest impact in the Anglican church. Prior to the 1987 coup, the regime was antagonistic towards the church, Christians suffered and expatriate priests were expelled. All the churches are involved in educational, medical and social work, but are crippled by poverty. One of the major concerns is for reconciliation and the healing of the deep and long-standing ethnic divisions.

Intercessions and Prayers

We bless you for sending your Spirit into the hearts of
the men, women and children of Burundi,
so that they recognize Jesus as Son of God and Saviour,
and are brought together in the church.

Through the fraternal charity which overcomes divisions,
through baptism and confirmation which plunges them into Christ
and makes them witnesses of the faith,
and through the grace of ordination which gives them their
own bishops and priests,
confirm your children in their faith through all trials
and persecutions.

Prayer for Burundi Christians:
Louis Lochet of the Foyers de Charité

We give thanks

for the Roman Catholic contribution to this land; for the devotion and fortitude of early missionaries; for schools and Christian education, and for courageous outspokenness in times of need for the message of the cross at the heart of the East African revival, and for its continued power to speak to a new generation of African Christians

We pray

for all in need in this country; for widows and orphans, refugees and those displaced

for those who suffered in past conflicts, and those who inflicted suffering on others; for forgiveness and healing

for church leaders and catechists, and all engaged in town and countryside in nurturing Christian congregations

Let us identify with Christians in this region in repeating the words of a well-known devotion, *Salvator mundi*:

> *O Saviour of the world,*
> *who by your cross and precious blood*
> *has redeemed us;*
> *Save us and help us,*
> *we humbly beseech you, O Lord.*

Of this prayer it has been observed that sometimes an element of superiority enters our prayers for others, "but when we ask a third person to help us both, that element is eliminated, and we see ourselves at the same level of dependence and need as the ones for whom we pray."

Rwanda

Population: 5.8 million.

Languages: French, Kinyarwanda.

Government: Single-party republic.

Religion: Christians 73% (Roman Catholics 55.5%, Protestants 11.5%, Anglicans 6%), adherents of traditional beliefs 18%, Muslims 8.6%.

This landlocked country faces many problems. It is the most densely populated country in Africa, with 95% of people living in rural areas where there is not enough agricultural land. In October 1982, 44,000 refugees together with 50,000 head of cattle streamed across the border from Uganda. Although all of the same ethnic group, many of these were Ugandan citizens; others were Rwandans who had fled from earlier strife in their country. The problems of refugees, overpopulation and poverty continue. "As the credibility of the church's message depends on its response to a situation of misery, poverty, hunger, illness, ignorance and illiteracy, it" (in this case referring to the Presbyterian Church of Rwanda, but applicable to others also) "tries to maintain a balance between social engagement and the teaching of the biblical message." The churches provide much-needed services to the country in hospitals, primary health care, education and vocational and agricultural training; but the churches also are poor in material terms.

The experience of the psalmist of having a new song put upon his lips, and that of St John that "if we walk in the light as he is in the light, we have fellowship with one another, and the blood of Christ cleanseth us from all sin" continue to be central themes of the East African revival. Beginning in Rwanda in 1929, this movement spread into eastern Africa, parts of Zaïre and beyond. For the most part remaining within the mainline churches it has had a profound influence. The movement's greatest challenge today lies in relating faith to matters of social justice. In Rwanda itself some of the fire has died down in the older generation, but there are signs of a fresh response among younger people.

Intercessions and Prayers

We pray

for the spiritual, social and economic wellbeing of Rwanda

for refugees in this country — those in camps, and those integrated into the community yet denied citizenship; and for Rwandan refugees in Burundi and elsewhere

for the Twa pygmy people, and all who seek to proclaim the gospel among them

and for the fruitful and harmonious contact between Christians and the growing Muslim community

for those preparing for the ministry in different centres in Africa and elsewhere, and for the congregations which will eventually receive and support them

for the Christian community life of hospitals and clinics, vocational training schools and agricultural projects; that all such communities may be adaptable and sensitive to changing needs and circumstances

that in this nation which has been torn by ethnic strife, Christians may
continually live the gospel of reconciliation

May the brokenness of our Lord Jesus Christ
and the Calvary love of God
and the fellowship of the Holy Spirit
be with us all. Amen.

Revival grace

Zaïre

Population: 30.4 million.

Languages: French and over 400 Sudanese and Bantu languages.

Government: Single-party republic.

Religion: Christians 94% (Roman Catholics 48%, Protestants 29%,
African indigenous 17%), adherents of traditional beliefs 3.5%, Muslims 1.5%.

With considerable agricultural, mineral and energy resources Zaïre is
potentially a rich country; but poor roads, corruption and smuggling,
inflation and foreign debt have impeded development. The many refugees
in the country are mostly from Angola. The Christian church, which has
grown from 1% to 90% of the population within a century continues to
play a very significant role in schools, hospitals, development work and
social service.

As in many other countries in Africa the Roman Catholic pastoral plan
for small Christian communities is operating in Zaïre. This represents a
shift from effort concentrated in large institutions to the nurture of small

communities of lay people working out their faith in daily life. The training and support of lay leaders and catechists is a high priority.

Formed in 1970 at the Assembly of the Congo Protestant Council, and without referring back to participating churches, the Church of Christ in Zaïre is the only Protestant church recognized by government. The government stance has forced other Protestant bodies to join this church, which now consists of over 60 member communities, each retaining its previous traditions and structures. This united church has its own theological faculty, and works with government and other bodies in a national rural health project.

Financially self-supporting from the beginning, the Kimbanguist Church, also recognized by government, has built churches, schools, clinics, workshops and agricultural colonies. These provide jobs for the unemployed, and young offenders are accepted in some. Kimbanguists are active in counselling those who suffer from AIDS and their families. The voluntary pastoral support system and sense of togetherness within this church are replacing the traditional family community in situations where this is disrupted by social change.

Intercessions and Prayers

We give thanks

for the courage and devotion of the many who have given their lives in the service of the gospel

for the rapid growth of the church in this century

for all who sing the praises of God in this African setting

for the positive gains and enrichments enjoyed by the Protestant denominations united in L'Eglise du Christ au Zaïre

for all who combine a strong faith in the unique relevance of Christ for Africa with a wider ecumenical vision

> *I thank you, Almighty God,*
> *maker of heaven and earth,*
> *that heaven is your throne and the earth your footstool,*
> *and that your will is done on earth as it is in heaven.*
> *Bless all the peoples of the earth,*
> *great and small, men and women, whites and blacks.*
> *May the blessing of heaven fall on the whole world*
> *so that we all may enter heaven.*

We pray to you, trusting that you will receive us,
in the name of Jesus Christ our Saviour.

A prayer said to have been used daily
by Simon Kimbangu

We pray

for the unity of this vast country

for all small Christian communities, and the women and men who provide
the leadership

for growing urban areas, and their need of churches sensitive to their
situation

for seminaries and colleges training people for the ordained ministry; and
for all local Bible schools and lay training programmes

for the church's expanding ministries of evangelism, education, health
and development

"In Zaïre, evangelism and social action are one. The life of the spirit is
fully as real as physical life. In a situation of extreme poverty and
injustice 'courageous Christians build churches, clinics, schools, lib-
raries, water wells, fish ponds, dormitories, roads and bridges.'"

Bless, O Lord,
all such courageous Christians,
and all work undertaken in your name and in your spirit
in Zaïre today. Amen.

God, bless Africa
Guard her children
Guide her leaders
And give her peace.

Conference of European Churches

The Geneva-based Conference of European Churches (CEC) is a fellowship of non-Roman Catholic churches whose 118 members are from every European country, both East and West, except Albania. The Roman Catholic Church, although not a member, cooperates closely. In an area of immense cultural, political and religious diversity, CEC provides a forum for the churches to reach across the barriers which divide them, and enables them to work out together their place in the Europe of today and in the future. Its main thrusts, therefore, are ecumenism in Europe, peace with justice, and concern for human rights.

Grant us prudence in proportion to our power,
wisdom in proportion to our science,
humaneness in proportion to our wealth and might.
And bless our earnest will to help all races and peoples
to travel, in friendship with us,
along the road to justice, liberty and lasting peace:
but grant us above all to see that our ways
are not necessarily your ways,
that we cannot fully penetrate the mystery of your designs,
and that the very storm of power now raging on this earth
reveals your hidden will and your inscrutable decision.
Grant us to see your face in the lightning of this cosmic storm,
O God of holiness, merciful to your creatures.
Grant us to seek peace where it is truly found.
In your will, O God, is our peace. Amen.

Prayer for Peace, Conference of European Churches,
Gloria Deo Worship Book, 9th Assembly, 1986

1.	Iceland		
2.	United Kingdom	17.	Switzerland
3.	Republic of Ireland	18.	Liechtenstein
4.	Norway	19.	Austria
5.	Sweden	20.	Italy
6.	Finland	21.	Poland
7.	USSR	22.	Czechoslovakia
8.	Denmark	23.	Hungary
9.	The Netherlands	24.	Romania
10.	Belgium	25.	Yugoslavia
11.	Federal Republic of Germany	26.	Albania
12.	German Democratic Republic	27.	Bulgaria
13.	Luxembourg	28.	Malta
14.	France	29.	Greece
15.	Spain	30.	Turkey
16.	Portugal	31.	Cyprus

Week 44

Federal Republic of Germany
German Democratic Republic

Graciously comfort and tend all who are imprisoned, hungry, thirsty, naked, and miserable; also all widows, orphans, sick, and sorrowing. In brief, give us our daily bread, so that Christ may abide in us and we in him for ever, and that with him we may worthily bear the name Christian. Amen.

Martin Luther

Lying in the centre of Europe, and with few natural frontiers, Germany has always been exposed to a variety of cultural and political influences. Christianity spread gradually into this area, from south and west to north and east, between about the 3rd and 12th centuries. Martin Luther's Reformation, beginning at Wittenberg in 1517, has had a profound influence both within Germany and throughout the world. The name of Germany is associated with great achievements in music, literature, philosophy and science; but also with the memory of two dreadful wars. In the present century immense suffering has been inflicted, particularly to European Jewry, but also to others. Christians of the Confessing Church, who resisted the fascist regime, were persecuted. Germany itself lost vast territories and was divided. There are now two German states: the Federal Republic of Germany and the German Democratic Republic. The FRG is a federal republic; the GDR a socialist republic. They belong to the two great power blocs which were constituted in Europe after the war, and are now distanced from each other by definite socio-political and military barriers. The demarcation line runs through the middle of a once united Germany, and is a painful reminder of the unhappy past.

Population, language, government and religion

FRG: 61 million. German. Federal republic.

Christians 86.6% (Roman Catholics 43.5%, Protestants 42.4%, Orthodox 0.7%), Muslims 2.8%, a very small Jewish community.

GDR: 16.1 million. German. Socialist republic.
Christians 53.6% (Protestants 46.1%, Roman Catholics 7.2%), substantial numbers of atheists and those of no religion.

Both German republics have made remarkable recoveries, after the second world war, partly as a result of foreign aid, but also because of their own achievements in reconstruction. The FRG is one of the wealthiest countries in the world, but like other densely populated and highly industrialized countries it faces various difficulties: increasing unemployment, many migrant workers, and problems of environmental protection. In the GDR a communist political and economic system operates. It has the most successful economy in the Soviet bloc.

The churches in the FRG share many of the same concerns, and work in friendly partnership with the state, but are legally separate. The Roman Catholic Church, once in the minority, has increased numerically in recent decades largely because of an influx of migrant workers from southern Europe. The 17 Landeskirchen (regional churches), Lutheran, Reformed and United, have since 1948 constituted the Evangelical Church in Germany. They are heavily involved in social service both at home and overseas. Various free church bodies (Baptist, Methodist, Free Evangelical, Moravian, Pentecostal and others), as well as the Old Catholic Church and Orthodox churches, are small but vigorous. Most are full or associate members of the Federation of Christian Churches of which the Roman Catholic Church is a full member. In recent decades there has been greater contact between Roman Catholics and Protestants.

As the GDR is a socialist society, the situation for the various churches is different, and limits have been set with regard to the work they do publicly. The eight regional churches have come together to form the Federation of Evangelical Churches in the GDR, and this body has expressed its readiness to look upon itself as "the church in a socialist society". Important conversations between church (both Protestant and Roman Catholic) and state have resulted in opportunities for freer contacts with the wider church.

The great gatherings of laity, the Kirchentag (Protestant) and Katholikentag (Catholic), which take place every two years in both parts of Germany and attract many thousands of participants, are an important feature of church life in both states.

Intercessions and Prayers

God, our Father, we thank you for putting new life into your people,
so that they never die. Prevent us from being paralysed with wrong
worries. Let us enjoy all new things, which show us that you are still at
work in our world. Amen.

Prayer of East German woman

We thank God

for the awakening of the church at the time of the Reformation, and for all movements of renewal in more recent times

for all men and women who have worked to enlarge the kingdom of God over the centuries

for the interpretation of the biblical story offered by poets, musicians, painters and theologians

We pray

for increasing understanding and better relations between the two states

for the Christians of Berlin, and for the continuing process of prayer, reflection and action directed towards overcoming the city's divisions

for the churches in the two states, that they may bear witness to the hope of the gospel, give support and encouragement to each other, and be a channel for reconciliation and peace in Europe

for all members of minority groups, immigrants and migrant workers, that they may experience tolerance and consideration

for all those involved in programmes to combat racism, to promote peace with justice, and to provide bread for a hungry world

> *Almighty and eternal God*
> *we pray for the unity of your church on earth:*
> *We have all resigned ourselves too long*
> *to the division of the church.*
>> *Let us pray*
>> *that our eyes may see the offence we thus give*
>> *as Christians in the world — Silence*

We are still not free from pettiness and prejudice.
  Let us pray
  that God will give us the Spirit of his love,
  a love that knows no bounds — Silence

We talk of "separated brethren"
heedless of the contradiction lying in these words.
  Let us pray
  that love and fellowship be not mere words
  but that we act to seek togetherness
  in word and work — Silence

We have all burdened ourselves with guilt
and given in too easily to difficulties.
  Let us pray
  that we do not passively sit and wait,
  as if unity would be bestowed upon us from outside,
  but rather we become friends and trust each other
  so that in us unity may grow and mature.

From a Roman Catholic Agape Celebration

I believe
that God both can and will bring good out of evil.
For that purpose God needs men and women
who will make the best use of everything.

I believe
that God is willing to provide us in any emergency
with all the powers of resilience that will be necessary for us.
But he does not give in advance
lest we should rely upon ourselves and not on him alone.
It is such a faith that will overcome all anxiety and fear of the future.

I believe
that God is not a timeless fate,
but that he is attending and responding
to sincere prayers as well as to responsible action.

Letters and Papers from Prison, Dietrich Bonhoeffer

Week 45

Austria • Liechtenstein • Switzerland

Lord, save us from being self-centred in our prayers,
and teach us to remember to pray for others.
May we be so bound up in love with those for whom we pray
that we may feel their needs as acutely as our own,
and intercede for them with sensitiveness,
with understanding and with imagination.
This we ask in Christ's name. Amen.

Prayer based on words of John Calvin

These three alpine countries, whose geographical situation makes them an important link between Eastern and Western Europe, all pursue a policy of active neutrality, and are thus well placed to facilitate international consultation. A number of well known international organizations have their headquarters in Austria and Switzerland.

The region came under Roman rule very early in the Christian era, and Christianity was slowly introduced, first into what is now Austria and later into Switzerland. The mountainous terrain which prevented the rapid spread of Christianity also helped isolated groups of believers to maintain their faith during the repeated invasions of the next thousand years. In the Middle Ages the monasteries were important centres of scholarship and mission.

Austria

Population: 7.6 million.

Languages: German. Various minority languages are also spoken.

Government: Federal republic.

Religion: Christians 96% (Roman Catholics 89%, Protestants 6%, Orthodox 1%), Muslims 1%, Jews 0.1%.

The origins of Christianity in Austria date from before the time of Constantine. A sermon preached by Paul Speratus in St Stephen's Cathedral in Vienna on 12 January 1522 was influential in the Reformation. For some 150 years the systematically conducted counter-Reformation of the 17th and 18th centuries forced Protestant Christians to go underground as secret communities. The decree of tolerance issued by Emperor Josef II in 1781 allowed the re-establishment of small Lutheran and Reformed congregations with limited religious freedom. Similar provisions were also made for Orthodox Christians and for Jews. Both these religious communities had been present in Austria for centuries. It was not until after the second world war that the motto of a "free church in a free state" became a reality for all the minority churches.

Ecumenical cooperation has also increased. The federal capital Vienna, in particular, has become a centre of ecumenical relations. The two Protestant churches, the Old Catholic, Methodist, Anglican, five Eastern Orthodox and four Oriental Orthodox churches work together ecumenically. Although the Roman Catholic Church officially has observer status only in the Ecumenical Council of Churches in Austria, it plays a full part in the Council's work. The Pro Oriente Foundation is a forum for encounter between Eastern and Western churches. Austrian radio broadcasts a regular ecumenical Sunday morning service.

Liechtenstein

Population: 27.1 thousand including resident foreigners.

Language: German.

Government: Constitutional principality.

Religion: Christians 98.5% (Roman Catholics 88%, Protestants 10.5%).

The Principality of Liechtenstein has been an independent state since 1719. Rapid industrialization since the second world war has created a demand for labour and there is virtually no unemployment. Nowadays about a third of the resident population are foreigners and many more cross each day from Austria and Switzerland to work in the Principality. The Roman Catholic Church is the state church, and administratively is part of the Swiss diocese of Chur. The inter-denominational Evangelical Church was formed in 1881 by skilled textile workers, mostly members of the Lutheran or Reformed churches, immigrating from neighbouring countries, and was broadened by those who came more recently to meet the needs of industrial expansion. In 1954 a separate Lutheran congregation was formed. Lively ecumenical cooperation exists in many fields.

Switzerland

Population: 6.5 million.

Languages: German, French, Italian. Romansch in some areas.

Government: Federal republic.

Religion: Christians 96%, Jews 0.3%, Muslims 0.3%.

Reformation influences were strong in Switzerland, especially in Zurich through Zwingli and Bullinger, and in Geneva where Calvin and Farel were notable figures. Some cantons became strongly Protestant; others remained strongly Catholic. Rivalry between the two persisted for centuries, but more recently migration patterns have altered the balance and furthered closer cooperation. Overall, among Swiss citizens, Protestants are in the majority (approximately 50.5% Protestants, 43.5% Roman Catholics), but if resident foreigners are included, the balance is reversed.

The Protestant churches are cantonal churches, each being autonomous. Their legal status varies from canton to canton, and there is diversity in liturgy and constitution. Together with the Free Evangelical churches and the Methodist Church they join in the Federation of Protestant Churches of Switzerland, through which a number of activities and issues are dealt with jointly. The Federation is concerned about human rights, religious liberty, peace and disarmament, social justice and development in the third world. Nearer home there is concern about alcoholism and drug abuse, and work among ethnic minorities.

More than 3 million Roman Catholics are spread throughout the country in 6 dioceses. Bridging the linguistic and cultural characteristics particular to each canton is a problem for some of the larger dioceses, and local feelings arising out of the historical rivalries between Protestants and Catholics make reorganization difficult. As in most western countries this church is concerned to find ways and means of presenting the gospel in a way which touches people in their daily lives. The Conference of Swiss Bishops and the congregations are active in the continuous search for ways towards Christian unity.

Intercessions and Prayers

O God, the giver of life,
we pray for the church throughout the world:
Sanctify its life; renew its worship;
empower its witness; restore its unity.
Remove from your people all pride
and every prejudice that dulls their will for unity.
Strengthen the work of all those who strive to seek
that common obedience that will bind us together.
Heal the divisions which separate your children from one another,
that they may keep the unity of the spirit in the bond of peace.

Prayer used in the Ecumenical Centre, Geneva,
on the occasion of the visit of Pope John Paul II

Let our chief end, O God, be to glorify thee,
and to enjoy thee for ever,
and let our second endeavour be to share with others
what we so richly enjoy.

After Calvin's Catechism

We thank God

for the long centuries of Christian tradition in Austria, Liechtenstein and Switzerland

for the Catholic tradition of devotion, pilgrimage and scholarship, and for all contemporary manifestations of an ecumenical spirit

for the faith of the Reformation emanating from Zurich and Geneva

for the faithfulness of Christian minorities in Austria in hard and oppressive times

for the saints, scholars, ecumenists and ordinary Christians of these countries

for the stand taken by these countries in defence of human rights and in upholding the dignity of human life

for all places of great natural beauty

We thank you, gracious God, for the beauty of the earth and of its
continents and oceans; for the abundance of mountains and plains; for
the song of birds and the loveliness of flowers.

For all these good gifts we praise you. Help us, we beseech you, to
protect and conserve them for those who follow us. Help us to grow in

gratitude for the riches of your creation, and increase our joy in you,
to your glory and the praise of your name.

From the Liturgy of the German-speaking Evangelical
Reformed Church of Switzerland, 1986

We pray

that Christians will be open to one another and that trust may grow among
the churches

that the churches in East and West may derive mutual enrichment and
fulfilment from their contacts

that new ecumenical initiatives may be taken and sustained

for the World Council of Churches and other international Christian
organizations with their headquarters in Geneva, for their members and
concerns in every part of the world

for priests and missionaries from Austria and Switzerland, sacrificially at
work in many parts of the world

that migrants and asylum seekers may find a refuge and a welcome in
these lands

for the Red Cross, sections of the United Nations based in Geneva, and
other international organizations concerned with the rights and welfare of
people

that the natural environment of these parts of Europe may be conserved
and continue to be a source of refreshment, recreation and renewal for
many people

Upheld by the prayers of St Nicholas von Flüe,
we humbly beseech you, O Lord,
that you will constantly protect us;
and to those who lead us give the light of your grace.

Prayer for the Feast Day of the 15th century soldier-saint
Brother Nicholas von Flüe, revered in Switzerland as a figure of
reconciliation and unity

Dear heavenly Father,
Send your Holy Spirit on us all, we pray, now and ever anew, that the
Spirit may awaken us, illumine us, encourage and give us the strength
to dare to take the small yet gigantic step, to leave behind the comfort
with which we can comfort ourselves and to step forward into the hope
that is in you. Turn us to yourself. Do not let us hide ourselves from

you. Do not accept it when we try to do everything without you. Show us how magnificent you are, and how wonderful it is that we may trust and obey you. This we ask also for all people:

That nations and their governments may submit to your Word and be willing to strive for justice and peace on earth

That, through word and deed, your Word may be rightly told to all who are poor, all who are sick, all prisoners, all who are in distress, all those who are oppressed, all who do not believe; that they may hear it and understand it and heed it as your answer to their groans and cries

That Christians of all churches and confessions may understand your Word with new eyes and learn to serve it with renewed faithfulness

That its truth may shine forth here and now and stand firm amidst all human confusion and chaos until at last it illumines all people and all things.

Praise be to you who in your Son, Jesus Christ, set us free to confess and affirm always that our hope is in you. Amen.

Prayer at Pentecost, Karl Barth

Week 46

Italy • Malta

All-powerful and ever-living God,
today we rejoice in the holy men and women
of every time and place.
May their prayers bring us your forgiveness and love.

Solemnity of All Saints: The Roman Missal

Italy

Well known for its historic association with the apostles Peter and Paul, it was the presence and witness of faithful members of the Christian church in Italy in the early centuries, which gave the universal church its first taste of being "a church of the catacombs". In later years, and with a growing desire to express the intercommunion of the living and the dead in the Body of Christ, Roman Christians were led to commemorate all those who had professed faith in the living Christ in days past, and to observe a Feast of All Saints. Significant early saints from this region were Ambrose of Milan, and Benedict, regarded as the founder of Western monasticism. The great medieval movements of renewal gave rise to the mendicant orders such as the Franciscans, and also to the Waldensian movement which originated in France in the 13th century and spread into the valleys of the Pinerolo region of Italy. Identifying with the Reformation, Waldensians were severely persecuted in the counter-Reformation.

The country was finally unified in 1870, with the Holy See remaining a separate state. Since the second world war there has been rapid economic development and industrialization especially in the north which is relatively well off, while the south remains poor and under-developed.

Population: 57.3 million

Language: Italian

Government: Multi-party republic

Religion: Christians 84% (Roman Catholics 83.4%, Protestants 0.5%, Orthodox 0.1%). Atheists and non-religious 16%. Small communities of Jews and Muslims, and some Buddhists.

Since the Concordat of 1984 Roman Catholicism is no longer the state religion, but the Roman Catholic church continues to have a strong influence in the daily lives of very many Italians. Communism is growing, especially in the north, and an increasing number of people are largely ignoring the church. Within the church, however, there are movements of renewal and a growing concern about social problems. The mainstream Protestant churches, like the Waldensians, are also heavily involved in social action. Since Vatican II the ecumenical climate has been changing, leading to a much greater openness and understanding. In the Waldensian valleys, where Roman Catholics and Waldensians have been living together for centuries, local ecumenism is growing.

Malta

Population: 341,200 excluding foreign residents.

Languages: Maltese, English, Italian

Government: Multi-party republic

Religion: Christians 99%. There is a small Jewish community and some atheists.

St Paul's shipwreck on the island of Malta marks the coming of Christianity, and it is no exaggeration to say that his arrival was the greatest event in Maltese history. The country was later occupied by the Arabs before being captured by the Normans. It was subsequently given to the Knights of St John of Jerusalem. It became a British Crown Colony in 1814 and gained independence in 1964.

"The faith brought by Paul, preserved, protected and propagated down the centuries, is very much alive in Malta today. It is reflected in the elaborate architecture of heavily ornate churches studded in profusion all over the island, as well as in the rhythmic tolling of bells calling the faithful to prayer at regular intervals." Virtually all Maltese nationals are baptized Roman Catholics, and this church has exercised significant institutional power. Through the Missionary Society of St Paul a considerable number of Maltese priests and religious are working outside the islands. A number of other denominations serve the expatriate community.

Intercessions and Prayers

We thank God

for the witness of many Christians, known and unknown, who through the ages have risked their lives for their faith

for the rich spirituality and the missionary contribution of the Roman Catholic Church

for the faithful witness of the Protestant churches, and their work of Christian service

for all signs of renewal in the Body of Christ in these countries

for two thousand years of art, architecture, thought, devotion and common life inspired by the Christian faith:

> *Blessed are you, O Lord our God, King of the universe,*
> *Who has given the wisdom of your hands to flesh and blood*
> *that beautiful cities might rise to your glory.*
>
> Rabbi Moshe Hakotun: said to have been written in Venice

We pray

for a joint Christian witness for justice, peace and the integrity of creation in the face of increasing militarization of the Mediterranean

for growing trust between members of all churches, and wisdom for their leaders in furthering the process of reconciliation and common action

for the Bishop of Rome and members of the Curia

for leaders of the Protestant and Orthodox churches

for the people of Italy and Malta, at their work and in their worship, seeking to live out their faith in daily life

> *Lord*
> *may I ever speak*
> *as though it were the last word that I can speak.*
> *May I ever act*
> *as though it were the last action that I can perform.*

May I ever suffer
as though it were the last pain that I can offer.
May I ever pray
as though it were for me on earth
the last chance to speak to you.

Prayer of Chiara Lubich, founder of The Focolare Movement

O God, Creator, Redeemer, and Sanctifier,
we thank you that we may be together
to hear your word of life and hope.
We are all equal before you.
You know our life in its deepest recesses.
You have not forgotten us;
you love us, and again and again you fill the empty hands
which we stretch out towards you.
Through the suffering and death of your Son Jesus Christ,
you took our darkness and fear upon yourself
in order that we might know light and joy.

Prayer of the Waldensian Church

O Lord, you have said to us "Peace I leave with you".
This peace that you give is not that of the world:
it is not the peace of order, when order oppresses;
it is not the peace of silence, when silence is born of suppression;
it is not the peace of resignation, when such resignation is unworthy.
Your peace is love for all people
is justice for all people, is truth for all people,
the truth that liberates and stimulates growth.
Lord, it is this peace we believe in because of your promise.
Grant us peace, and we will give this peace to others.

From the Waldensian Liturgy

Week 47

Bangladesh • Bhutan • Nepal

Dear Jesus,
as a hen covers her chicks with her wings
to keep them safe,
protect us this dark night
under your golden wings.

Prayer from the region

Bangladesh

Situated on the Ganges delta and very low-lying, Bangladesh is subjected annually to devastation from natural disaster — cyclone, flood, drought and tidal wave. At the same time, the climate and fertility of the land are such that it is extraordinarily green and lush and abounding with life of all kinds.

Population: 98.7 million, 80% of it below the poverty line.

Languages: Bengali, English. Santali, Garo, Bawm, Khashia and many others are spoken in some areas.

Government: Presidential form of government.

Religion: Muslims 86.6%, Hindus 12.1%, Buddhists 0.6%, Christians 0.3%.

Before 1947 Bangladesh was part of India. With the partition of that country and the creation of Pakistan, the state of Bengal was divided; the predominantly Muslim east becoming East Pakistan, and the predominantly Hindu west remaining part of India. Subsequent unrest between East and West Pakistan developed into a war of liberation and Bangladesh declared itself an independent country in 1971. The first sustained Christian communities date from the late 15th century.

At present there is liberty to practise any religion, but not the freedom to evangelize. About three-fifths of Christians are Roman Catholics, and

Baptists form the largest Protestant group. Anglicans, Presbyterians, Methodists and Lutherans united in 1970 to form one of the dioceses of the Church of Pakistan, but were cut off when Bangladesh became independent, and now form the United Church of Bangladesh. The Roman Catholic and Protestant churches are meeting together on matters of common witness and service. Christians come mainly from poor Bengali communities and minority tribes, and the church is therefore a church of the poor.

Intercessions and Prayers

"People generally can only see Bangladesh in material terms. They are prepared to think of it as an impoverished society. To feel sorry for it, and do what they can to help. But they aren't prepared to see its beauty and respect its strength."

Therefore let us give thanks for
the teeming burgeoning life of Bangladesh
the strength of family life, and a life-style which encourages conversation and friendship
the hospitality of the people, with their seemingly infinite capacity for suffering, survival — and song

> About prayer — what people commonly do whenever any of the household is seriously ill is to invite a whole lot of friends for a prayer meeting. If the evening is fine and warm we sit in the courtyard on rush mats, the men on one side and the women on the other. The host will say what he has called the meeting for, and while he is about it he will add a number of supplementary biddings, Mary is taking an important examination, Peter is away catching turtle, Uncle is going for a journey, and so on. We start with a hymn, a lilting ragtime sung to drum and cymbal. There follows the Bible reading with a brief (or not so brief) sermon attached. Then begin the prayers, the president first and then others, often repeating each other, and the good Lord is informed of a lot of things that he knows very well already. Then sometimes we go on far into the night with hymn after hymn. Usually at about 1 or 2 a.m. the final prayer is said, some light refreshments

are served, and everyone trails off across the fields to their own homes.

A former bishop of Dacca

Therefore let us pray

for ordinary folk preoccupied with keeping body and soul together

for Christian leaders facing immense need with few resources

that opportunities may be given to local people to exercise leadership, so that the church may be strengthened

for the search for deeper unity of thought and action among members of the different churches

for those who seek to alleviate poverty, illiteracy and injustice

for wisdom and compassion for those in authority in Bangladesh, and for the maintenance of peace

> *Grant, O Lord, that we may expect great things of thee,*
> *and attempt great things for thee.*

from the well-known words of William Carey of Serampore,
Bible translator, and founder of the Baptist Church in Bengal

The village women of Bangladesh frequently embroider pillows with Bengali words meaning *an end of tiredness*. Whether on behalf of its very many poor people who wearily go to sleep under constant threat of cyclone, flood or famine, or of minority groups in endemic fear of violence and robbery by night, it is a country which stands in special need of the night prayers of Christians everywhere:

> *Save us O Lord waking; guard us sleeping:*
> *That awake we may watch with Christ,*
> *and asleep we may rest in peace.*

from Compline, and used as a night prayer
by the religious communities of Bangladesh

Bhutan

Bhutan is a small independent country in the Eastern Himalayas. The mountainous north borders on Tibet with which the country has cultural and trade links. In the south, the land sweeps down to plains adjoining India.

Population: 1.3 million, scattered and consisting mainly of Bhotias but also a considerable number of Tibetan refugees and some Nepalis.

Languages: Dzongkha, Nepali, English.

Government: Monarchy with elected National Assembly.

Religion: Buddhists 70%, Hindus 24.8%, Muslims 5%.

Bhutan was impenetrable to foreigners until 1965, but has recently been developing links with other countries, and became a full member of the United Nations in 1971. It has had agreements first with the British and then with India, in matters of foreign affairs. Since 1966 certain Christian agencies have been permitted to enter the country to engage in medical and educational work.

The government of Bhutan is concerned that the Buddhist religion should be maintained, not least for the sake of cultural stability at a time when significant social change is taking place through development. There are Christians among the many Indians working for the government, and several groups among the Nepali minority in southern Bhutan. There are very few Bhotia Christians. All these groups are independent. Christians are free to worship, but not to preach or evangelize.

Intercessions and Prayers

We pray

for the king and government, and all who work for the development and welfare of this kingdom

for Christians who celebrate the Lord's presence here, and work hand in hand with all who fight illiteracy and disease.

One of the Christian agencies of the country describes its role as "simply loving and serving the people, just as Christ loves and serves both us and them"

O Servant Lord,
teach us how to serve.

Nepal

This small mountainous landlocked country in the Himalayas is the only Hindu kingdom in the world, and is incredibly beautiful. Most people live on subsistence farms, and 23% are literate. None are starving, but they are continuously undernourished.

Population: 16.7 million.
Languages: Nepali, Gorkhali and other tribal languages, English.
Government: Constitutional monarchy.
Religion: Hindus 90%, Buddhists 7%, Muslims 2%, others 1%.

Nepal was closed to the rest of the world until 1951 when the first Westerners were invited to enter the country and establish medical ministries. However over the years Nepalis themselves have crossed the borders in search of work, thus encountering Christian congregations, and some have returned as Christians. For many years there have been small groups of Christians in border areas praying for the country.

The church is indigenous and self-supporting, and scattered over the country. The preoccupation of Christians in the villages is with health and general wellbeing, and the need to claim the power of Christ for deliverance from the main uncontrollable influences in life; and in the towns, with the need to resist the temptations that come with Western influences. Christians are frequently harassed by police action against any who are baptised or who dare to witness to their faith. This can lead to gaol sentences, as conversion is not allowed by the constitution.

Traditional missionary work is not permitted, but at the invitation of the Nepalese government and for specified periods of time a number of Christian agencies are carrying out projects in areas of education, health, and land, water and electrical development.

God is here
God is present in Nepal
God has called us to be his servants here
We respond in faith, willing to accept our vulnerability.

So affirms one such agency, involving Christians of many different denominations and nationalities.

Intercessions and Prayers

We pray
for the king, and the government and councils of Nepal
that the country may be saved from corruption and the abuse of power
that religious freedom may come
for support and strength for Christian pastors under persecution

that God will confirm and strengthen all that is for the good of the nation
and the welfare of its most needy people

Using the words of Nepali Christians, sometimes out of tune with each
other, and often facing strong local opposition, *we pray:*

> *Lord, give us the strength that comes from your living presence*
> *to remain true to you, to honour you,*
> *and to witness to you in our land of Nepal. Amen.*

> *O Lord, hear our petitions,*
> *Open the door of salvation for the Gorkhalis.*
> *Father, Son, Holy Spirit, hear our petition,*
> *Show us the way by a cloudy fiery pillar.*
> *Peoples of different regions are to the east, west, and south;*
> *Tibet is north, and Nepal our home in the middle.*
> *There are cities: Thapathali, Bhatgaon, Patan, Kathmandu:*
> *Our desire is to make them your devotees.*
> *Up! we must go, ignoring hate and shame,*
> *Leaving wealth, people, comfort, to do the holy task.*

Prayer-hymn originally sung on the borders of Nepal,
and now a favourite among Nepali Christians

"Nepal has often been described as the picture-postcard paradise of
clear streams, alpine hiking trails, and snowy peaks" — *for this we
give thanks and praise.*

"But the country is also traversed by barefooted people trudging miles
every day with heavy loads supported by slings across their foreheads.
They lead a hard life which lasts on average only about 40 years" —
for them we pray.

If the carrying of enormous loads is a
common feature of life in the mountains of
Nepal, so also is the provision of burden
benches on which heavy loads may be
rested. Used in one church as the design
for its Lord's Table, the "chautara" stands
as a very local reminder for Christians of
the promise of Jesus:

Come to me, all who labour and are heavy laden, and I will give you
rest. — *Amen, so be it Lord.*

Week 48

Afghanistan • Pakistan

Almighty God, whose dominion is in the hearts of people and nations, set, we beseech you, in our Christian hearts a care for our Muslim brothers and sisters, and so foster love that understanding follows. And if, as understanding deepens, a need for penitence appears, then, Lord, do not withold it.

Prayer for Christian/Muslim understanding

Afghanistan

In this high, landlocked country, about 6% of the land is cultivable, the remainder being mountain or desert. The vigorous tribal people are mostly farmers or herders, and some are entirely nomadic.

Population: 18.2 million.

Languages: Pushtu, Dari, and many others, both tribal and European.

Government: Marxist republic.

Religion: Almost all are Muslims, Hindus 0.6%, very few Christians.

Before sea routes were developed this territory was at the centre of Asian trade, and a Christian bishop from Herat was at the Council of Selucia in 424. There is mention of the Nestorians in the Middle Ages, but the Christian presence was terminated in the 14th century. A tribal confederation, with the beginnings of a monarchy, emerged in 1747, but subsequently broke up. Unity was eventually restored and the monarchy strengthened. This ended in 1973 with increasing unrest, and the entry of forces from the Soviet Union in 1979.

Afghan freedom fighters resisted Soviet domination and there was a long period of strife. A quarter of the population fled the country or were killed, and famine resulted in some areas. With the withdrawal of Soviet troops and negotiations for the return of refugees, there are signs of hope for the future. Expatriate Christians working with the government in aid agencies and in embassies have remained in the country. As well as service to the people of Afghanistan they see their role as a token representative presence for Christ in the land. Afghan Christians are few and scattered.

Intercessions and Prayers

We pray

for the land and people of Afghanistan

for those who suffer the horrors and hardships of war, and all who are refugees

for all efforts to bring about a just and lasting peace

"In the absence of Afghan Christians able to come together publicly to give thanks to God for their own country, should there be no thanksgiving for its mountains, its streams, its antiquity, its history, its poetry and music?" asks a frequent traveller in Afghanistan.

O Creator God,
we rejoice that the ruggedness of this land
has produced a people
of great resourcefulness and tenacity,
of hospitality and diversity;
and we ask for them
a share in your new creation.

Pakistan

Population: 97.7 million and growing rapidly.

Languages: Urdu, regional languages, English.

Government: Islamic republic.

Religion: Muslims 96%, Christians 1.8%, Hindus 1.3%.

Conceived as a land for the Muslims of the subcontinent, Pakistan came into being in 1947 when British rule in India ended. It originally included Bangladesh which later became an independent state. History in the area can be traced back to the Indus civilization of about 2000 BC. Traceable Christianity dates from the 8th century, but owes its more recent growth to the work of 19th century missionaries. A small but significant flow of Christian converts from the major religions of the area, and the great mass movement among landless labourers formed the beginnings of today's church. Christian schools, colleges and hospitals have made a widely acknowledged contribution to the life of the country.

Of today's Christians approximately half are Roman Catholics. The Church of Pakistan, formed in 1970 by a union of Anglicans, Lutherans, Methodists and some Presbyterians, is the largest Protestant body. Among a number of other denominations the United Presbyterian is the most significant. Current government policy favours a programme of Islamization which particularly affects education, banking, the position of women and courts of law. This has implications for the Christian community, and has resulted in the nationalization of schools and colleges. The church promotes Christian-Muslim dialogue and is involved in a range of social and developmental projects, and theological education. Some Christians face problems of identity and discrimination. Many are very poor, doing menial jobs in the cities and labouring work in rural areas. The church struggles with internal factions, but can also rise to heights of great vitality, and simple, sincere faith.

Many Pakistanis, both Christian and Muslim, work overseas and their earnings constitute the second main source of foreign exchange. Some 3 million Afghans in the country, almost three quarters of them women and children, constitute the largest refugee population in the world.

Intercessions and Prayers

Discovered locally, and adopted as the symbol of the Church of Pakistan, the ancient Taxila cross serves as a reminder of a very early Christian presence in this area.

Present-day Christians, using the refrain of a well-known convention hymn, pray that they may remain firm in this long and sometimes very costly tradition:

Yisu ke pichhe main chalne laga, na lautunga, na lautunga...
I have begun to follow Jesus, no turning back, no turning back...

With them we pray

for faithful following of Jesus in situations of great hardship and difficulty

for alertness to the possibilities of Christian service and self-giving (renewal, lay training and development are among the stated priorities of the church)

for village people, whose livelihood is dependent on the availability of water and on the goodwill of landowners and government officials

for the church in rural areas and semi-literate communities, relying much on the local catechist or teacher and the occasional visit of a priest

for the Christian women of Pakistan, often the backbone of families and of new ventures of one kind or another

for refugees from Afghanistan, the Pakistani communities who accommodate them, and the international agencies that support them

for all meeting between Muslims and Christians at the neighbourhood level, and for study centres and seminars which facilitate specialized discussion and understanding

for wise, compassionate and stable leadership in church and in state

O Creator and Mighty God,
you have promised
strength for the weak
rest for the labourers
light for the way
grace for the trials
help from above
unfailing sympathy
undying love.
O Creator and Mighty God
help us to continue in your promise. Amen.

Prayer from Pakistan

O Heavenly Father,
open wide the sluice gate into my heart
that I may receive your living water and be fruitful.

Prayer of Punjabi Christian

Look graciously, O Lord, upon this land.
Where it is in pride, subdue it
Where it is in need, supply it
Where it is in error, rectify it
Where it is in default, restore it
And where it holds to that which is just
and compassionate, support it.

Based on the words "O Lord, be gracious to our land"
from Morning and Evening Prayer, Church of Pakistan

Week 49

India • Sri Lanka

Almighty God, who to your holy apostle St Thomas our patron, revealed your incarnate Son in his risen glory; draw, we beseech you, the peoples of our lands to know and confess him as their Lord and God, that coming to you by him they may believe and have life in his name. Amen.

Collect for the commemoration of St Thomas

Holy Apostle Thomas,
your memory is exalted here.

India

At heart this vast country, with widely varying terrain and climate, is an agricultural nation, with about two-thirds of the people living in villages. Industrial development in the cities is advanced.

Population: Nearly 800 million.

Languages: Hindi, English and 13 others officially recognized. Over 1500 others are "mother tongue" for various groups of people.

Government: Parliamentary federal republic.

Religion: Hindus 79%, Muslims 12%, Christians 3%, Sikhs 2%, adherents of tribal religions 1.5%, Buddhists 0.8%.

India's diverse population is largely the result of a succession of invasions which have occurred in the long history of the subcontinent.

Early invaders came from the north-west. Europeans came later by sea, and the subcontinent eventually became part of the British empire. Independence was gained in 1947, with partition of the country.

Tradition holds that the apostle Thomas came to India in 52 A.D. and preached the gospel in the south of the country. Certainly a church was established in the south by the year 200. The Mar Thoma Church, the Malankara Orthodox Syrian Church and the Syrian Orthodox Church all trace their origins to this ancient church. Together they have over two million members, the Syrian Orthodox Church having more members in India than anywhere else. Roman Catholics came with the Portuguese, and Anglicans with the East India Co., but it was not until the 18th and 19th centuries that Protestant work really began. The formation of the Church of South India in 1947 uniting Anglicans and British Methodists with an already united body of Congregationalists and Presbyterians was the first such union in the world. The Church of North India, incorporating a slightly wider grouping, came into existence in 1970.

In today's secular state increasing religious rivalries have resulted in communal conflicts which continue to erupt in violence and loss of life. Caste discriminations, though legally banned, continue to cause hardship for many.

Following rapid growth in the last century, the church continues to grow in some areas. Catholics join with others in promoting inter-faith dialogue. The CSI, CNI, and Mar Thoma Church have entered into a conciliar union, bringing together Eastern and Western traditions for the first time. The Methodist Church in India is also seeking to join. Having undertaken a stringent self-examination, the CSI and CNI have gained a new determination to fight against social evils and to serve the real needs of those around. Christians are a small minority in the north, and consequently the CNI has tended to be somewhat inward-looking, but the moderator has recently launched a comprehensive programme of renewal and outreach. He says: "Because the church is poor, its wealth is people .... Our sense of insecurity, of being a minority, and our financial weakness are our greatest assets."

Intercessions and Prayers

O Lord, let me rest the ladder of gratitude against your cross, and mounting, kiss your feet.

Prayer of an Indian Christian

Gratitude

for the CSI and CNI, and for continuing efforts to bring about greater and more fruitful unity of the churches

for the freedom enjoyed by the church in its life and activities, and for recent movements of renewal and outreach

for the faithfulness in poverty of pastors and congregations in hundreds of villages and towns

for progress achieved in the fields of food production, medical care, literacy and social welfare

for the women of India, their contribution in many spheres of care and development, and their participation in movements for peace, environmental protection and economic justice

Intercession

for peace and communal harmony, and for all victims of conflict

for the building up of awareness in the church and in society of justice, peace and the integrity of creation in the Indian context

for the National Council of Churches in India, and for the ongoing negotiations towards a broader union of churches

for inter-faith ventures between Christians and Hindus, Muslims, Sikhs and others

for ashrams, religious communities, church institutions and all Christian households

for the growing cities of India

Cities are springing up like mushrooms
Cities which have come in the wake of industry
Cities that portray vivid and striking contrasts.
   Lord, look at those young men and women
   standing in line from morning till evening
   in front of the army office for recruiting
   waiting to get a patient hearing.
   Look at those beggars sitting
   with bowls in hands, complaining.
   Look at the mansions of those money-lenders;
   guarded by watchers to keep out
   street dogs and job-hunting callers.

The motorists come and go in pomp and splendour;
the hotels are crowded, six-course dinners served.
The church bells toll, and the pews are filled.
But Christ is sitting at the gate with the beggars,
a bowl in hand, complaining.
Why Lord? Why must there be this difference?
Why must there be this gap
this gap that is widening instead of narrowing;
this gap that has no bridge?
And still they come from village to city,
from farming to industry.
Lord, do you have a message for the city?

M. A. Thomas, Bangalore

O God, we would pray at this time for all those who suffer, for all who are in want, for those who have no home, for widows and orphans, for refugees, for prisoners, for those who are in despair and on the verge of madness or violence, for those who are tortured or persecuted, for the aged, the sick, for those about to undergo operations, for the hungry and the poor, for those who are discriminated against on account of race or of caste, and for all who have need of our prayers.

Daily prayer suggested for use by members of the
Syrian Orthodox Church, dispersed abroad

Sri Lanka

In the tropical island of Sri Lanka 70% of people work on the land and are poor, but they are relatively well nourished and educated. Unemployment is high in towns.

Population: 16.2 million, made up of Sinhalese (74%), Sri Lankan Tamils (13%), Indian Tamils (5.1%) and other minority groups.

Languages: Sinhalese, Tamil, English and others.

Government: Democratic socialist republic with an executive president.

Religion: Buddhists 69.3%, Hindus 15.5%, Muslims 7.6%, Christians 7.5%.

Sri Lanka, the oldest centre of Theravada Buddhism, flourished as one of the small but important ancient civilizations of Asia. From the 16th century it came into trading relationships with European nations, and was a British colony from 1802 until independence in 1948. The Roman Catholic Church dates from the Portuguese period and most Protestant churches from the Dutch and British periods. There is archaeological evidence of an early Nestorian Church, and a tradition that St Thomas visited the island's sacred mountain, a centre of pilgrimage for the four religions.

Each ethnic group maintains its own beliefs and customs. Differences and inequalitites between the Sinhalese and Tamil communities have led to armed conflict, with the worst violence in the north where groups of Tamils fight for a separate state. Transport and trade between north and south are disrupted, and there is an acute refugee problem. The churches, embracing all areas and ethnic communities, work for reconciliation and peace with justice.

The vast majority of Christians are Roman Catholics. Conversations are taking place between the Roman Catholic and Anglican churches to promote greater cooperation. Taking the view that if Sri Lanka was to have a united church it must work out its own scheme, the Anglican Church did not join in the union scheme with South India. However the Congregational Church in the north, which owes its origins to the work of the American Board and is predominantly Sri Lankan Tamil in membership, became the Jaffna diocese of the CSI. The other major Protestant body is the Methodist Church. There are efforts to re-activate the scheme for church union thwarted earlier by legal opposition. The Ecumenical Institute for Study and Dialogue in Colombo brings Buddhists and Christians together for inter-faith programmes, and a similar institute in Jaffna seeks to work among Christians and Hindus.

Intercessions and Prayers

We give thanks

for the deep capacity for worship and devotion of the people of Sri Lanka

for all who work lovingly and courageously for reconciliation and peace, and the just ordering of community life

> *What we need, Lord, is mercy from all, and forgiveness wherever there has been wrong, and the infusion of intrinsically Christian attitudes in all who have anything whatever to do with Sri Lanka.*
>
> Petition of Sri Lankan church leader

We pray

for those affected by ethnic conflict, that mutual respect, justice and peace may prevail

that Christians may be given a new spirit of prayer and praise, and ever fresh inspiration, vision and vitality

for the National Christian Council of Sri Lanka, and all efforts to promote unity

for all in any community who set their faces against exploitation, violence, and corruption in business and public life, and seek to build up trust

> *Lord Jesus, you were awakened by the cry of your disciples on a storm-tossed sea. Hear also our cry for help. There is no justice in our land for the weak and the powerless, because the powerful and the strong have decided what is and what is not right and just. We, the minority of the humble and weak, are tired of crying for justice and peace. How much longer must the strong dominate and the weak suffer? Bring your justice and grant us your peace. Let your kingdom become a reality on this earth.*

A prayer from Sri Lanka

> *Remembering St Thomas, we invoke the blessing promised to those who have not seen the nailmarks of your hands, and the spear thrust in your heart, and yet believe; that leading others to confess you as their Lord and God, they may together find life in you. Amen.*

Week 50

Angola • Mozambique

We pray for Africa with all its richness of spirit, that its peoples may be strengthened as they build their own nations and work for peace and justice: that they may be delivered from the terrors of famine and drought, of disease, of conflict, and of discouragement.

Christian prayer for peace, Pope John Paul II, Assisi, 1986

These two countries, on opposite sides of Africa, each experienced nearly 500 years of Portuguese rule before becoming independent in 1975, after a prolonged armed struggle. In Angola a period of civil strife followed; and Mozambique suffered as a result of the war in neighbouring Rhodesia. Continuing unrest in the south of Angola, together with incursions of South African forces, and persistent guerilla activity throughout Mozambique, supported by various outside governments and agencies, place heavy burdens on the respective governments.

Population, religion, language and government

Angola: 8.6 million. Christians about 80% (Roman Catholics 61%, Protestants 18%, African indigenous 1.5%), adherents of tribal religions 15%.

Mozambique: 13.5 million. Adherents of tribal religions 47%, Christians 39% (Roman Catholics 31.5%, Protestants 6.8%, Anglicans 0.7%), Muslims 13%.

In both countries Portuguese is the official language although numerous African languages are also spoken.

Both are single party republics.

Angola

The Roman Catholic Church has been continuously present since 1560 when Jesuits accompanied the first Portuguese to the Ndongo Kingdom.

Early progress was seriously reversed by the ravages of the slave trade, and it was not until 1940 onwards that the church began to grow rapidly. Baptists came in 1878, followed by Congregationalists, Methodists and others; each working among different ethnic groups. Protestants were prominent in the independence movements, and the church was under suspicion from the Portuguese authorities.

Now strong throughout the country, the Roman Catholic church is frequently in conflict with the Marxist government, and has itself a problem of living down its early association with the colonial regime. However, wherever it is active in social work it has the approval of the government. The main Protestant churches continue for the most part to work in different areas. Though its membership is divided in political allegiance, the Christian church worships and acts as one in serving the spiritual and human needs of the Angolan people. In a situation of continuing conflict and uncertainty about the future, it ministers to a growing Christian community, meeting often in the simplest of buildings and shelters, praying and working for unity and reconciliation.

Intercessions and Prayers

We pray

for the work of the Christian Council of Angola in coordinating evangelism and social service projects; and for growing contact and goodwill between the Roman Catholic and Protestant churches

for the training of leaders, educators, and pastors

for all those who help scattered groups and congregations in their Christian life and witness

for refugees from Namibia, South Africa and Zaïre, and all displaced Angolans harassed by the ongoing war

for peace in this huge and troubled land

We sincerely thank you, O God, for your powerful gift of hope in the face of seemingly hopeless situations. We thank you for your peace in the hearts and minds of men and women in this part of Africa who believe you are the living God, quick to save in time of danger. You reign above all, directing the course and destiny of the universe.

João Makondekwa, Bible Society of Angola

Mozambique

Roman Catholic missionary orders came with the first Portuguese, and worked in the areas of the southern coast and the Zambesi river. Not until the late 19th century did work begin further north. At about this time Protestant missionaries began to arrive, and many more came after the first world war. Prior to independence the Roman Catholic Church was closely identified with the state, although some individuals protested. Protestants were under suspicion and suffered considerable persecution.

Coordinating the work of some two dozen churches the Christian Council of Mozambique has done much to break down the hostility between the Marxist government and the church. Beginning with aid given to Zimbabwean refugees, the church has gone on to build health centres and schools in the villages, to establish agricultural projects, and to make available emergency food aid in times of drought. Most church buildings are now reopened, and the church continues to grow. Many Mozambican men go to neighbouring countries to find work; and poverty and family breakdown cause enormous hardship. Poor communication and terrorist attacks make pastoral care extremely difficult. In remote areas of the north practical ecumenism finds Anglican and Roman Catholic priests ministering to the same congregations, in which members of both denominations are baptized, confirmed, and receive communion together.

Intercessions and Prayers

We pray

for reconciliation and peace

for Christians seeking to prove their loyalty to the socialist state while remaining true to their faith

for pastors making frequent, hazardous and exhausting journeys from village to village to minister and encourage

for the women of Mozambique, that they may be able to sustain a Christian family life amidst the strains imposed by the migratory labour system

for those who serve others through medicine, education and social service

O Lord,
we pray for justice, peace and stability throughout Southern Africa,
for the end of apartheid and racial intolerance,
of tribalism and all exclusive nationalism.
We pray that in Africa and in each and every country
men and women may honour and respect
their fellow beings of every race and colour.
We pray that those who abuse power may be humbled,
and the meek inherit the earth.

Prayer for Mozambique

I wonder if we are aware of the deep implication, in matters of faith, of belonging to the Christian era....in all these years since Christ's birth, a new, not just style, but essence of life, a life which cannot be crushed down by pressures, physical or spiritual, has begun...We are in 19.. of the Era *of* Christ, not after Christ as if Christ is overdue, outdated. We are in Christ, and "the disciple is not above his teacher"...Christ's Era means that we are to be ready to face what Christ had to face.

Dinis Sengulane, Bishop of Lebombo, Mozambique

Week 51

Botswana • Zimbabwe

Almighty God,
as your Son our Saviour
was born of a Hebrew mother,
but rejoiced in the faith of a Syrian woman
and of a Roman soldier,
welcomed the Greeks who sought him,
and suffered a man from Africa to carry his cross;
so teach us to regard the members of all races
as fellow heirs of the kingdom of Jesus Christ our Lord. Amen.

Botswana

Population: 1.2 million.

Languages: English, Setswana.

Government: Multi-party republic.

Religion: Christians approximately 50% (Protestants 26.5%, African Indigenous 12%, Roman Catholics 9.5%, Anglicans 2%), adherents of traditional beliefs 50%.

The people of Botswana mostly belong to a group of Bantu who migrated here in the early centuries of the Christian era. Bushmen, who also live here, may have been in southern Africa since the Middle Stone Age. As Bechuanaland, the country became a British protectorate in 1885, and obtained independence in 1966. Largely savannah and desert, the land is increasingly afflicted by drought. Most of the people live along the eastern border, which is both more fertile and close to the main railway line. Social and economic patterns are changing as a result of the discovery of minerals.

The United Congregational Church is the traditional church of Botswana, although other Protestant bodies have been present since the early

19th century. The first Roman Catholic mission was established in 1895. Today the Botswana Christian Council coordinates the work of over 20 member churches, including the Roman Catholic, and an increasing number of African independent churches. In this large, thinly populated country, pastoral work is not easy to sustain. Through a programme of theological education by extension, Christians of many professions — teachers, nurses, government servants and others — are undertaking courses. The growing mining townships constitute a challenge to provide welcoming Christian communities especially for the many young people who, in the absence of jobs and social structures, are subject to new temptations and sometimes drift into delinquency. Drought has decimated the country's cattle, and the churches are involved with the government in projects aimed at more long-term solutions as well as giving immediate aid.

In response to the plight of Hambukushu refugees from Angola the Christian Council embarked on one of its most imaginative projects, which led to the emergence among these people of a lively church, ecumenical from the beginning. A visitor writes:

"To those brought up in the ordered life of the traditional church, the life of a Christian community devoid of accumulated traditions presents the faith in Christ both vividly and starkly... For the Hambukushu Christians the god of their exodus from Angola has been rediscovered in the Christ whose presence they celebrate at the eucharist, whose gospel they walk miles to hear, and whose spirit now dwells exuberantly among them."

Sadly, even here dissensions have occurred, and the prayer of our Lord *that they all may be one* needs to be said for this community also.

Intercessions and Prayers

Let us pray

for local catechists and members of the ecumenical team who live and work in the New Testament ambience of the Hambukushu Christian community

for the Christian Council of Botswana with its diverse membership tackling new problems in the country

for priests and pastors ministering to congregations in villages and in growing townships for young people drifting into towns, and the church's response to their needs

for the success of projects to combat drought, and for the many who suffer from its effects. "There are children in Botswana who have never seen rain"

> *O God,*
> *we pray for those places in the world*
> *made awful by climatic conditions;*
> *places of intense cold, and heat and drought,*
> *places of great hardship and privation,*
> *where man, woman and beast are constantly endangered*
> *by the elements and environment.*
> *We give thanks for all that sustains and helps them,*
> *and pray that such may be multiplied*
> *in the hands of Jesus Christ and those who serve in his name. Amen.*

Zimbabwe

Population: 8.2 million.

Languages: English, Shona, Sidebele.

Government: Multi-party Republic.

Religion: Christians 58% (Protestants 21%, Roman Catholics 16%, African Indigenous 16%, Anglicans 5%), adherents of traditional beliefs 41%, Muslims 1%, a small Hindu community.

Occupied by Shona-speaking peoples, who have probably been in this area for over a thousand years, and the Ndebele, who came from the south, Zimbabwe achieved legal independence in 1980. Both Shona and Ndebele were at the mercy of the manipulations of the British South Africa Company which took control of their land. Colonization followed (the country was then known as Southern Rhodesia), and then an influx of white settlers mainly from Britain and South Africa. This minority white community exerted political and economic control, while African political organizations were successively banned, and their leaders exiled or imprisoned. The long struggle for a just independence with majority rule involved warfare and immense suffering.

Although Portuguese Jesuits had contact with the Shona in the 16th century, a sustained Christian presence dates from the work of 19th century missionaries who initially worked in close cooperation with the white regime. In this century many Christian leaders, both Roman Catholic and Protestant, protested against government repression and segregation, and some missionaries were expelled. Now church and state are seeking to work out their relationship with each other; for although the majority political party is committed to the eventual creation of a Marxist-Leninist one-party system, religious freedom is respected and many members of government are practising Christians. Tensions and unrest within the country have persisted, and are the subject of Christian prayer and concern.

During the years of military struggle church membership declined greatly, but many, especially young people, are now returning. The largest single body is the Roman Catholic Church. Within the Protestant community there is no one predominant denomination. The African Apostolic Church, the first indigenous to the country, was established in 1906, and there are now many others, some with a large membership. Through its Department of Christian Care, the Zimbabwe Christian Council provides technical assistance to farming cooperatives and small farmers, and an emergency committee responds to the needs of refugees. Individual churches are involved in medical, educational, social and development work, and a united theological college trains candidates for the ministry. Pastoral care and the nurture of new Christians are priorities.

Intercessions and Prayers

We pray

for those in government facing the many problems common to developing countries

for peace and stability in the region

for reconciliation, love, unity and peace where there has been violence and enmity between those of different communities and political allegiances

for the young people of Zimbabwe

for those who train pastors, priests and lay leaders

for God's blessing on all efforts on the part of the Zimbabwe Christian Council and individual churches to bring help to the poor and needy

O God, friend of the poor,
help us to be their friends as well...

A pastor's prayer

Open my eyes that they may see
the deepest needs of people;

Move my hands that they may feed the hungry;
Touch my heart that it may bring warmth to the despairing;
Teach me the generosity that welcomes strangers;
Let me share my possessions to clothe the naked;
Give me the care that strengthens the sick;
Make me share in the quest to set the prisoner free;

In sharing our anxieties and our love,
our poverty and our prosperity,
we partake of your divine presence.

Reverend Canaan Banana, First President of Zimbabwe

O God of all nations and people, we come before you remembering
and interceding for the people of Africa. You know the struggles and
predicaments of our continent and the hopes of its people. We pray for
justice, peace and reconciliation in Africa. We remember the All
Africa Conference of Churches, the member churches, the Christian
councils and the Organization of African Unity, as they struggle to
bring peace, reconciliation and unity in Africa.

African bidding

Week 52

Lesotho • Namibia
South Africa • Swaziland

Lord Jesus Christ,
you are the truth and rule over all the nations of the earth:
give us wisdom to discern the truth
among all the conflicting voices that claim to be true.
Protect us from the violence
of words, fire, bullet, stone and quirt*.
Make us agents of your truth, righteousness and peace,
and give us boldness to be ambassadors for you.
For you reign supreme
with the Father and the Holy Spirit for ever.

Prayer from South Africa

Lesotho

Population: 1.6 million.

Languages: Sosotho, English.

Government: Hereditary monarchy.

Religion: Christians 92% (Roman Catholics 43%, Protestants 30%, Anglicans 11%, African indigenous 8%). The remainder are mostly adherents of traditional beliefs.

Formerly known as Basutoland, Lesotho became a British protectorate in 1868 and, following a gradual process of increasing self-government, obtained independence in 1966. The country is completely surrounded by, and economically dependent on, South Africa. In 1984 approximately half the adult male labour force was working in South African mines.

By arrangement with King Moshoeshoe I of the Basuto, the Paris Mission sent missionaries to Lesotho in 1833. The Lesotho Evangelical

---

* The quirt is a short handled whip with a braided leather lash.

Church, now the second largest Christian denomination in the country, emerged out of this work. Roman Catholic missionaries followed in 1862 and then Anglicans. The Roman Catholic Church is a full member of the Christian Council of Lesotho, which is concerned with refugees and matters of peace and justice, and maintains an ecumenical agricultural school. The Christian church is greatly involved in educational and medical work, and there are a number of ecumenical ventures in these fields.

Intercessions and Prayers

We pray

for the church in Lesotho, asking — at the request of the Christian Council — that the Spirit of forgiveness may "blow through the churches in this country, that Christians may work together for unity, justice, and peace"

for religious communities, maintaining a chain of prayer for the needs of the world, and South Africa in particular, while providing centres of refreshment in an often parched and needy environment

for Christian congregations in the lowland towns, where a steady inflow of people is exacerbating the problems of loneliness, crime, alcoholism and violence

for those who grow food in the mountain areas, where crops may fail because of drought or be destroyed by flood

> *Lord, we think you know our land, it is so like the country you once lived in — mountains and sometimes snow contrasting with the thirsty lowlands.*
>
> *You, who often went alone upon hillsides, know the mysterious peace and beauty to be found there. You know also the clamouring crowds waiting down below.*
>
> *We wait for you today. We pray that you will have compassion on the poor — those who have no chance of school, no work, no place to belong. Give strength to those in exile and the thousands who work in mines far from home. We remember those who live in fear, and any who have been threatened or attacked.*

*Give courage to your people. Enable our Christian leaders to inspire
hope and unity. Help all who are striving for justice. And let your
peace descend again and wash over the land.*

Prayer prepared by staff and students of Roma Theological Seminary

Namibia

Population: 1.2 million.

Languages: Afrikaans, English, Oshiwambo, Herero, Damara and other
African languages, German.

Government: Illegally occupied by South Africa which holds administrative power.

Religion: Christians over 90% (Protestants 60%, Roman Catholics 20%,
Anglicans 11%). Others adhere to traditional beliefs.

Formerly known as South West Africa, this land, much of it now desert
but with rich mineral resources in some areas, became a German colony
in 1884. South African forces entered the country in the first world war,
and in 1920 it was entrusted to Britain under a League of Nations
Mandate, which then passed to South Africa. After the second world war,
when other mandated territories became United Nations Trust Territories,
South Africa refused such an agreement for Namibia, and a prolonged
dispute with repeated recourse to the International Court of Justice began.
The UN General Assembly voted to terminate the Mandate in 1966, and
in 1971 the ICJ ruled that South Africa's presence in the territory was
illegal.

From the beginning of white occupation the indigenous peoples of
Namibia have been made to suffer. Under German rule unscrupulous
cattle trading deals and appropriation of land resulted in an uprising which
was brutally crushed. The Herero-Nama communities, with a combined
population of 120,000, were reduced to less than 40,000 in just four
years. During the Mandate period a rush of white South Africans took
possession of the best land and all of the mines. Dispossessed of their
land, Africans were increasingly forced to sell their labour under the
contract labour system, in which men have to work on a migrant basis for
prolonged periods. In 1966 the South African security and apartheid laws
were formally extended to Namibia. Meanwhile nationalist movements
campaigning to end racial discrimination and secure independence had

been formed. In 1966 the South West African Peoples' Organization (Swapo), disappointed by the failure of the international community to secure any progress, and feeling that peaceful means had been exhausted, decided that there was no alternative to armed struggle. In 1973 Swapo was recognized by the UN General Assembly as "the sole and authentic representative of the Namibian people".

The Christian church in Namibia owes its origins to 19th-century missionaries, and initially the only education available for Africans was that undertaken by the churches. Under South African rule the church, like everything else, has been segregated, and the government has imposed its own system of Bantu education. Today Lutherans make up more than half the population, followed by Roman Catholics, Anglicans, Methodists and others, all active in their support for independence. Among the white population the Dutch Reformed Church is strong. The Council of Churches in Namibia, of which the Roman Catholic Church is a member, was formed in 1978.

The suffering of the Namibian people has escalated in recent years, and the north is virtually a war zone. Under the pretext of curbing Swapo "terrorism" the military and security forces seemingly stop at nothing. Beatings, torture, rape and killings occur, and the local population lives in constant fear and dread. Some 75,000 Namibians are refugees in Angola, Zambia and Botswana. The struggle for liberation continues, the churches being actively involved in it.

> We wail and cry, not in self-pity or in despair, but in hope and hard labour of preparing for a new nation with a constitution based on the love of God and respect for a human person. We cry to God because the road to that new Namibia and just society is full of pains, trials, detentions and deaths. We refuse to be consoled until we finally reach there as a nation of black, white and brown, of all Namibians.
>
> Abisai Shejavali, general secretary of the CCN

Intercessions and Prayers

Let us thank God

that in the midst of incredible difficulties and suffering, courage, determination and resurrection life still burst through *and let us affirm our solidarity* with Christians in all such situations as we declare our common faith that "the third day he rose again from the dead", and all that that belief implies for life now.

To you, O God, we lift our outstretched hands.
Give us your justice and peace in Namibia.

We pray

for those many people who suffer harshly at the hands of the South African security forces, or who are in prison for their vision of a new Namibia

O God, I am oppressed: undertake for me.

Ascribed to Hezekiah, King of Judah in 707 BC

for bereaved families; that God will comfort the widows, protect the orphans and provide company for the lonely

for those who live in constant fear of being picked up or killed

O Christ, who hast known fear,
be with all who are afraid today.

for all who have fled from Namibia, and for those who are uprooted in their own land

O Lord, help us who roam about. Help us who have been placed in Africa and have no dwelling place of our own. Give us back our dwelling place, O God, all power is yours in heaven and earth.

Chief Hosea Kutako of the Hereros

for thousands of Black pupils and students whose education discriminates against them, and who see few prospects for the future

for the Council of Churches in Namibia, and for all who unite to stand together against forces of division and destruction

Lord Jesus Christ, voice of the voiceless and comforter of the oppressed; bless and strengthen the people of Namibia in their trials and quest for justice and peace. Grant to all the people of Namibia and their Christian leaders a sense of your presence; and lead them, Prince of Peace, to the reality of your eternal love.

From *Kulimukweni*, adapted

South Africa

Population: Over 32 million.

Languages: Afrikaans, English, Xhosa, Zulu, Sosotho and others.

Government: Republic.

Religion: Christians 79% (Protestants 39%, African Independent 22%, Roman Catholics 11%, Anglicans 7%), adherents of traditional religions 16%, Hindus 2%, Muslims 1.5%, Jews 0.6%.

> The time has come. The moment of truth has arrived. South Africa has been plunged into a crisis that is shaking the foundations and there is every indication that the crisis has only just begun and that it will deepen and become even more threatening in the months to come. It is the kairos or moment of truth not only for apartheid but also for the church.
>
> Kairos Document, Braamfontein, 1985

The chain of historical events which led up to this crisis began in 1652 when the first European settlers arrived in South Africa. These first settlers were Dutch, but nearly a century and a half later Great Britain gained control of the Cape. Dissatisfied with British rule Dutch settlers trecked northwards and fought the Bantu states of the region to occupy the Orange Free State, Natal and Transvaal. Later Britain gained control of these territories also. The four states merged in 1910 to form the Union of South Africa which became independent in 1934 but under exclusively white rule. The present ruling party gained control of government in 1948 and began to legalize the policy of apartheid.

One of the most painful aspects of this policy is the forced removal of African people into so-called homelands (Bantustans). Between 1960 and 1984 an estimated 3.5 million people were forcibly resettled, and the process continues. It involves concentrating 75% of the population on 13% of the land. It means that the migrant labour system is reinforced; and the granting of "independence" to the Bantustans means that those who live there are technically foreigners in South Africa. Some 50% of children in the Bantustans die before they are 5, and thousands suffer from malnutrition. Government expenditure on education for Black children is minimal. Stringent security laws have resulted in detention without trial and a very large prison population including increasing numbers of children; and there are many instances of torture. The main African political organizations have been banned since 1960. Increasing unrest has resulted in violence and deaths, and strongly repressive measures.

Proponents of apartheid claim to be "upholding Christian civilization", and for some change is unthinkable. For a few, even the 1984 constitution, which provided for parliamentary representation for Coloured and Indian people, but not for Africans, was going too far. On the other hand, the president, without giving specific details, has announced proposed legislation to allow two of the three black races to have some limited representation in parliament. However, the government attitude to more progressive groups remains unchanged, and the banning of 17 organizations simultaneously prompted the historic march to parliament by church leaders. Black Africans do not gain from South Africa's considerable mineral and agricultural resources which continue to provide wealth for those who are economically powerful, but hardship and misery for those exploited by unjust economic systems.

"The moment of truth has arrived... not only for apartheid but also for the church." The oldest and largest group of churches in South Africa is the Dutch Reformed. Organized on racial lines and with a large membership among Afrikaaners, this church did much to promote and support the concept of apartheid. This stance led to its withdrawal from the WCC in 1961, and the severance of relations with the Netherlands Reformed Church in 1978. There have been notable dissenting voices for some time, and now the church has acknowledged that there is no scriptural justification for apartheid. Other churches, united in their opposition to apartheid, are committed to working for peaceful change. They are increasingly outspoken and active, and thus come into critical confrontation with the government.

There are over 3,000 African independent churches with a combined membership of some 5 million, representing the second largest group of Christians in the country. African in their expression of Christianity, these bodies have always been independent of financial support from abroad. Of the mainstream Protestant churches the Methodist Church is the largest, but there are significant Presbyterian, Lutheran and Congregational bodies, and a smaller Moravian community. At this time of crisis social justice and an end to apartheid are over-riding concerns. Within the Christian church there are a growing number of examples of the coming together of those of different races and social backgrounds.

Intercessions and Prayers

In word and deed,
in loving and caring, in sharing and compassion,
in participation and confrontation;
Lord, speak your word to us all,
give us ears to listen
and willingness to be involved with and for one another
and a spirit of obedience.

A multi-racial group in Johannesburg

We pray

for the Republic of South Africa, that it may experience freedom, justice and the peace of God's kingdom soon

for the South African Council of Churches and all church leaders, that God will give them wisdom, courage and protection as they witness for justice and the dignity of all people

for local congregations struggling to break free from the assumptions of apartheid

for those forced to live in the Bantustans — described by a recent visitor as "a sea of shacks reaching to the horizon, aluminium latrines, no electricity or proper roads, and only scattered single water taps — in short, organized poverty"; "Martin Luther King had a dream," said another, "well, what we saw was a nightmare."

Thank you God, that you care.

for those in detention or prison, and those banned and silenced as a consequence of their struggle to see right prevail

Now, God, will you please open all prison doors.

Arrow prayers of Archbishop Desmond Tutu

for all who have been wounded, tortured, bereaved or made homeless in South Africa

for all who are refugees from South Africa, elsewhere in Africa or in the world

Almighty God,
you whose own son had to flee the evil plans of King Herod

and seek refuge in a strange land,
we bring before you the needs of the many refugees
throughout the world, particularly those in Africa.
We pray for those known personally to us
whom we now name before you...
We pray for them in their need for the necessities of life —
for shelter and food.
Grant that they may have the skills and equipment
to build shelters and to grow food.

South African Council of Churches

for Black young people, involved in the struggle, deprived of a decent education

Loving Father, your young and lovable Son was found
amidst the teachers of the law listening and enquiring of them;
Have pity on South African young people who,
in quest of freedom and a better future,
have been shot at, maimed and killed
and have fled from home and country.
Sustain them in all danger; give them your wisdom and protection,
and let their every sacrifice
yield peace, justice and freedom in their day.
Through Jesus Christ, our Lord.

Simeon Nkoane CR, Bishop Suffragan of Johannesburg East

for those in authority

O God, whose righteous wisdom governs the heavens and controls
also the destinies of men and women; teach the rulers of this and other
nations the things that belong to peace.
Save, Lord, by love, by prudence and by fear, for Jesus Christ's sake.
Amen.

From a service called by the Christian Council
to pray for families in the Crossroads Camp

A litany of rejoicing

Leader: *For rebirth and resilience,*
People: *Blessed be God.*
Leader: *For the spiritually humble,*
People: *Glory to God, Hallelujah.*

Leader:	*For all who are hungry and thirsty for justice,*
People:	*Praise him and magnify him forever.*
Leader:	*For all who are banned for speaking the truth,*
People:	*Blessed be God.*
Leader:	*For all who triumph over their bitter circumstances;*
People:	*Glory to God, Hallelujah!*
Leader:	*For all who risk reputation, livelihood and life itself for Christ's sake and the gospel,*
People:	*All praise and all glory; this is God's kingdom; praise him and love him for ever.*

A service of celebration, Cape Town

Swaziland

Population: 706,200 excluding absentee workers.

Languages: siSwati, English.

Government: Absolute monarchy.

Religion: Christians 75% (Protestants 33%, African Independent 28%, Roman Catholics 10.5%, Anglicans 3.5%), adherents of tribal religions 23%, Bahais 2%.

The Swazi people migrated into what is now Swaziland in the late 18th century. Many of the scattered groups of people already there were of the same ancestry, and all were formed into a nation. At one time a British protectorate, it became independent again in 1968. Two-thirds of the land is held in trust by the king as Nation Land, and used for subsistence farming. The remainder is privately owned by Europeans or commercial companies. Under-employment forces many men into South Africa's migrant labour system, and the tourist industry at home brings the usual problems. This small country is also host to some 26,000 refugees, most of them from Mozambique.

Methodist missionaries came into the country in 1825 at the invitation of King Sobhuza I, and today the African Methodist Episcopal Church is the largest Protestant body. There are some forty African independent churches. Roman Catholics began work in 1913 and the church is a member of the Council of Swaziland Churches. Incorporating nine member churches the CSC is concerned with development and educational projects, and involved in assisting refugees, providing water to rural people and initiating a legal aid education programme.

Intercessions and Prayers

Let us pray

for the king, that he may rule the country with wisdom, justice and peace, so that love and concern for one another may increase

for this and other countries living in proximity and in close dependence on their powerful neighbour, that they may be enabled to maintain their own integrity and their constant witness to a fellowship of people transcending race and colour

for the Council of Swaziland Churches, for its development and education programmes, and its particular concern to help families cope with problems of alcoholism and teenage pregnancy

for young people

for the planting of new churches and the renewal of old ones

O God, may this great, carefully wielded thread of worldwide prayer and concern serve the healing and salvation of our brothers and sisters in Swaziland; through Jesus Christ our Lord. Amen.

As the earth keeps turning, hurtling through space;
and night falls and day breaks from land to land;
Let us remember people — waking, sleeping, being born,
and dying — of one world and of one humanity.
Let us go from here in peace. Amen.

Closing prayer, WCC Assembly, Vancouver

Index

Calendar 1989-1996

In order that all may use the same material each week we offer here a calendar for 1989-1996.

It will be noted that the prayer cycle starts each week on a Sunday, and that Week 1 always includes 1 January. Because the calendar year does not divide into 52 weeks exactly, there is at intervals an extra week. In the span covered by this calendar this occurs once; at the turn of the year 1994-95. It is suggested that Jerusalem be prayed for during this week, as well as at other appropriate times and seasons.

	1989	*1990*	*1991*	*1992*
Week 1	1 Jan.	31 Dec. (89)	30 Dec. (90)	29 Dec. (91)
Week 2	8 Jan.	7 Jan.	6 Jan.	5 Jan.
Week 3	15 Jan.	14 Jan.	13 Jan.	12 Jan.
Week 4	22 Jan.	21 Jan.	20 Jan.	19 Jan.
Week 5	29 Jan.	28 Jan.	27 Jan.	26 Jan.
Week 6	5 Feb.	4 Feb.	3 Feb.	2 Feb.
Week 7	12 Feb.	11 Feb.	10 Feb.	9 Feb.
Week 8	19 Feb.	18 Feb.	17 Feb.	16 Feb.
Week 9	26 Feb.	25 Feb.	24 Feb.	23 Feb.
Week 10	5 March	4 March	3 March	1 March
Week 11	12 March	11 March	10 March	8 March
Week 12	19 March	18 March	17 March	15 March
Week 13	26 March	25 March	24 March	22 March
Week 14	2 April	1 April	31 March	29 March
Week 15	9 April	8 April	7 April	5 April
Week 16	16 April	15 April	14 April	12 April
Week 17	23 April	22 April	21 April	19 April
Week 18	30 April	29 April	28 April	26 April
Week 19	7 May	6 May	5 May	3 May
Week 20	14 May	13 May	12 May	10 May

	1989	*1990*	*1991*	*1992*
Week 21	21 May	20 May	19 May	17 May
Week 22	28 May	27 May	26 May	24 May
Week 23	4 June	3 June	2 June	31 May
Week 24	11 June	10 June	9 June	7 June
Week 25	18 June	17 June	16 June	14 June
Week 26	25 June	24 June	23 June	21 June
Week 27	2 July	1 July	30 June	28 June
Week 28	9 July	8 July	7 July	5 July
Week 29	16 July	15 July	14 July	12 July
Week 30	23 July	22 July	21 July	19 July
Week 31	30 July	29 July	28 July	26 July
Week 32	6 Aug.	5 Aug.	4 Aug.	2 Aug.
Week 33	13 Aug.	12 Aug.	11 Aug.	9 Aug.
Week 34	20 Aug.	19 Aug.	18 Aug.	16 Aug.
Week 35	27 Aug.	26 Aug.	25 Aug.	23 Aug.
Week 36	3 Sept.	2 Sept.	1 Sept.	30 Aug.
Week 37	10 Sept.	9 Sept.	8 Sept.	6 Sept.
Week 38	17 Sept.	16 Sept.	15 Sept.	13 Sept.
Week 39	24 Sept.	23 Sept.	22 Sept.	20 Sept.
Week 40	1 Oct.	30 Sept.	29 Sept.	27 Sept.
Week 41	8 Oct.	7 Oct.	6 Oct.	4 Oct.
Week 42	15 Oct.	14 Oct.	13 Oct.	11 Oct.
Week 43	22 Oct.	21 Oct.	20 Oct.	18 Oct.
Week 44	29 Oct.	28 Oct.	27 Oct.	25 Oct.
Week 45	5 Nov.	4 Nov.	3 Nov.	1 Nov.
Week 46	12 Nov.	11 Nov.	10 Nov.	8 Nov.
Week 47	19 Nov.	18 Nov.	17 Nov.	15 Nov.
Week 48	26 Nov.	25 Nov.	24 Nov.	22 Nov.
Week 49	3 Dec.	2 Dec.	1 Dec.	29 Nov.
Week 50	10 Dec.	9 Dec.	8 Dec.	6 Dec.
Week 51	17 Dec.	16 Dec.	15 Dec.	13 Dec.
Week 52	24 Dec.	23 Dec.	22 Dec.	20 Dec.

	1993	*1994*	*1995*	*1996*
Week 1	27 Dec. (92)	26 Dec. (93)	1 Jan.	31 Dec. (95)
Week 2	3 Jan.	2 Jan.	8 Jan.	7 Jan.
Week 3	10 Jan.	9 Jan.	15 Jan.	14 Jan.
Week 4	17 Jan.	16 Jan.	22 Jan.	21 Jan.
Week 5	24 Jan.	23 Jan.	29 Jan.	28 Jan.
Week 6	31 Jan.	30 Jan.	5 Feb.	4 Feb.
Week 7	7 Feb.	6 Feb.	12 Feb.	11 Feb.
Week 8	14 Feb.	13 Feb.	19 Feb.	18 Feb.
Week 9	21 Feb.	20 Feb.	26 Feb.	25 Feb.
Week 10	28 Feb.	27 Feb.	5 March	3 March
Week 11	7 March	6 March	12 March	10 March
Week 12	14 March	13 March	19 March	17 March
Week 13	21 March	20 March	26 March	24 March
Week 14	28 March	27 March	2 April	31 March
Week 15	4 April	3 April	9 April	7 April
Week 16	11 April	10 April	16 April	14 April
Week 17	18 April	17 April	23 April	21 April
Week 18	25 April	24 April	30 April	28 April
Week 19	2 May	1 May	7 May	5 May
Week 20	9 May	8 May	14 May	12 May
Week 21	16 May	15 May	21 May	19 May
Week 22	23 May	22 May	28 May	26 May
Week 23	30 May	29 May	4 June	2 June
Week 24	6 June	5 June	11 June	9 June
Week 25	13 June	12 June	18 June	16 June
Week 26	20 June	19 June	25 June	23 June
Week 27	27 June	26 June	2 July	30 June
Week 28	4 July	3 July	9 July	7 July
Week 29	11 July	10 July	16 July	14 July
Week 30	18 July	17 July	23 July	21 July
Week 31	25 July	24 July	30 July	28 July
Week 32	1 Aug.	31 July	6 Aug.	4 Aug.
Week 33	8 Aug.	7 Aug	13 Aug.	11 Aug.
Week 34	15 Aug.	14 Aug.	20 Aug.	18 Aug.
Week 35	22 Aug.	21 Aug.	27 Aug.	25 Aug.

	1993	*1994*	*1995*	*1996*
Week 36	29 Aug.	28 Aug.	3 Sept.	1 Sept.
Week 37	5 Sept.	4 Sept.	10 Sept.	8 Sept.
Week 38	12 Sept.	11 Sept.	17 Sept.	15 Sept.
Week 39	19 Sept.	18 Sept.	24 Sept.	22 Sept.
Week 40	26 Sept.	25 Sept.	1 Oct.	29 Sept.
Week 41	3 Oct.	2 Oct.	8 Oct.	6 Oct.
Week 42	10 Oct.	9 Oct.	15 Oct.	13 Oct.
Week 43	17 Oct.	16 Oct.	22 Oct.	20 Oct.
Week 44	24 Oct.	23 Oct.	29 Oct.	27 Oct.
Week 45	31 Oct.	30 Oct.	5 Nov.	3 Nov.
Week 46	7 Nov.	6 Nov.	12 Nov.	10 Nov.
Week 47	14 Nov.	13 Nov.	19 Nov.	17 Nov.
Week 48	21 Nov.	20 Nov.	26 Nov.	24 Nov.
Week 49	28 Nov.	27 Nov.	3 Dec.	1 Dec.
Week 50	5 Dec.	4 Dec.	10 Dec.	8 Dec.
Week 51	12 Dec.	11 Dec.	17 Dec.	15 Dec.
Week 52	19 Dec.	18 Dec.	24 Dec.	22 Dec.

Sources and Acknowledgments

We wish to thank all those who have granted permission for the use of prayers, texts and music in this book. We have made every effort to trace and identify them correctly and to secure the necessary permissions for reprinting. If we have erred in any way in the acknowledgments, or have unwittingly infringed any copyright, we apologize sincerely. We would be glad to make the necessary corrections in subsequent editions of this book.

Photos and illustrations

p. xvi: WCC/Bruce Best

p.2: Pelican: from "Seasons and Symbols: a Handbook for the Church Year", by Robert Wetzler and Helen Huntington, 1962 Augsburg Fortress Publishers, Minneapolis, USA.

pp.43, 132, 139, 262: WCC/Peter Williams

p.47: Brush stroke figure of Christ: from "Your Will Be Done", 1984 Christian Conference of Asia Youth, Quezon City, Philippines.

p.56: Franklin Ishida

p.104: Marc Vanappelghem

p.125: WCC

p.167: WCC/John Taylor

p.268: Guns: used on the order of service at the 1985 Oscar Romero memorial service, Newcastle-on-Tyne, England. Source untraced.

p.277: WCC/A. Sommerfeld

p.336: WCC/John Taylor

Prayers, texts and music

Page 1: *Lord, dear Lord, I long for Jerusalem*, from "I Sing your Praise all the Day Long: Young Africans at Prayer", edited by Fritz Pawelzik, © 1966 Friendship Press, New York, USA.

Lord God, then I would see, in my mind, from "I Sing your Praise all the Day Long: Young Africans at Prayer", edited by Fritz Pawelzik, © 1966 Friendship Press, New York, USA.

Page 2: *Blessed Jesus*. Source unknown.

Page 3: *Lord Jesus, we pray for the church*, from "Network", winter 1978, USPG, London, UK. Adapted.

Jesus comes to Benares as he does to Mecca, from "Jesus Christ the Life of the World: a Selection from Asia", 1982 Christian Conference of Asia, Hong Kong.

Jesus, ride again into our cities, from "Prayers for Peace", New Being Publishers, Palo Alto, California, USA.

Page 4: *O God of the ever present crosses,* Coptic Orthodox Patriarchate, Cairo, Egypt.

O Master, Lord God, Almighty, the Father of our Lord, Coptic Orthodox Patriarchate, Cairo, Egypt.

Page 5: *Lord, give us such a faith,* from "The Wisdom of the Suffis" (p.88), by Kenneth Cragg, 1976 SPCK, London, UK.

We pray, Lord, for the rising of the water of the Nile this year, from "Another Day: Prayers of the Human Family" (p.12), compiled by John Carden, 1986 Triangle Books/SPCK, London, UK.

Page 6: *Accept, our Lord, from us,* Coptic Orthodox Church, Cairo, Egypt.

God of grace and providence, by Kenneth Cragg, from "Morning, Noon and Night", compiled by John Carden, 1976 Highway Press/Church Missionary Society, London.

Pray not for Arab or Jew, by a Palestinian Christian. Source untraced.

Page 8: *As Christians, especially do we pray,* Christian prayer for peace with representatives of the church and ecclesial communities and of world religions at the invitation of Pope John Paul II, Assisi, 27 October 1986, published jointly by the British Council of Churches and Catholic Truth Society, London, in "Together in Prayer for Peace".

For all peoples, that thy light, Melkite petition translated from the Arabic by Kenneth Cragg.

Page 9: *Lord, after all the talking.* Source unknown.

O Lord Jesus, stretch forth your wounded hands, prayer for the unity of the Middle East, from "Morning, Noon and Night", compiled by John Carden, 1976 Highway Press/Church Missionary Society, London, UK.

Page 10: *We commend to thy fatherly goodness,* from the prayer book of the Arab Evangelical Episcopal Church.

O God, send into the hearts of the people of Jordan, from "The Book of Common Prayer". Extracts from the Book of Common Prayer 1662, the rights of which are vested in the Crown in perpetuity within the United Kingdom, are reproduced by permission of Eyre & Spottiswoode Publishers, Her Majesty's Printers, London, UK.

Page 12: *Come in peace, prophets of the Spirit,* Maronite liturgy.

Lord Christ, give me some of your Spirit, by Terry Waite, from "Lent for Busy People", The Bible Reading Fellowship, Warwick House, 25 Buckingham Palace Road, London SW1W OPP, UK. © Shelagh Brown.

Page 13: *Lord God, lover of peace and concord,* from "Another Day: Prayers of the Human Family", compiled by John Carden, 1986 Triangle/SPCK, London, UK.

Page 14: *O glorious apostle Paul,* "At the Apistchon" (first tome), from the Melkite Prayer Book, translated from the Arabic by Kenneth Cragg.

Page 15: *To me, who am but black cold charcoal,* a prayer after St John of Damascus.

In peace let us make our supplication to the Lord, divine liturgy of St James.

Page 16: *O God, I haven't recognized thee,* prayer of Muhammed.

Page 18: *O God, who by a star guided the wise men,* Epiphany Collect from the Church of South India Prayer Book (adapted). Courtesy Christian Literature Society, Madras, India.

How often it happens, preface to "Christians in the Arab East", by Robert Brendon Betts, 1978 SPCK, London, UK.

Page 19: *We pray, O Father, for the land that nurtured the prophet Mohammed,* from "Quarterly Intercession Paper", No. 318, USPG, London, UK.

Page 20: *God protect this country,* ancient prayer of Darius in "Morning, Noon and Night", compiled by John Carden, 1976 Highway Press/Church Missionary Society, London.

Thou who didst spread thy creating arms, Armenian liturgy.

O God, thou hast not endowed conscience, from "City of Wrong", by Kamil Hussein, translated by Kenneth Cragg, published by Geoffrey Bles, Garnstone Press Ltd, Petworth, West Sussex, UK.

Our condition is very much like the condition of Peter, quotation from "Bible Lands", by the Jerusalem and East Church Aid Association, 20 August 1982.

The cross of our Lord protect those who belong to Jesus, a blessing by Bishop Simon of Iran. Source untraced.

Page 21: *Litany for Iraq.* Source unknown.

Page 22: *You, Lord of all, we confess,* Chaldean liturgy.

O Lord, we beseech you grant your blessing and guidance. Source unknown.

Page 23: *Lord, who through a vision to your servant John on Patmos.* Source unknown.

Page 24: *O God of peace, good beyond all that is good,* liturgy of St Dionysius.

Page 25: *O Barnabas, who art equal unto the angels,* from the service of St Barnabas the Apostle, founder of the Church of Cyprus.

Page 26: *For the land and people of Greece.* Source unknown.

Page 27: *Lord Jesus Christ,* Orthodox.

Grant, O God. Source unknown.

Page 28: *Our thoughts rest for a few moments with them,* Week of Prayer for World Peace, Centre for International Peacebuilding, Wickham House, 10 Cleveland Way, London E1 4TR, UK.

Page 29: *For our Muslim brethren who repeat your name of grace,* from the Melkite liturgy in "Byzantine Daily Worship", The Byzantine Seminary Press, Pittsburg, Pennsylvania, USA.

To God be glory, a prayer from the old Syriac.

Page 30: *Lord of the lovers of humankind,* by Kenneth Cragg, from Provisional Calendar, Grace Cup, Quarterly Study Paper, Easter 1981, published by the Central Synod of the Episcopal Church in Jerusalem and the Middle East.

Page 33: *Lord, let me offer you in sacrifice,* by St Augustine of Hippo.

Another day of sand and prayer. Source: Meditations on the Sand in "God the Difficult" (p.75), by A. Pronzato, St Paul Publications, UK. Origin: "Meditazioni sulla sabbia" by Alessandro Pronzato, Piero Gribaudi Editore, © 1981.

Page 34: *My brother, bridge the Christian centuries and touch us now,* by Randle Manwaring, in "Another Day: Prayers of the Human Family", compiled by John Carden, 1986 Triangle/SPCK, London, UK.

Page 35: *Almighty God, whose son our Saviour Jesus Christ taught us,* by Kenneth Cragg, from Provisional Calendar, Grace Cup, Quarterly Study Paper, Easter 1981, published by the Central Synod of the Episcopal Church in Jerusalem and the Middle East.

Islam... takes God with awful seriousness, quotation from Hendrik Kraemer. Source untraced.

Almighty God, grant that we may listen, from "Quarterly Intercession Paper", USPG, London, UK.

As the needle naturally turns to the north, prayer to Jesus by Raymond Lull. Source untraced.

Give, O God, peace and harmony to the Islamic nations of North Africa. Source unknown.

Page 37: *"The 12 million or so Christians",* by David Kerr, from "MECC Perspectives", Geneva, Switzerland.

God bless the countries of the Middle East. Source unknown.

Page 38: *Christ look upon us in this city,* by Thomas Ashe. Source untraced.

Page 39: *Heavenly Parent,* from "World at One in Prayer", edited by D.J. Fleming, Friendship Press, New York, USA.

Page 40: *Pray for us, brothers and sisters in Christ,* a plea from Hong Kong, Anglican Diocese of Hong Kong, Bishop R.O. Hall. Source untraced.

O God our Father, by Raymond Fung, World Council of Churches, Geneva, Switzerland.

Page 41: *God the Father the voice of John the Baptist,* Mass, Feast of St John the Baptist, Patron Saint of Macau, Roman Missal.

Page 44: *We reverently worship the mysterious person, God the Father,* ancient Chinese ascription, used in worship by the Nestorian Church.

Help each one of us, gracious God, prayer from China. Source untraced.

Page 45: *O God, teach us to be understanding friends,* Amity Foundation, Eugene, Oregon, USA.

God, creator of heaven and earth and giver of human life, a contemporary prayer from China. Source untraced.

Page 46: *Now may the God of peace,* Hebrews 13:20-21.

Page 47: *If the Lord is in prison with me, what do I fear?*, by Hsu T'ien Hsien, from "Testimonies of Faith: Letters and Poems from Prison in Taiwan", studies from the World Alliance of Reformed Churches, Geneva, Switzerland.

Gracious God, let your will for Taiwan be known, prayer from Taiwan, from "Calendar of Prayer 1986-1987" (p.77), United Church of Christ Board for World Ministries, New York, USA. Used with permission.

Page 48: *You have shown us, O God, what is good*, prayer based on Micah. Source untraced.

Page 49: *If I had not suffered*, by Mizuno Genzo, from "Your Will Be Done", 1985 Christian Conference of Asia Youth, Quezon City, Philippines.

Page 50: *"As a Catholic I feel that fingerprints are given by God"*, by Kim Myong Shik, Japan, CIIR News, November 1986, reprinted in "Now", September 1987, Methodist Church Overseas Division, London. © CIIR News, London.

Page 51: *Eternal God we say good morning to you*, by Masao Takenaka, from "Your Will Be Done", 1985 Christian Conference of Asia Youth, Quezon City, Philippines.

Page 52: *Lord, touch with your fingers those who are so demeaned.* Source unknown.

O God, we do not protest, by Tohoyiko Kagawa, from "Your Will Be Done", 1985 Christian Conference of Asia Youth, Quezon City, Philippines.

Lord, bless the work of the National Christian Council of Churches in Japan. Source unknown.

Page 53: *O God, you have made us glad*, thanksgiving for Korean martyrs, from the "Prayer Book" of the Anglican Church of Korea.

Page 54: *Christians in North Korea*, by Erich Weingärtner, from "One World", April 1986, © World Council of Churches Publications, Geneva, Switzerland.

Our Father hallowed be your name, in Korea. Source unknown.

Page 55: *We give thanks O God, for the rapid growth of the church in Korea*, from the Quarterly Intercession Paper, No. 317, USPG, London, UK. Paraphrased.

We must not forget that today, Park Hyung Kyu. Source untraced.

O Christ, whose loving eyes. Source unknown.

Page 57: *The story is told*, by Erich Weingärtner, from "One World", November 1986, © World Council of Churches Publications, Geneva, Switzerland.

Lord, with Korean Christians. Source unknown.

Lord, thanks to you the dividing wall. Source unknown.

Lord, break down the walls that separate us, chorus of the theme song Fifth Assembly, WCC, Nairobi 1975, from "Break Down the Walls", lyrics by Fred Kaan, music Peter Janssens, © Peter Janssens Musik Verlag, Telgte, Federal Republic of Germany.

Page 58: *United through grace with all the members of your universal church,* offering of the day, prayer used in the Philippines. Prayer to Christ the King, Cursillo in Christianity Prayer Book.

Page 60: *As you annointed kings and called prophets of old,* prayer from the Philippines.

We pray that we may be truly sensitive, "Prayers for Asia Sunday", Christian Conference of Asia, Hong Kong.

Page 61: *Your death, O Lord, we commemorate,* acclamation as used by Filipino members, Cursillo in Christianity Prayer Book.

Page 62: *May the peaceful nature of multi-racialism in our lands,* prayer of a Malaysian Christian, from "The World at One in Prayer", Friendship Press, New York, USA.

Page 65: *O God of many names,* Christian prayer for peace with representatives of the church and ecclesial communities and of world religions at the invitation of Pope John Paul II, Assisi, 27 October 1986, published jointly by the British Council of Churches and Catholic Truth Society, London, in "Together in Prayer for Peace".

Page 66: *Just call me by my name,* "Alone I am not yet alone", words and music by Samuel Liew, from "New Songs of Asian Cities", No. 18, Christian Conference of Asia/URM, Hong Kong.

Thank you Father, for your blessing upon this land, by Lim Swee Cher, from "The Light of the World", CWM Prayer Handbook, 1981 Council for World Mission, London, UK.

In the brightness of your Son, opening recollection and benediction, from "Your Will Be Done", 1985 Christian Conference of Asia Youth, Quezon City, Philippines.

Page 67: *Destroy O Lord, the spirit of self-seeking in individuals,* prayer from Sweden. Source untraced.

Page 70: *O Lord, I have come into your house,* from the "Danish Church Service", Church of Denmark, Council on Inter-church Relations, Copenhagen.

Father in heaven, from "The Prayers of Sören Kierkegaard 1813-55", edited by Percy D. Le Fevre, © 1956 University of Chicago. All rights reserved.

Oh God, our Father and Mother, taken from a prayer by Kerstin Lindqvist and Ulla Bardh, Sweden, "Accept Our Deep Longing to Live", from "No Longer Strangers: a Resource for Women and Worship", 1983 World Council of Churches Publications, Geneva, Switzerland.

Page 72: *God, grant that in my mother tongue,* Hallgrimur Petersson, "Hymns of the Passion", 1674.

Lord our God, who taught wisdom to Solomon, the blessing of a computer, Finnish Orthodox.

Page 73: *Heavenly Father, we thank you that in the building of this home,* from "The New Lutheran Manual in Finland". Adapted.

Lord, we bring you thanks for the care and attention you gave to women, prayer used on the Norwegian Radio, 6 March 1987.

Page 74: *God, our creator, as we join the large spectrum of Christians,* prayer from Finland. Source untraced.

Page 75: *O Holy Spirit, giver of light and life,* slightly adapted after a prayer by Monica Furlong, c/o Movement for the Ordination of Women, London, UK.

Page 76: *Lord Jesus Christ, you are the way of peace,* from "Unity", newsletter of the Irish School of Ecumenics, Dublin, Eire.

Page 77: *Three things are of the Evil One,* 15th century Irish benediction.

Page 79: *We are tired, Lord,* by T.A. Patterson, N. Ireland, written for "With All God's People".

God our Mother and Father, we come to you as children, from "Corrymeela Worship", © 1987 Corrymeela Press, Belfast, N. Ireland. Used with permission.

Page 80: *All-merciful tender God,* Janet Berry, South West Manchester Group of Churches, UK.

Lord God, we thank you, prayer for the interchurch process by Jamie Wallace, British Council of Churches, London, UK.

Page 81: *O Lord Jesus, let not your word,* Thomas à Kempis, from "Prayers for the Future of Mankind" (p.212), Wolfe Publishing Ltd, London, © Pyramid Communications Inc.

Page 83: *Grant to us, O Lord,* Thomas à Kempis, from "Prayers for the Future of Mankind" (p.56), Wolfe Publishing Ltd, London, © Pyramid Communications Inc.

Page 84: *Let us pray to God who calls us in Jesus Christ to unity,* from "Fürbitten und Kanongebete der holländischen Kirche" (p.266), edited by A. Schilling, 1972 12th edition, Verlag Hans Driewer, Essen, Federal Republic of Germany.

O Holy Spirit of God, who with thy holy breath, Erasmus of Rotterdam, from "The Oxford Book of Prayer", No. 506, edited by George Appleton, 1985 Oxford University Press, London.

Page 85: *God in heaven, we beg you,* from "Fürbitten und Kanongebete der holländischen Kirche", edited by A. Schilling, 1972 12th edition, Verlag Hans Driewer, Essen, Federal Republic of Germany.

Go now, all of you, in peace, from "Prayers, Poems and Songs", by Huub Oosterhuis, 1975 Sheed & Ward Ltd., London, UK.

Page 86: *Lord, grant that Christians may again find visible unity,* from "Praise in all Our Days: Common Prayers at Taizé", 1975. Mowbray's & Co. Ltd., © Cassell Plc, London, UK.

Page 89: *Blessed are you, Lord God of the universe,* prayer from the Roman liturgy.

You are always with us, Lord, by Fr Pierre-Etienne, French in "Nos cœurs te chantent", 1977 Taizé, 71250 Cluny, France. English source unknown.

Page 91: *Lord God, you accepted the sacrifice of St James,* from the Roman liturgy.

O heavenly Father, we bend the knee before Thee, prayer from the Mozarabic sacramentary "Prayers for the Future of Mankind" (p.18), published by Wolfe Publishing Ltd, London, © Pyramid Communications Inc.

You are my family, an African, affirmation of Patrice, from "Expressions of Faith from the Universal Church" (p.33), Département évangélique français d'action apostolique.

Page 92: *Our God, we are one in solidarity,* One in Solidarity, from "100 prières possibles", by André Dumas, 1982 Editions Cana, Paris, France.

Page 93: *O God you who are from generation to generation the Creator of the ends of the earth,* Francis Ibiam, All Africa Conference of Churches. Source untraced.

Almighty and eternal God, we fervently lift up our eyes to you, prepared by women students in the Pan-African leadership course, Kitwe, Zambia, from "Journey of Struggle, Journey in Hope: People and their Pilgrimage in Central Africa", edited by Jane Heaton, Friendship Press, New York, USA.

Page 96: *And in a random scorching flame of wind,* Somali prayer, by Allen Lane, from "Heart of Prayer: African, Jewish and Biblical Prayers", by Anthony Gittins CSS (p.113), Wm B. Collins, London, UK.

Page 97: *Lord, I am not worthy that you should come under my roof,* prayer before communion, Western rite.

Page 98: *O Lord our good and life-giving God,* prayer from liturgy of the Ethiopian Orthodox Church, published by the Continental Printery, Kingston, Jamaica. Also the "Liturgy of the Ethiopian Church", translated by Marcos Daoud, The Egyptian Book Press.

Page 99: *Yes Lord, you are the God of all,* acclamation, Anaphora of St Dioscorus, prayer from liturgy of the Ethiopian Orthodox Church, published by the Continental Printery, Kingston, Jamaica. Also the "Liturgy of the Ethiopian Church", translated by Marcos Daoud, The Egyptian Book Press.

Remember, Lord, the sick among your people, evening prayer of the Covenant, prayer from liturgy of the Ethiopian Orthodox Church, published by the Continental Printery, Kingston, Jamaica. Also the "Liturgy of the Ethiopian Church", translated by Marcos Daoud, The Egyptian Book Press.

Page 100: *Give comfort, O Lord, to all who are torn away from their homes,* from the "Quarterly Intercession Paper", No. 322, USPG, London, UK.

Page 101: *O God, give us rain,* from "The Prayers of African Religion", by John S. Mbiti (p. 162), SPCK, London, UK.

Page 102: *O God, give us peace,* from "The Prayers of African Religion", by John S. Mbiti (p.162), SPCK, London, UK.

Lord God, there are places in this world some of us will never visit. Source unknown.

Page 103: *O Thou, who art the Lion of Judah,* a prayer for Africa by George Appleton, from "In His Name", Lutterworth Press and Macmillan Publishers. © George Appleton.

Page 105: *O God, make speed to save us,* versicle and response, Prayer Book of the Church of the Province of Sudan.

These are the new songs of worship, quotation from Christian Missionary Society source.

Page 106: *The Father of our Lord in Heaven,* hymn from Christian Missionary Society source.

All the problems of the rest of Africa. Source unknown.

O Lord Christ, who as a boy, "Quarterly Intercession Paper", No. 316, USPG, London, UK. Adapted.

O God, our Creator, Redeemer, Fellowship of the Least Coin. Used with permission.

God bless Sudan, "Quarterly Intercession Paper", No. 316, USPG, London, UK.

Page 108: *Martyrs gave birth to that great dynamic family of Christ,* Canon Samuel Van Culin, secretary general of the Anglican Consultative Council, speaking of Archbishop Janani Luwum.

O God, by your providence the blood of the martyrs, collect for the martyrs of Uganda, Anglican Church of Uganda, Kampala.

Tukutendereza, Yesu — Glory, glory, Hallelujah, from "Breath of Life", by Patricia St John, Ruanda Mission CMS, London, UK.

Page 109: *O Father God, I cannot fight,* prayer from Africa, from "Light of the World Prayer Book", Highway Press/Church Missionary Society, London, UK.

Keep us, Sovereign Lord, from panic, prayer from Uganda, from July/September 1984 issue of "Yes", Church Missionary Society, London, UK.

O Lord, stablish, strengthen and settle all Christians in Uganda. Source unknown.

Page 110: *Grant that the peoples of East Africa.* Source unknown.

Page 111: *We beg you, O God, to rule,* prayer from Kenya, from "The UNICEF Book of Children's Prayers", by William I. Kaufman, The Stackpole Company, Harrisburg, Pennsylvania, USA. © with the permission of William I. Kaufman.

Page 112: *From a wandering nomad,* from the draft eucharistic liturgy, Church of the Province of Kenya.

Let us pray to the God of our fathers, from the draft eucharistic liturgy, Church of the Province of Kenya.

Page 114: *Heavenly Father, thank you for the peace you have given us in Tanzania,* prayer from Tanzania, by W.F. Darby, from "Network", January 1986, USPG, London, UK. Adapted.

Good Lord: just as you were pleased to relax, Richards & Richardson, "Home Meeting", in "Prayers for Today", first published 1977 by Uzima Press Ltd, Nairobi, Kenya.

Page 115: *Here in Tanzania,* quote from the Christian Council of Tanzania.

O God forgive us for bringing this stumbling block, prayer of an African minister, from "Morning, Noon and Night" (p.83), compiled by John Carden, 1976 Highway Press/Church Missionary Society, London, UK.

Page 116: *Let your love,* a Malagasy petition. Source untraced.

Page 117: *Gracious Lord, in this season of fullness,* "The Greater Family", from "A Book of Family Prayer", edited by Gabe Huck, 1979 Seabury/Continuum Publishing Co., New York, USA.

O God, who calls us to your service, Fellowship of the Least Coin. Used with permission.

God of goodness and love, Christian Aid, London, UK.

Page 118: *Heavenly Father, you who taught your Son all he knew,* by Eleri Edwards, from "Proverbs for Today", CWM Prayer Handbook, 1984 Council for World Mission, London, UK. Adapted.

Page 120: *We must see ourselves,* quote from Ecumenical Press Service on Lusaka, 1988 World Council of Churches, Geneva, Switzerland.

May Africa praise you, you the true God, by Jerome Bala, from "Prayers for Mission" (p.18), USPG, London, UK, and "Another Day: Prayers of the Human Family", compiled by John Carden, 1986 Triangle/SPCK, London.

Page 121: *We pray for Zambia — your people tremble, wonder and are perplexed,* by John Banda, from "The Light of the World Today", CWM Prayer Handbook, 1984 Council for World Mission, London, UK.

Dear God in heaven, we pray for the tens of thousands of refugees, from Zambia, a prayer for refugees. Adapted. Source untraced.

Merciful God, from the sky you send the rain on the hills, by Jean Hall, from "Proverbs for Today", CWM Prayer Handbook, 1984 Council for World Mission, London, UK.

Page 122: *At last, O God, the sun's heat has given away to the cool evening,* Richards & Richardson, "Evening", in "Prayers for Today", first published 1977 by Uzima Press Ltd, Nairobi, Kenya.

Page 123: *O God of all youth, we pray to you,* from "Calendar of Prayer 1986-1987", United Church of Christ Board for World Ministries, New York. Used with permission.

Page 124: *But their potential,* quote from "Now" (p.5), February 1987, Methodist Church Overseas Division, London, UK.

Page 126: *You know, O God, how hard it is,* Rubem A. Alves. Source untraced.

Lord, no matter what we Christians get called. Source unknown.

Page 127: *I truly believe in the new humanity,* by Dom Pedro Casaldaliga, Rio de Janeiro, 1978, from "Confessing Our Faith Around the World IV: South America" (pp.32/33), 1985 World Council of Churches Publications, Geneva, Switzerland.

Page 128: *O God, to those who have hunger give bread,* prayer from Latin America. Source untraced.

Page 131: *True evangelical faith cannot lie dormant,* Menno Simons, 16th century founder of the Mennonites, from "Bible Lands Society Magazine", © The Bible Lands Society, High Wycombe, UK. Used with permission.

Page 133: *It must be the hardest thing,* Bernard Thorogood, from "Prayers for the Disappeared", Latin American Federation of Relatives of Disappeared Prisoners, London, UK.

Page 134: *After 11 years of military government,* from "Network", January 1985, USPG, London, UK. Adapted.

We pray to you, O Lord, prayer for use on Rogation Sunday, Evangelical Church of the River Plate, Argentina, from "Confessing Our Faith Around the World IV: South America" (p.10), 1985 World Council of Churches Publications, Geneva, Switzerland.

Page 136: *Why on earth had the Spaniards dragged enormous mirrors,* from "Like a Mighty River", by Lois Wilson, 1981 Wood Lake Press, Winfield, Canada.

Page 141: *For the deep sense of gratitude,* by John Carden.

The Christ of the Andes, by Max Warren, from "I Believe in the Great Commission", © Hodder & Stoughton, London, UK. Wm B. Eerdmans Publishing Co, Grand Rapids, for USA and Philippines.

Our Father... here and now, quoted from "We Believe", 1986 Uniting Church in Australia, Sydney, Australia.

Page 142: *Lord of mystery,* by Louis Espinal, quoted in "We Drink from Our Own Wells" (p.165), by Gustavo Gutierrez, 1974 SCM Press Ltd, London, UK, British and Commonwealth rights. For USA and Canada: Orbis Books, New York, USA.

O Lord, in times of weariness and discouragement, excerpted from "L'Amérique latine en prière", compiled by Charles Antoine, 1981 Editions du Cerf, Paris, France.

Page 143: *Lord God, gracious and merciful,* from "The Eucharistic Liturgy of Lima", Faith and Order 1982, World Council of Churches Publications, Geneva, Switzerland.

Page 145: *Paragraphs 1-4* quotes from "Signs of the Times", © CLAI (Latin American Council of Churches). Excerpted from "Prayer Manual 1986-1987" (p.19), Methodist Church Overseas Division, London, UK.

Almighty God, we come to your presence with the awareness of your gracious love, Emilio Castro, World Council of Churches, Geneva, Switzerland.

Page 146: *Solidarity is another name,* by Jon Sobrino, from "Theology of Christian Solidarity", by Jon Sobrino and Juan Hernandez Pico, © 1985 Orbis Books, Maryknoll, USA.

Page 148: *To you, Creator of nature and humanity,* from a prayer by Pope John Paul II during his visit to Hiroshima 1981, in "Prayers for Peace", by Robert Runcie and Basil Hume, 1987 SPCK, London, UK.

Page 150: *When I'm down and helpless,* Czech litany. Source untraced.

Page 151: *Bless, O God, the diligent work of all people,* from the Czech Hussite Church, Sunday eucharist.

Page 152: *We are two hands,* from Poland, translated from the German "Wir sind zwei Hände". Source untraced.

May the Lord accept our prayers, by Karol Wojtyla, prayer for ecumenical understanding. Source untraced.

Page 153: *As the bread which we break was scattered.* Didache, 2nd century.

Page 154: *You, O God, have made us human beings for yourself,* after the words of St Augustine.

Page 155: *O Lord, in you have I trusted,* from Te Deum Laudamus, 5th century, Yugoslavia.

Page 156: *Lord, we have sinned against you and against each other,* from "Week of Prayer for Christian Unity 1986", British Council of Churches, London, UK.

Page 157: *Grant, O Lord, that with your love,* Mother Teresa of Skopje and Calcutta. Source untraced.

Lord, you sent your Son Jesus Christ into the world, from "Week of Prayer for Christian Unity 1986", British Council of Churches, London, UK.

Page 158: *Remember, Lord, the city in which we dwell,* from the Divine Liturgy of St Chrysostom, commemoration of the diptychs of the living.

Page 159: *O Heavenly King, Comforter, Spirit of truth,* Orthodox invocation of the Holy Spirit.

Page 161: *O Christ, our God, who for us and for our salvation,* prayer for unity by Ion Bria, © World Council of Churches, Geneva, Switzerland.

Page 162: *Almighty God, in your majesty and nearness,* a Hungarian teacher's prayer from "Die Schönsten Gebete der Erde" (pp.75-76), © 1964 Südwest Verlag GmbH & Co. KG, Munich, Federal Republic of Germany.

O Lord our God, we thank you for the peace of our country and our homes, prayer from the Reformed Church of Hungary. Adapted.

Page 164: *Khristos voskress! Christ is risen!* Russian Orthodox prayer from "The Oxford Book of Prayer", No. 658, by George Appleton, 1985 Oxford University Press, London, UK.

Page 165: *O God, that we may receive your blessing,* prayer from Mongolia, from "Die Schönsten Gebete der Erde", © 1964 Südwest Verlag GmbH & Co. KG, Munich, Federal Republic of Germany.

Page 166: *Lord, through the shedding of the blood of your saints,* Armenian Orthodox liturgy, in "La prière oecuménique", collection of litanies put together by the Faith and Order Commission and published by Taizé, 71250 Cluny, France.

Page 168: *When my soul sheds its tears,* prayer by Lithuanian prisoners in Northern Siberia, 1960 Paulist Press, New Jersey, USA, quoted by Cicily Saunders in "Beyond all Pain", SPCK, London, UK.

Russian believers, quote from "Sojourners", November 1983, Washington DC, USA.

age 169: *Good Jesus, patient as a lamb,* by E.B. Pusey. Source untraced.
Kyrie eleison, Orthodox liturgy, USSR.
O Lord, I do not know what to ask of you, by Metropolitan Philaret of Moscow (1553-1633), from the "Russian Orthodox Liturgy".

Page 171: *More than anything else,* from "Unfinished Agenda" by Lesslie Newbigin, 1985 World Council of Churches Publications, Geneva, Switzerland.

Page 173: *There are literally two Liberias,* Anglican bishop of Liberia.

Page 175: *If Mary and Joseph,* by Dorothy R. Gilbert, Bo, Sierra Leone, excerpted from the 1985 Prayer Calendar (p.18), General Board of Global Ministries, The United Methodist Church, New York, USA. Used by permission.
Lord, we pray that in all the contacts. Source unknown.
May God give you a long life, a Krio blessing, excerpted from the 1985 Prayer Calendar (p.60), General Board of Global Ministries, The United Methodist Church, New York, USA. Used by permission.

Page 176: *May the word of God,* a prayer from Guinea. Source untraced.

Page 178: *I saw a child today, Lord,* prayer of an African Christian, quoted in "Prayers for Harvest Leaflet 1986", Christian Aid, London, UK.
Grant, O God, to your children in Guinea. Source unknown.

Page 179: *Bless, O Lord, the independent nations of Africa,* "Quarterly Intercession Paper", No. 324, USPG, London, UK.

Page 181: *We thank you Lord.* Source unknown.
O God, in whom we live and move, prayer from the Roman liturgy.
O God, our Heavenly Father, prayer for use in the Muslim world, by Oliver Allison, Diocese of the Sudan, quoted in "New Threshold", by David Brown, 1976 British Council of Churches, London, UK.
Lord, you want everybody to live in your Truth, prayer of a Senegalese Christian. Source untraced.

Page 182: *Years ago our Elders said,* from "Calendar of Prayer 1986-1987", United Church of Christ Board for World Ministries, New York, USA. Used with permission.

Page 183: *Lord our God,* prayer from Benin. Source untraced.

Page 184: *Our heavenly Father, we in Ghana,* general secretary of the Christian Council of Ghana, from "Calendar of Prayer 1986-1987", United Church of Christ Board for World Ministries, USA. Used with permission.
O God, we implore you, prayer of a young Ghanaian, "Make us your people", from "I Lie on My Mat and Pray" (p.56), edited by Fritz Pawelzik, © 1966 Friendship Press, New York, USA.

Page 185: *God of all nations,* prayer from Ghana. Source untraced.
Hallelujah, in Ewe Ghana, as taught by Alexander Gondo, in "African Songs of Worship", edited by I-to Loh, © 1986 Renewal and Congregational Life, World Council of Churches Publications, Geneva, Switzerland.

Page 186: *O God, most mighty among the heavens,* excerpt from a prayer o: confession recorded in an African Independent Church by Akin Omoyajowo, for a symposium on Christian theology in Nigeria, 1981.

Page 187: *Let us pray for those who foster violence,* prayer from the Ivory Coast. Source untraced.

Page 188: *Lord, you told the apostles,* prayer for unity from Togo. Source untraced.

Page 189: *O Almighty God, we humbly ask you,* prayer used in Yoruba parishes in Nigeria, from "Morning, Noon and Night" (p.87), compiled by John Carden, 1976 Highway Press/Church Missionary Society, London, UK.

Page 190: *Creator of heaven and earth accept our thanks,* excerpt from a prayer of thanksgiving recorded in an African Independent Church by Akin Omoyajowo, for a symposium on Christian theology in Nigeria, 1981.

Page 191: *Lord, we were brought up together.* Source unknown.

O Lord, we beseech thee to deliver us from the fear of the unknown future, prayer of Francis Akanu Ibiam. Source untraced.

Page 192: *Ezigbo hwannem, nyem aka gi,* Ibo chorus of farewell, Nigeria. Source untraced.

Page 193: *We pray for the churches where many suffer,* from prayers used at the 8th Assembly of the Christian Conference of Asia in Seoul, Korea, 1985.

Page 196: *God of peace, help us to be committed as Christians,* Fellowship of the Least Coin. Used with permission.

Our Father, we thank you that in Jesus Christ, prayer by two members of the Fellowship of the Least Coin. Used with permission.

Page 198: *With all my heart I take refuge in God,* from the Norwegian of Karl Ludvig Reichelt, Buddhist/Christian Centre, Hong Kong.

Page 199: *God came down to us like the sun at morning,* from "Your Will Be Done" (p.156), 1985 Christian Conference of Asia Youth, Quezon City, Philippines.

Page 201: *We cannot go post-haste,* quoted from "Fides", April 1987.

Page 202: *Look with mercy, O Lord, on the suffering people of Indo-China,* "Quarterly Intercession Paper", No. 326, USPG, London, UK. Adapted.

Dear God, we thank you for your love shown to us, prayer of a Cambodian Christian refugee woman, Fellowship of the Least Coin. Used with permission.

Page 203: *We remember, O Lord, those who suffer,* from "Week of Prayer for World Peace", Centre for International Peacebuilding, London, UK.

We pray for the peoples of Asia, Christian prayer for peace with representatives of the church and ecclesial communities and of world religions at the invitation of Pope John Paul II, Assisi, 27 October 1986 published jointly by the British Council of Churches and Catholic Truth Society, London, in "Together in Prayer for Peace".

As we are together, praying for peace, by Thich Nhat Hanh, a Buddhist litany for peace, from "Oxford Book of Prayer", No. 935, edited by George Appleton, 1985 Oxford University Press, London, UK.

Page 204: *May the grace of our Lord Jesus Christ,* benediction, Christian Conference of Asia, Hong Kong.

Page 205: *Dear Lord, you wanted all people to live in unity,* prayer of a Burmese Christian woman, Fellowship of the Least Coin. Used with permission.

Page 206: *Good Shepherd, we ask that you will seek the lost,* by Gwen Rees Roberts, from "Psalms for Pilgrims", CWM Prayer Handbook (p.19), 1983 Council for World Mission, London, UK.

Page 207: *Staying in Bangkok briefly,* a tourist, Joyce Peel, Church Missionary Society, London, UK.

O God, our Father, the fountain of love, by Koson Srisang, Thailand, from "Your Will Be Done", 1985 Christian Conference of Asia Youth, Quezon City, Philippines.

Page 209: *O God, be with us in this new day,* prayer of a Thai Christian woman, Fellowship of the Least Coin. Used with permission.

Lord, we take refuge in your compassionate name, by John Carden, prayer prompted by a thought in Bishop Neill's "The Supremacy of Jesus" (p.52), "The Hodder Book of Christian Prayers", by Tony Castle, Hodder & Stoughton, London, UK.

Page 211: *I believe in God, who is love,* an Indonesian creed, Christian Conference of Asia, Hong Kong.

Page 212: *Give us strength, give us courage,* Fridolin Ukur, Indonesia. Source untraced.

Page 213: *O God, who sent the Holy Spirit,* prayer of an Indonesian Christian woman, Fellowship of the Least Coin. Used with permission.

Page 214: *O God, who has bound us together in this bundle of life,* by Reinhold Niebuhr, from "Hymns of Worship", edited by Ursular Niebuhr, 1939 Association Press, New York, USA.

Page 215: *Grandfather, Great Spirit,* Dakota Indian prayer, from "The Gift is Rich", by E. Russell Carter, 1955 and 1968 Friendship Press, New York, USA.

God of our weary years, by James Weldon Johnson, third verse of hymn "Lift Every Voice and Sing", © 1927 Edward B. Marks Music Corporation, USA.

Page 217: *We pray that our neighbourhoods, cities and nation,* prayer by Lyman Ogilby. Source untraced.

O God, you are like a weaver-woman in our lives, "The Weaver Woman", prayer from the USA. Source untraced.

Page 218: *Almighty God, we offer our prayers,* by Joan Campbell, used by permission of the National Council of the Churches of Christ in the USA, October 1983.

Lord, I could use some help. Source unknown.

God, help everyone living with AIDS, Grant M. Gallup, Episcopal Diocese of Chicago, Illinois, USA.

Let those who have no home to go to in the evening, John Fandel "AM/PM", Forward Movement Publications, Cincinnati, Ohio, USA.

Page 219: *Lord, we know that you'll be coming through the line today,* Mary Glover, quoted in "Sojourners", Washington DC, USA, in Jim Wallace's "The Rise of Christian Conscience".

Thank you, Lord, for counting me one of your sheep, Albert Newton, All Saints Episcopal Church, Montgomery, Alabama, USA.

Lord, one of the problems I have with praying is that you always get too personal, Albert Newton, All Saints Episcopal Church, Montgomery, Alabama, USA.

You are the healing, the loving, the touching, "God is a Verb", by Marilee Zdenek, excerpted from 1985 Prayer Calendar (p.39), General Board of Global Ministries, The United Methodist Church, New York, USA. Used by permission.

Let us pray for the world that is immeasurable, Pax Christi, USA. Source untraced.

Page 222: *Lord, in creation you have revealed your awesome power,* "Ecumenical Prayers", © Paulist Press, Ramsey, New Jersey, USA.

Page 223: *You have come from afar,* "Prières d'Ozawamick", Canadian Indian liturgical text. Source untraced.

For human contact, for courage and vision, Alyson Huntly, Canada, reprinted with permission from "Faithful Reflections on Our Experience", published by the Women's Inter-Church Council of Canada, 1984.

Page 224: *You, O God, have spoken to us through the story of Ruth,* United Church of Canada, Toronto. Adapted.

O God, through the image of a woman crucified on the cross (By His Wounds You Have Been Healed), Canada, from "No Longer Strangers: a Resource for Women and Worship" (p.33), edited by Iben Gjerding and Katherine Kinnamon, 1983 World Council of Churches Publications, and "Ecumenical Decade 1988-1998: Churches in Solidarity with Women — Prayers and Poems — Songs and Stories" (p.23), 1988 WCC Publications, Geneva, Switzerland.

Page 225: *Jesus, make our hearts ever gentler and more humble,* Jean Vanier in "Eruption to Hope" (p.50), 1971 Griffin House Publishers, Toronto, Canada. Used with permission.

The blessing of the God of Sarah and Hagar, as of Abraham, by Lois Wilson, Toronto, Canada, from "No Longer Strangers: a Resource for Women and Worship" (p.45), edited by Iben Gjerding and Katherine Kinnamon, 1983 World Council of Churches Publications, Geneva, Switzerland.

Page 226: *O God, you are my God,* "As Dolphin and Eagle", from "Australian Prayers", by Bruce D. Prewer, used by permission of Lutheran Publishing House, Adelaide, South Australia.

Page 227: *You must think me silly, God,* from "Australian Images", by Aubrey Podlich, used by permission of Lutheran Publishing House, Adelaide, South Australia.

God of our ancient people, first stanza of "Our Black People", from "Australian Prayers" (p.122), by Bruce D. Prewer, slightly modified, used by permission of Lutheran Publishing House, Adelaide, South Australia.

Dear God, you have forgiven us our sins, by Arthur Malcolm, Australia.

Page 228: *Give wisdom to those in authority,* copyright Anglican Church of Australia Trust Corporation, from the text of "An Australian Prayer Book", published by the Anglican Information Office, reproduced with permission.

Page 229: *Lord God of all Peoples,* from an offertory prayer, New Zealand.

Gracious God, we pray for the peoples of New Zealand-Aotearoa, T.W., a prayer from the Conference of Churches in Aotearoa-New Zealand, Wellington.

Page 231: *O Jesus, be the canoe that holds me up in the sea of life,* an islander's prayer for Melanesia, from "Melanesia News" and "Morning, Noon and Night" (p.95), compiled by John Carden, 1976 Highway Press/CMS, London, UK.

Page 233: *Almighty God, your word of creation caused the water,* prayer from Samoa, quoted from "We Believe" (p.49), Uniting Church in Australia, Sydney, Australia.

Page 235: *Keep the ocean clean,* from the West Caroline island of Palau, a fifth-grader's cry of protest, excerpted from the 1985 Prayer Calendar (p.104), General Board of Global Ministries, The United Methodist Church, New York, USA. Used by permission.

The environment of the small but vivacious communities, from "To Live Among the Stars: Christian Origins in Oceania", by John Garrett, 1982 World Council of Churches, Geneva, Switzerland.

We believe that creation is a gift of God, taken from a creed "Women of the Pacific: Worship Workshop", JPIC women's meeting "Caring for God's Creation", Tonga, September 1987.

Page 236: *We ask you, dear God,* "Southern Cross Prayer", © The Bible Society of Papua New Guinea, Port Moresby.

Page 237: *Lord, in your mercy,* litany by Jabez L. Bryce, Fiji. Source untraced.

We pray for the peoples of Oceania, Christian prayer for peace with representatives of the church and ecclesial communities and of world religions at the invitation of Pope John Paul II, Assisi, 27 October 1986, published jointly by the British Council of Churches and Catholic Truth Society, London, in "Together in Prayer for Peace".

O God our Father, save our shores from the weapons of death, by Sione Amanaki Havea, Tonga, excerpted from Prayer Calendar 1986-1987 (p.43), Methodist Church Overseas Division, London, UK.

Page 238: *O Lord, our palm trees can no longer hide us,* prayer of Tahitian pastor. Source untraced.

Page 239: *O God, we pray that you will give us enough wisdom and faith,* prayer from Seychelles. Source untraced.

Page 242: *O God of all the people and all the nations of the earth,* Brian Crosby, Beau Bassin, Mauritius.

Page 243: *Lord Jesus, we claim your promise.* Source unknown.

Almighty God, always you have wished for the unity of all humanity, by kindness of Jean Margeot, Bishop of Port-Louis, Mauritius.

Page 244: *Red eyes, batons, red fire, red blood,* E. Anthony Allen, Bethel Baptist Healing Centre, Kingston, Jamaica.

Page 245: *We are weary of the years of sowing and reaping,* from a litany of justice, hope and peace, Caribbean Conference of Churches. Used with permission.

Page 246: *O Lord, lead us not into imitation!,* prayer of the East Asia Youth Assembly, 1984.

Page 247: *We believe in you, O God,* affirmation from Cuba. Source untraced.

Page 248: *Thank you, O Lord our God, for all that you have done to sustain us,* 4th Assembly, Caribbean Conference of Churches, 1986. Used with permission.

Lord, how glad we are that we don't hold you, prayer from Haiti, from "God is no Stranger", by Sandra L. Burdick, Baker Book House, Grand Rapids, Michigan, USA.

O God, in baptism you have called us by name, prayer for family life and vocations, from "Praise Yahweh my Soul: Hymnbook of the Roman Catholic Diocese of Kingston, Jamaica".

Page 249: *We pray that thou wilt watch over us in St Lucia,* schoolgirl's prayer from St Lucia, from "Network", April 1986, USPG, London, UK. Adapted.

Loving Creator, may those who visit the Caribbean, 4th Assembly, Caribbean Conference of Churches, 1986. Used with permission.

O God, we pray that you will keep together those you have united, opening service, 4th Assembly, Caribbean Conference of Churches, 1986. Used with permission.

Page 251: *Loving God, we are concerned about the spread of hatred in our time,* 4th Assembly, Caribbean Conference of Churches, 1986. Used with permission.

Page 252: *The right hand of God is writing in our land,* words by Patrick Prescod; music by Noel Dexter; from "Sing a New Song", No. 3, edited by Patrick Prescod, Caribbean Conference of Churches, Barbados.

Page 254: *Give us, Señor, a little sun, a little happiness and some work,* prayer on a church wall in Mexico, from "Calendar of Prayer 1986-1987" (p.53), United Church of Christ Board for World Ministries, USA. Used with permission.

Page 255: *Grant, O Lord, that the people of Belize may have peace and prosperity,* from "Quarterly Intercession Paper", No. 328, USPG, London, UK. Adapted.

Page 256: *The message that the poor Christian from Latin America,* testimony given before the US House of Representative Subcommittee on Human Rights and International Organizations, Committee on Foreign Affairs. Source: "A Vision of Hope", by Trevor Beeson, 1984 Fontana/Collins, London, UK.

Captivate me, Lord, from "Confession", in "Threatened with Resurrection", Julia Esquivel, © 1982 Brethren Press, Elgin, Illinois, USA. Used with permission.

Page 257: *Jesus, we believe that you are living,* prayer of an Indian woman member of the Guatemalan Committee for Justice and Peace, in "Prayer Manual 1984/1985" (p.22), Methodist Church Overseas Division, London, UK.

Page 258: *We still pray, we still sing,* "Maryknoll Magazine" (p.22), June 1987, Maryknoll, New York, USA. Used with permission.

Page 259: *By his coming to the world in the form of a stranger.* Source unknown.

Page 260: *God of our daily lives,* Jan Pickard, "Prayer Manual 1987-1988", Methodist Church Overseas Division, London, UK.

Page 261: *Lord, if this day you have to correct us,* prayer from Mexico. Source untraced.

Page 263: *Señor, sálvanos de caer en el pecado,* Tómas H. Téllez, Baptist Convention of Nicaragua, Managua.

Page 265: *We live in a world of division,* Oscar Romero, in "Prayer Manual 1984-1985", Methodist Church Overseas Division, London, UK.

I believe in you, companion, human Christ, Misa Campesina Nicaraguense de Carlos Mejia Godoy.

Page 266: *Nicaragua is as weak and fragile,* © Division of World Outreach, United Church of Canada, Toronto, quoted in "United Church Observer".

Blessed be God, who is always renewing the church, act of praise following Vatican II.

Page 267: *Loving Lord, you will the health and wholeness of all your people,* Christian Aid, London, UK. Adapted.

Page 268: *And now, when I fall down,* Jerjes Ruiz, Seminario Teologico Bautista de Nicaragua, Managua.

Our Father, who are in this our land, Lord's prayer adapted from Christian communities in Nicaragua. Source untraced.

Page 269: *Blessed be God,* the Divine Praises, Roman Catholic Church.

Page 271: *O Christ, as the spear opened a passage to your heart.* Source unknown.

Page 273: *O God, we bring before you the people of Latin America,* Felipe Adolf, from "Calendar of Prayer 1987-1988" (p.76), United Church of Christ Board for World Ministries, USA. Used with permission.

We believe in a loving God, creed of Camilo Torres, Colombia, from "The Revolutionary Priest: the Complete Writings and Messages of Camilo Torres", edited by © John Gerassi, 1969 Penguin Books.

Page 274: *O Lord, I don't want to be a spectator,* a tourist's prayer, Freda Rajotte, World Council of Churches, Geneva, Switzerland.

I hunger and I eat, three times a day — or more, John Fandel from "AM/PM", Forward Movement Publications, Cincinnati, Ohio, USA.

O God, we find ourselves dealing in death and deprivation, by John Poulton, 1983 "Week of Prayer for Christian Unity", British Council of Churches Publications, London, UK.

Page 289: *He comes to us as one unknown*, Albert Schweitzer, from "The Quest for the Historical Jesus", by Albert Schweitzer, 1968 The Macmillan Publishing Co Inc. © A. & C. Black Ltd., London, UK.

I will follow you, Jesus, Congolese hymn, from "Simon Kimbangu: an African Prophet and his Church", by Marie-Louise Martin, 1975 Wm. B. Eerdmans Publishing Co., Grand Rapids, Michigan, USA.

Page 292: *Jesus, we want to grow in knowledge*, children's prayer, in "Journey of Struggle, Journey in Hope: People and their Pilgrimage in Central Africa", by Jan Heaton, Friendship Press, New York, USA.

Page 293: *Lord Jesus Christ, you said to your apostles*, the Roman Mass.

O God: enlarge my heart, prayer of an African Christian. Source untraced.

Page 294: *The cross is the hope of Christians*, 10th century African hymn, used in the prayer manual of the Methodist Church Overseas Division, London, UK.

Page 296: *We bless you for sending your Spirit*, prayer for Burundi Christians, Louis Lochet, Foyers de Charité.

Page 297: *O Saviour of the world*, Salvator mundi.

Page 299: *May the brokenness of our Lord Jesus Christ*, revival grace. Source unknown.

Page 300: *I thank you, Almighty God, maker of heaven and earth*, a prayer said to have been used by Simon Kimbangu, from "Simon Kimbangu: an African Prophet and his Church", by Marie-Louise Martin, 1975 Wm. B. Eerdmans Publishing Co., Grand Rapids, Michigan, USA.

Page 301: *Bless, O Lord, all such courageous Christians*. Source unknown.

God, bless Africa, prayer for Africa, Trevor Huddleston.

Page 302: *Grant us prudence in proportion to our power*, prayer for peace, Conference of European Churches, Gloria Deo Worship Book, 9th Assembly, 1986.

Page 304: *Graciously comfort and tend all who are imprisoned*, Martin Luther, reprinted by permission from "Luther's Prayers", © 1967 Augsburg Publishing House, Minneapolis, USA.

Page 306: *God, our Father, we thank you for putting new life into your people*, prayer of East German woman, Fellowship of the Least Coin. Used with permission.

Almighty and eternal God, from a Roman Catholic agape celebration, edited by A. Schilling, "Fürbitten und Kanongebete der holländischen Kirche", 1972 12th edition, Verlag Hans Driewer, Essen, Federal Republic of Germany.

Page 307: *I believe that God both can and will bring good out of evil*, an extract from Dietrich Bonhoeffer, "Letters and Papers from Prison", enlarged edition, 1971 SCM Press, London, UK. British Commonwealth rights including Canada. For USA: Macmillan Publishing Company Inc., New York, USA.

Page 308: *Lord, save us from being self-centred in our prayers,* prayer based on words of John Calvin, "Contemporary Parish Prayers" (pp.106-107), by Frank Colquhoun, 1975 Hodder & Stoughton, London, UK.

Page 311: *O God, the giver of life,* prayer used in the Ecumenical Centre, Geneva, on the occasion of the visit of Pope John Paul II, 1984.

Let our chief end, O God, be to glorify thee, after Calvin's catechism.

We thank you, gracious God, for the beauty of the earth, from the liturgy of the German-speaking Evangelical Reformed Church of Switzerland, Taschenausgabe, p.16, No. 4, 1986 Zurich. Adapted from a prayer of the Episcopal Church, USA, by H. Bernoulli.

Page 312: *Upheld by the prayers of St Nicholas von Flüe,* the prayer for the Feast of Nicholas von Flüe, Swiss Missal.

Dear heavenly Father, send your Holy Spirit on us all, we pray, Aus: Barth, Karl: Gebete. 4 Aufl. 1974 (München). Rechte: Theologischer Verlag Zürich.

Page 314: *All-powerful and ever-living God,* Solemnity of All Saints, the Roman Missal.

Page 316: *Blessed are you, O Lord our God, King of the universe,* Rabbi Moshe Hakotun, said to have been written in Venice, from "God of a Hundred Names" (p. 115,) compiled by Barbara Greene and Victor Gollancz, 1962 Victor Gollancz Ltd, London, UK.

Lord, may I ever speak as though it were the last word that I can speak, prayer of Chiara Lubich, founder of The Focolare Movement, "Spiel mit gottlichen Rollen" (p.130), Neue Stadt Verlag, Munich, Federal Republic of Germany. © Città Nuova Editrice, Rome, Italy. Used with permission.

Page 317: *O God, Creator, Redeemer, and Sanctifier,* prayer from the Waldensian liturgy.

O Lord, you have said to us "Peace I leave with you", prayer from the Waldensian liturgy.

Page 318: *Dear Jesus, as a hen covers her chicks with her wings,* Indian origin. Source unknown.

Page 319: *About prayer,* a former bishop of Dacca. Source untraced.

Page 320: *Grant, O Lord, that we may expect great things of thee,* William Carey of Serampore.

Save us O Lord waking, from Compline.

Page 321: *O servant Lord, teach us how to serve,* Episcopal Church of Scotland, Mission Department. Used with permission.

Page 322: *God is here.* Source unknown.

Page 323: *Lord, give us the strength that comes from your living presence.* Source unknown.

O Lord, hear our petitions, prayer-hymn originally sung on the borders of Nepal. Source untraced.

Page 324: *Almighty God, whose dominion is in the hearts of people and nations,* from "Empty Shoes" (p.27), Highway Press/Church Missionary Society, London, UK.

Page 325: *In the absence of Afghan Christians,* traveller in Afghanistan. Source untraced.

O Creator God, we rejoice that the ruggedness. Source unknown.

Page 326: *Yisu ke pichhe main chalne laga.* Source unknown.

Page 327: *O Creator and Mighty God,* prayer from Pakistan from "Now", December 1987, Methodist Church Overseas Division, London, UK.

O Heavenly Father, prayer of a Punjabi Christian. Source untraced.

Page 328: *Look graciously, O Lord, upon this land,* based on the words "O Lord, be gracious to our land", from "Morning and Evening Prayer", Church of Pakistan.

Page 329: *Almighty God, who to your holy apostle St Thomas our patron,* collect for the commemoration of St Thomas.

Page 330: *O Lord, let me rest the ladder of gratitude against your cross,* prayer of an Indian Christian. Source untraced.

Page 331: *Cities are springing up like mushrooms,* "Message for the City", from "About You and Me" (p.44), by M.A. Thomas, courtesy Christian Literature Society, Madras, India, 1975.

Page 332: *O God, we would pray at this time for all those who suffer,* daily prayer suggested for use by members of the Syrian Orthodox Church dispersed abroad, from "Prayer Book for Young People", Sophia Publications, Orthodox Seminary, Kottayam, Kerala, India.

Page 333: *What we need, Lord, is mercy from all,* petition of Sri Lankan church leader. Source untraced.

Page 334: *Lord Jesus, you were awakened by the cry of your disciples,* prayer from Sri Lanka, Fellowship of the Least Coin. Used with permission.

Remembering St Thomas, we invoke the blessing, Olive Hitchcock. Source untraced.

Page 335: *We pray for Africa with all its richness of spirit,* Christian prayer for peace with representatives of the church and ecclesial communities and of world religions at the invitation of Pope John Paul II, Assisi, 27 October 1986, published jointly by the British Council of Churches and Catholic Truth Society, London, in "Together in Prayer for Peace".

Page 337: *We sincerely thank you, O God, for your powerful gift of hope,* João Makondekwa, © Bible Society of Angola, used in "Prayer Manual 1984-1985" (p.13), Methodist Church Overseas Division, London, UK.

Page 339: *O Lord, we pray for justice, peace and stability throughout Southern Africa,* prayer for Mozambique, USPG, London, UK.

I wonder if we are aware, by Dinis Sengulane, Bishop of Lebombo, Mozambique, courtesy of "Lebombo Leaves", spring 1979, chronicle of the Diocese of Lebombo, published by the Lebombo Association, London, UK.

Page 340: *Almighty God, as your Son our Saviour was born of a Hebrew mother,* Toc H, quoted from George Appleton's "The Oxford Book of Prayer", No. 218, 1985 Oxford University Press, London, UK.

Page 341: *To those brought up,* Chris Race, a South African priest, reported in "13/Background to Mission, Botswana, Partners in Mission with the Province of Central Africa", USPG, London, UK.

Page 342: *O God, we pray for those places in the world made awful by climatic conditions.* Source unknown.

Page 344: *O God, friend of the poor,* a pastor's prayer, "Prayer Manual 1985-1986", Methodist Church Overseas Division, London, UK.

Open my eyes that they may see the deepest needs of people, Canaan Banana, first president of Zimbabwe, from "The Gospel According to the Ghetto" (p.21), 1981 Mambo Press, Gweru, Zimbabwe.

O God of all nations and people, African bidding. Source untraced.

Page 345: *Lord Jesus Christ, you are the truth and rule,* prayer from South Africa. Source untraced.

Page 346: *Lord, we think you know our land,* prayer prepared by staff and students of Roma Theological Seminary, from "Network", April 1986, USPG, London. Adapted.

Page 348: *We wail and cry,* Abisai Shejavili, Council of Churches in Namibia.

Page 349: *To you, O God, we lift our outstretched hands.* Source unknown.

O God, I am oppressed: undertake for me, ascribed to Hezekiah, King of Judah in 707 BC, "An Anthology of Prayers", A.S.T. Fisher, Longman, Green & Co., London, UK.

O Christ, who hast known fear, "Network", USPG, London, UK.

O Lord, help us who roam about, prayer used in 1947 by the late chief of the Hereros, Hosea Kutako, in entrusting Michael Scott with the mission of persuading the UN to take up Namibia's case... Source untraced.

Lord Jesus Christ, voice of the voiceless and comforter of the oppressed, from "Kulimukweni. © Council of Churches in Namibia. Adapted.

Page 350: *The time has come,* Kairos Document, Braamfontein, 1985.

Page 352: *In word and deed,* prayer of a multi-racial group in Johannesburg. Source untraced.

Thank you God, that you care, by Desmond Tutu, South Africa.

Now, God, will you please open all prison doors, by Desmond Tutu, South Africa.

Almighty God, you whose own son had to flee the evil plans of King Herod, South African Council of Churches, Refugee Sunday liturgy.

Page 353: *Loving Father, your young and lovable Son was found amidst the teachers of law,* Simeon Nkoane CR, "Spirituality in a Violent Society", Eric Symes Abbot Memorial Lecture, Kings College, London, May 1987.

O God, whose righteous wisdom governs the heavens, Crossroads Camp prayer, in "Cry Justice", by John de Gruchy, © 1986 Orbis Books, Maryknoll, USA. UK: Wm B. Collins, London, UK.

A litany of rejoicing, a service of celebration, Cape Town, in "Cry Justice" (pp.212-213), by John de Gruchy, © 1986 Orbis Books, Maryknoll, USA. UK: Wm B. Collins, London, UK.

Page 355: *O God, may this great, carefully wielded thread of worldwide prayer and concern.* Source unknown.

As the earth keeps turning, hurtling through space, closing prayer, WCC Assembly, Vancouver 1983, from "Let's Worship" (p.25), Risk Book Vol. 11, No. 2-3, 1975 World Council of Churches Publications, Geneva, Switzerland.